ORGANIZING
FOR YOUR
BRAIN TYPE

LANNA NAKONE, M.A.

ORGANIZING
FOR YOUR BRAIN TYPE

Finding Your Own Solution
to Managing Time, Paper,
and Stuff

ST. MARTIN'S GRIFFIN
≈ NEW YORK

www.stmartins.com

Book design by Jonathan Bennett

Library of Congress Cataloging-in-Publication Data

Nakone, Lanna.
    Organizing for your brain type : finding your own solution to managing time, paper, and stuff / Lanna Nakone.
        p. cm
    Includes bibliographical references.
    ISBN 0-312-33977-1
    EAN 978-0312-33977-7
        1. Home economics.   2. Time management.   3. Organization.
I. Title.

TX147.N33 2005
640—dc22

                                                    2004060159

10 9 8 7 6 5 4 3 2

To my mom and dad—
the world's greatest organizers.
Thanks for teaching me to live
with dignity and ease.
I love you!

Contents

Do not wish to be anything but what you are,
and to be that perfectly.
    —Saint Francis de Sales

It shows up early. We display a penchant for arranging our environment into some type of order in a way that works for us individually. Unfortunately, we often bump up against expectations that can be at odds with our own personal preferences. When what works easily for our brains doesn't match societal, family, school, church, or workplace expectations, we may hear comments such as:

What a mess!
That's not how you were raised!
You know, you're a real slob!
Do it like this!
What in heaven's name are you thinking of?
How do you ever expect to find anything?
That's not okay!
You really *do* need to get organized!
There's a right way and a wrong way and mine is the right way!
When are you going to get with the program?

When our attempts to manage our environment effectively don't meet expectations (ours or those of others), guilt and discouragement can kick in. When we try to meet expectations but our efforts don't match what our brains do easily, we can become exhausted, overwhelmed, or even immobile. Either way, the outcome is less than desirable.

In frustration or desperation we may contact a professional organizer (PO). Our assistant or partner may even make the appointment for us. Presto! In no time the environment gets "organized," usually in the style that works for the PO or that matches "current wisdom." However, two weeks or two months later, things are often pretty much back to where they were in the first place. Why? Because there is a huge difference between what we have learned to do and what our brains do easily.

When we try to sustain a style that is difficult for our brains, the resulting energy drain can sabotage our efforts. Fortunately, there is hope and help. Since your brain is as unique as your thumbprint, it is imperative to discard the old belief that there is only one acceptable way to manage your environment.

The twenty-first century is an especially exciting time in several arenas. For one, PET scans, MRI, and other brain-scanning modalities are making it possible for researchers to observe the way the brain works while the individual is alive. This study has led to the emergence of a new branch of science known as brain function. In short, the tissue inside your skull commonly referred to as the brain can be described in terms of functional layers. One of those layers, the thinking layer or cerebrum, is divided by natural fissures into four sections. Each section contains specific brain functions that can help us perform specific tasks (although, because the brain is so complex, there may be some overlap). Most human beings are believed to possess an innate, energy-efficient, biochemical brain preference for processing information in one of these four sections.

Take Eeny, Meeny, Miney, and Moe: In this allegory, they represent the four sections of the thinking layer and the challenges human beings often face when trying to manage their environment in a way that works for them—especially when their style differs from the "expected":

Eeny is the quintessential there's-a-place-for-everything-and-everything-in-its-place. So much so, that if one thing gets out of place, Eeny has been known to nearly fall apart. It can interfere with his thought processing for hours, even days. In fact, sometimes he can't get back on track until that one thing is back in its place.

Moe wants people (and pets) to be comfortable. He considers them to be far more important than things. Moe is much more interested in how people feel in the environment than in the details of managing inanimate objects. Of course, in the midst of his emphasis on harmony, *things* can get misplaced—even stay misplaced. Oh well, just as long as everyone is happy and there is no conflict . . .

Miney has his head in the proverbial clouds much of the time (at least that's what it seems like to others) doing what he does best: brainstorming, inventing, intuiting, and figuring out how to accomplish things in new ways. He likes to keep everything he is working on within his visual field, usually arranged in stacks and piles. And Miney can get out of sorts quickly if someone moves his stacks. Talk about irritation and energy drain: he has to go through everything again just to remind himself where things are!

Moe wants the environment arranged for functionality. Others need to fit inside his solutions. After all, what are people for but to help him attain goals? Meeny's emphasis is on how his surroundings can support him to set and achieve goals, one right after the other. He prefers to delegate organizational tasks and can get a bit testy and authoritative in an effort to make sure that others manage the environment in the style that works best for him.

Enter Lanna Nakone. She has taken some of the researched conclusions related to brain function, and applied them practically to the art of organizing. This is revolutionizing the typical one-size-fits-all approach to managing one's environment. When she showed up in my office to ask questions about the brain and brain function, her enthusiasm was contagious. We have collaborated, brainstorming ways in which information related to the science of brain function can assist individuals in managing their environments effectively in a style that can be sustained over time because it matches what their brains do easily.

That's what this book is all about. It is designed to help you identify the style that, overall, is easiest for your brain to maintain. Discover it and you'll still be managing your environment effectively two years from now. Lanna presents a plethora of strategies, realizing that even within one general style there will be variations resulting from such factors as gender, level of extroversion or introversion, and sensory preference, to say nothing of self-esteem issues, and the beliefs and attitudes that you absorbed early in childhood.

As the old saying goes: all roads lead to Rome. This holds true when applied to brain function and organizing styles. Recognize that your brain is unique and, therefore, the way in which you manage your environment most easily and successfully is likely to be somewhat unique as well.

The good news is there's plenty of room on this planet for Eeny, Meeny, Miney, Moe—and you. Identifying what your brain does easily can help you make choices toward increased success with reduced energy expenditures. Find your own style, live it, love it, and enjoy the journey.

—Arlene Taylor, Ph.D.
Napa, California

Welcome to Your Brain

It doesn't matter how well you walk the path, if it's not your path.
—Katherine Benziger, Ph.D.

How many times a day do you ask yourself:

Where is that piece of paper?
Where is that phone number?
Where is that other sock?
What did I do with my car keys?
Why do I let the incoming mail pile up unopened?
Why do I consistently procrastinate about certain things?
Why is there always so much to do?
Why do I despise working in that room?
Why can't I throw anything out?
Why does organizing seem so difficult?
Why do I feel that I work so hard every day and still get nothing accomplished?
Why am I so tired and feel like I have no solutions to make things easier?
Why am I always organizing, but still disorganized?

Does any of this sound familiar? You scramble from one project, appointment, or chore to another, only to realize that you are continuing to add more things to your infamous "to-do" list. You run around in circles, grab five minutes to sit down, catch your breath, and look around. You notice your messy office desk, bedroom closet, or kitchen table. Sometimes you have trouble finding things amid all the clutter; other times you purge to such a degree that not much is left. You're tired of doing the "quick tidying up before people come over for dinner" routine and spent from continually passing judgment on your less than perfectly organized environment. You panic just dealing with incoming mail, never mind voice mail and electronic mail. At the end of the day you feel frustrated living in surroundings that don't resonate with who you are. You throw up your hands and admit you don't know what the next step should be. And no, cloning yourself isn't an option, but shopping can be. It is the quick fix to feel better about your life, and yet we wonder why we are buried in things. *U.S. News & World Reports* estimates that the average child sees 40,000 commercials in a single year. As Michael Weiss, author of *The Clustered World*, maintains, "Americans are world-class consumers. It's our favorite indoor sport." Thus making organization kind of tricky.

Don't worry; most people are in your situation. My clients around the world are always so apologetic in requesting help. No matter where you live or how much money you make, the pressure is the same; no one escapes it. Writing this book in service not in judgment, let me indulge in a quick explanation as to why organizing can be such a challenge. One thing is for sure, and that is, wherever we are going as a collective, we are getting there faster and faster. Striving to keep up with ever-increasing societal changes without burning out or breaking down, we talk faster, eat faster, work faster, drive faster, and think faster. Forget multitasking, how about hypertasking? Even Carrie Fisher claims that "instant gratification" takes too long!

When you think back on your childhood, do you honestly remember your parents running around "multitasking"? Was your mom wearing a headset as she balanced the books, fed the baby, and pruned rose-bushes? Was your father on his cell phone driving home, closing deals and learning Russian? What's going on these days? We carry such heavy loads, with so many things to do and see and learn. So many of my clients have so much reading material, trade journals, and health newsletters on their bedside table that it becomes impossible for them to relax. Today it seems that many people have more money than time and prefer things to experiences. Another intrinsic reason for our disorganization is that many of us lack an immediate family support system. Since the average American moves five times in a lifetime, usually farther and farther away from their place of birth, there is less help from the extended family to manage the environment effectively. Added to this is the nature of modern life itself: it's more challenging, more chaotic, with more responsibilities, creating more angst and unease. As the authors of *Dot Calm* states, we all have access overload, information overload and work overload. Even taking a vacation can be stressful.

Clutter beats us up psychologically and physically. It clouds our minds, making it difficult to access what truly matters in our lives. According to Ab Jackson, a fellow organizer, "Are you a person that buys things that you don't need, with money that you don't have, to impress people that you don't even like?" Sound familiar? How reassuring would it be to get organized in a way that not only helps you cope with the basic demands of life but also gives you more energy and joy? How about a way that actually resonates with what is easy for your unique brain? We only have so much life force, so much chi, *pran*, or energy. Why spend it performing tasks that don't match your prewired tendencies? How can we learn to do this with less stress and more grace; even, dare I say, a sense of satisfaction and pleasure? Here is where your own organizing skills can greatly assist you in feeling intact, leading a life that is proactive rather than reactive, purposeful, and ultimately satisfying.

Have you ever considered that the environment you have created to support your needs really isn't that supportive and may even be a hindrance? Maybe the solutions you came up with don't make things easier for you but, perhaps, even harder. What little we know of organizing, we think that there is just one way that serves everyone equally well. I bet that some of you have been walking a path to organization that is *not your path!* Trying to get organized can be counterproductive if you don't use your natural bent or preference to conquer clutter.

As a professional organizer, I have helped all kinds of people find balance and order in their busy lives. I have dealt with every type of person in a variety of situations across the world. To be honest, I have the best career. It's intimate, provides instant gratification for me, but, more important, I help give my clients a brand-new life. Organizing is so much more than putting things in a box labeled "Christmas Decorations." My jobs have included reorganizing 8,000-square-foot mansions, tiny studio apartments, billion-dollar businesses, and companies leasing their very first office space. Behind all of these challenges are people just like you and me, with similar goals and desires. Everyone wants to accomplish more in less time, and everyone wants to have more control over their environment and to be able to live life on their own terms.

Being organized in your own unique style will change your life. You will not only save money and time, but will feel calm, and in more control to make the necessary decisions in life. So often your attempts have failed, and you can't understand why. You bought all the right storage gadgets and even that nifty label maker. And yet, you found yourself buried under old habits and assumptions that kept you from succeeding. That's because underneath all of your piles of paper and office supplies, you never uncovered the true source of your problem.

Here's my little secret: over the years I've realized that the problem isn't with the disorganized individual, or that there is just a lack of space. The actual problem is in the so-called solutions. We have all been told that there is only one way to create a home filing system or store long-term items. However, we all have different styles of thinking and doing. We all have different preferences and natural inclinations. Why do we even think we can squeeze everybody's style into a one-size-fits-all organizing package?

Organizing for Your Brain Type recognizes your innate need to match your style of organizing with your style of thinking. Traditional approaches assume that there is only one way to organize. The implication follows that if you can't do it, then something's wrong with you. You may be judged lazy, irresponsible, or denied a promotion because a superior thinks your desktop should look "neater." Many of my clients, who looked elsewhere for help before coming to me, found themselves lost inside an organizing maze that is foreign to their very being.

It is now time for a very important disclosure. Lanna's definition of being organized is:

"Being able to find what you need *in five minutes or less.*"

I don't care how your solution looks as long as it works for you. Nevertheless, an aesthetic environment, pleasing to the eye, will help you remain organized—as long as it matches your own sensory preference.

If you are searching for a system custom-designed to simplify your life that will actually work, you've come to the right place. This book will help you establish an energy-efficient organizing style that keeps you stimulated and efficient. After reading *Organizing for Your Brain Type*, you will be able to implement solutions that have a lasting impact. And you need look no further than yourself for the answers.

First, I invite you to take the organizing styles quiz on pp. xxi–xxxv and determine your brain function preference. Once you determine whether you are a *Maintaining, Harmonizing, Innovating,* or *Prioritizing Style*, you can make conscious, concerted efforts to rearrange and restructure some of your daily duties so they mirror who you really are. This first quiz will determine which organizing style comes most naturally to you. The following chapters give some guidelines to create a functioning, authentic, and successful organizing system in your home and office. Next, you will learn about your preferred sensory reception in a second quiz (p. 154–156). And, should you need some insight into your boss or spouse ("So *that* explains their behavior!"), you can also read the chapter on their type—but only once you've read, implemented, and mastered your own. So, join me now as I guide you into a more effective way to manage your environment.

What Is My Brain Style?

Instructions: Read each statement and select one answer that most resonates with what you would do in that given situation. Circle the bracketed letter. At the end of the quiz, add up the totals for each letter.

You'll notice that some of these scenarios might seem a little over the top. They are designed to help you clarify how you behave, so exaggeration is sometimes in order. Just have fun figuring out how you function.

1. **You have finally settled down to write your masterpiece. While typing, you notice your dog is looking at you with those huge hungry eyes. You:**
   a. Tell him that you'll feed him the same food, at exactly the same time of day, just like every day, end of discussion.
   b. Your dog never looks hungry because there's always a smorgasbord of food on the floor at all times—his happiness is your happiness.
   c. Throw him your half-eaten doughnut from breakfast and hope he's happy.
   d. Tell him to lie down and wait until you have accomplished what is on your to-do list.

2. **You are about to leave for a short vacation. You:**
   a. Check each item off your checklist as you place it in one of your suitcases. The suitcases are packed, ready to go in advance.
   b. Stay up most of the night packing and repacking, and there has to be room to bring back souvenirs for all your friends and . . . oh dear, it's so difficult to decide what to take and what not to take . . . and . . .
   c. Grab a few essentials and plan to buy whatever else you need when you get there.
   d. Know exactly what you hope to accomplish on this vacation and pack accordingly. It normally takes you a half an hour.

3. **Your daughter comes home from school with, yes, another art project. You:**
   a. Enter its title and the date in the book of "Olivia's Art Projects" and rotate her artwork on the refrigerator weekly.

   b. Try to find a new place to display it even though most everything she has brought home since day one is in its original place.
   c. Proudly display it for a few days and put the latest on top of the previous one.
   d. Analyze it and give her suggestions for improvement.

4. **You are reminded about going to the opera when:**
   a. You check your day planner a day in advance.
   b. You notice Post-its all over the house reminding you of the date and time.
   c. Your tuxedo-clad friend shows up at your doorstep and asks if you're ready to roll.
   d. Your PalmPilot's alarm goes off 15 minutes before you are due to leave.

5. **It is time to think about sending holiday greeting cards. You:**
   a. Retrieve last year's list that you updated the first week in January.
   b. Purchase a ton of cards and mail them to everyone you know, including some people you just met last week.
   c. Wait to receive the cards, then quickly respond by e-mail or with seasonal cards.
   d. Assemble a list of individuals who may be helpful to you in the New Year.

6. **Monthly bills are due. You:**
   a. Pay the bills that are in your tickler file postmarked two days in advance.
   b. Start by gathering all of your supplies, stamps, envelopes, checks, etc., which are all over the house. However, once you begin, you immediately become discouraged because you can't understand how you wracked up so many bills and can't believe you're overdrawn again. You decide to go shopping because you are feeling so stressed out!
   c. Know your bills are somewhere in the stacks that cover every flat surface in your home office and decide to just pay them when you receive past-due notices.
   d. Pay by automatic deduction.

7. **Your son has soccer practice. You:**
   a. Assign him a cubby by the door and label it with his name so he can remember to take his equipment to school with him.
   b. Already running late, quickly pick up anything off the floor that resembles "athletic" wear, throw it in your bag, and take it to the practice.
   c. Help him look for his equipment but get sidetracked onto something else and eventually arrive at practice a half hour late.
   d. Tell him he must be accountable for keeping track of his own equipment.

8. **It is Halloween night and the trick-or-treaters are fast approaching. You:**
   a. Decide to use up last year's candy first, since you only had fifty kids to the previous year's seventy-five, and purchase an additional twenty-five pieces of candy.
   b. When the doorbell rings, you *ooh* and *ah* over the costumes as you drop ten pieces of candy into each bag.
   c. Answer the door as Dracula and scare the kids out of their wits. (Hey, you like Halloween just as much as they do!) You then feel guilty at their terrified faces so give them seconds of candy.
   d. Turn out the house lights and work on a project in a back room so you don't have to deal with them.

9. **Your dinner guest has just rung the doorbell and you want some music on. You:**
   a. Turn on the player in which you have pre-selected six CDs.
   b. Open the door and start singing.
   c. Grab your favorite CD, and when you find the case is empty, switch on the radio.
   d. Tell them to make a selection while you finish preparations for dinner.

10. **Your term paper is due tomorrow. You:**
    a. Put finishing touches to your 20-page report, adding a few more details, and handing it in with the exact specifications of the instructor.
    b. Bribe three friends (with homemade ice cream) to come over and help you with your paper so you don't have to drop the class.
    c. Grab a dozen books; brew a pot of coffee; and pull something together that is quite passable, even brilliant.
    d. Finished your paper a week ago because it is not going to really help your career and immediately started another assignment.

11. **When you go to the library, the books you usually borrow are:**
    a. How-to books on a specific topic and only what you need at that given time.
    b. Nurturing for the soul, romantic novels, or any type of self-help book that makes you and the world feel better.
    c. The first things you see that appeal to your need for variety. After a couple of hours, you walk away with as many books as you can carry.
    d. Brief, to the point, written by the expert in the field. Cliffs Notes are sometimes ideal!

12. **The guests will be arriving shortly for your dinner party and your crème brûlée is overbaked. You:**
    a. Serve raspberry sorbet as you always have 2 pints on hand, just in case of a late night emergency.

   b. Call the deli to deliver something quick because you absolutely cannot serve your friends dinner without dessert.

   c. Bring out the crème brûlée, have a good laugh at its expense, and make a spontaneous trip to 31 Flavors part of the evening festivities.

   d. Announce that desserts are unhealthy and you crossed them off the menu.

13. You feel a bit under the weather and think about visiting your doctor. You:

   a. Call the office on your speed dial and ask to schedule an appointment as soon as possible.

   b. Have his number somewhere but are too sick to find it, so you phone a friend for some ideas on home remedies.

   c. Call the office and tell the receptionist that you are on the way and absolutely have to be seen, *now*.

   d. Take an aspirin and hope you feel better because you have too much to do today. After all, you can always go to the emergency room later.

14. It is finally time for a vacation. You normally:

   a. Prefer to go on an organized tour, or a trip that is planned well in advance, where a change is somewhat unlikely.

   b. Desire to travel in the company of close friends or family and prefer to visit people rather than just places.

   c. Pick a location that you have always wanted to explore. You will decide what to do when you get there.

   d. Enjoy an adventure that requires the use of some mental as well as physical skill—like hunting or even mountain climbing—where results can be measured.

15. When you go to a museum, you:

   a. Get a brochure immediately and go through the exhibit methodically and carefully, even taking notes if need be.

   b. Take a friend, tour the gift shop, and have a cup of coffee before you begin. You enjoy each other's company so much that you only have 15 minutes to view the art before the museum closes. Oh no, not again!

   c. Don't know where to begin. You may even get lost and see things five times, but you don't seem to notice. You always have so much fun even if you lose your friends along the way.

   d. If you can't avoid going, you pick out what you believe is the most important exhibit, view it, and move on.

16. It's the first day of January. You:

   a. Spend the day programming schedules for the entire year into your day planner, which you carry with you at all times.

b. Look at your Polaroids from last night and feel grateful for all your friends. Perhaps you should have the gang over for dinner tonight. Let's begin the year with what really matters!

c. Is it really the new year already? The time goes by so fast because the adventure was so amazing.

d. Nod "Happy New Year" to yourself and begin working on a project immediately. After all, you really want to make this year pay off!

17. You've been invited to your in-laws for a party. You:

a. Schedule the date on your calendar and purchase their favorite bottle of wine well in advance.

b. Bring their favorite dessert because you want everyone to have a great time while they look at the photos from the last family reunion.

c. Just bring yourself, isn't that enough? But you do have a few jokes up your sleeve.

d. Send the rest of the family because you're trying to complete a project and don't have time for socializing, or if you go you only want to spend an hour or so.

18. You just spilled some red wine on your living-room carpet. You:

a. Go to your supply closet, take out the wine stain remover, and clean it up, presto.

b. Start thinking about estimates for new floor covering because you can't possibly entertain your friends with a stained carpet! What would they think?

c. Spread a throw rug over the spot and pray nobody trips over it. And if someone moves the rug, start joking about changing the color scheme to match the spot.

d. Notify the cleaning service to take care of the problem.

19. Spring is here and it's planting time. You:

a. Purchase the same type of plants as last year.

b. Purchase eleven different types of flowers at the grocery store and have a planting party on Easter Sunday.

c. Enjoy designing a garden on paper and then get so busy with other things you realize that the leaves are changing and fall is here.

d. Hire a gardener.

20. You just bought a brand-new car. You:

a. Make a duplicate of the important papers and file them in a safe place.

b. You are so jazzed to show the car to your friends, you leave without the papers and have to go back for them.

    c. Paperwork? The dealer will mail what you need.

    d. Put the paperwork in the glove compartment.

21. You are hosting this year's Super Bowl party. You:

    a. Set up several garbage stations: one for items that can be recycled, one for paper trash, and one for everything else.

    b. Put a fancy garbage bin in the room, decorate it to match the theme of the party.

    c. Let the housekeeper clean up later. You're going to enjoy your friends and then go to bed when everyone leaves.

    d. Instruct everyone to dump their trash in the can at the end of the buffet table.

22. You don't have Tivo yet and it's time to tape your favorite show. You:

    a. Have all your tapes filed in alphabetical order and tape over the one that is the least important to save.

    b. Dash out to the store to buy a tape and miss the first 10 minutes. Rats!

    c. Start sorting through your tapes, only some of which are labeled, and have difficulty deciding which one to pop in—they're all so special!

    d. Have one blank tape, labeled and ready to go.

23. It's your best friend's birthday. You:

    a. Purchased a gift and wrapped it nearly a year ago.

    b. Arrange for dinner at a new restaurant.

    c. Go to your personalized gift box and take out several items. You decide to give all of them because you like them so much.

    d. Buy a gift certificate so the individual can choose his/her own gift.

24. It's tax season. You:

    a. Provide your accountant with the necessary documents/receipts that you have carefully grouped in order and had ready since early January.

    b. Ask for an extension because you just don't have time to go through fourteen shoe boxes filled with various receipts, returns, and other financial papers right now.

    c. Flee the country because you have absolutely no idea where those bits of paper are and hope your file gets lost at the IRS.

    d. Provide your accountant with a summary of your income and expenses and negotiate how you can pay the least possible amount and still be legal.

25. You are reading *Organizing for Your Brain Type*. Chances are, you will:

    a. Read the book in one sitting and immediately follow the directions, step by step.

b. Read it in bits and pieces, ask your friends to read it, and then plan a dinner party to discuss the ideas.
c. Start to read it. Get the gist with enthusiastic vigor and work around the clock getting your room organized.
d. Read key portions of the book and hire someone to implement your decisions.

26. **You're about to begin a new job clear across the country. You:**
a. Pack and move everything ahead of time so you can still take your annual two-week vacation.
b. Have a potluck and enjoy visiting with your friends as you pack.
c. Sell or donate nearly everything so you can start with new stuff, and move with your laptop and a few favorite essentials.
d. Decide on a moving company and instruct them to have everything at your new place on the specified date.

27. **Your boss wants you to be at the office tomorrow morning at 7 a.m. sharp. You:**
a. Set your one reliable alarm clock as you've done since the sixth grade.
b. Tune your clock radio to your favorite music station, set the alarm, and sleep fitfully all night worrying about waking up on time and not disappointing him.
c. Set four alarm clocks to go off 5 minutes apart just to make sure you wake up on time.
d. Program your wristwatch alarm although you're pretty sure you'll wake up without it.

28. **You got the job because of:**
a. Your attention to detail.
b. Your people skills and nurturing ability.
c. Your ability to start new projects with fervor and excitement.
d. Your financial skills and goal planning.

29. **At work, you are known for:**
a. Filing and keeping track of the centralized files.
b. Your capability to smooth over emotional discord.
c. Your creativity, foresight, and envisioning ability.
d. Your financial planning capability and ability to make cost-effective decisions.

30. **Your colleagues see you as someone:**
a. Who can be relied on at all times.
b. Who cares about other people than the job.

    c. Who has a great sense of humor and is full of ideas.
    d. Who will protect them and help them to be successful.

31. At work, you truly enjoy:
    a. Administrative duties.
    b. Planning special events, like the Christmas party, and throughout the year ordering the birthday cakes.
    c. Starting a project and inspiring others to follow in your footsteps.
    d. Making the final decisions for your department or company.

32. At work, you are good at:
    a. Maintaining standards and knowing what the rules are.
    b. Taking the time to listen to what people have to say and building consensus.
    c. Developing a new product line.
    d. Knowing how to win—at all costs!

33. At social events, others see you as:
    a. Showing up and quietly fitting in with the rules of the game.
    b. A chatterbox who talks to everyone present at least once, or twice, or . . .
    c. Off in another world or maybe from another planet.
    d. Missing altogether, unless you have to show up to meet expectations or achieve a goal.

34. To others, your style of managing your environment is seen as:
    a. Pretty close to perfect (at least that's what your mother would say).
    b. Homey, with a lot of personal mementos and inspirational quotes everywhere.
    c. Unique and creative, but how do you know where anything is?
    d. Spartan and functional.

35. During meetings, you often:
    a. Take notes so you can review them before you act upon anything.
    b. Make sure that your fellow colleagues are comfortable and that there are enough snacks for everyone.
    c. Doodle to amuse yourself and try to avoid boredom.
    d. Lead with precise, strategic steps to get the results your organization needs.

36. You normally try to avoid conversations that:
    a. Involve the future or imagining "what if?"
    b. Go into great length or great detail about a specific item.

   c. Deal with figures or strategies or budgets.
   d. Are too touchy-feely.

37. At work, you have a natural ability for:
   a. Bookkeeping and repetitive details.
   b. Being sensitive to the feelings of those around you.
   c. Taking risks and being intuitive.
   d. Logical and critical thinking.

38. Your desktop area can be described as:
   a. Containing all the goodies you use frequently (e.g., in-basket, tickler file, Post-its). Everything close to you has its space and needs to be in that space.
   b. Containing lots of items, but things help you to stay connected to the people in my office, to family at home, to nature . . .
   c. Completely covered with paper—but you know where everything is, you really do!
   d. Clear of everything except the item that you are working on right now.

39. Your filing system is:
   a. Up to date, labeled with computerized labels, and purged biannually.
   b. Color-coordinated with beautiful labels. Purging is *out* because you don't know when someone will request something and you want to be ready!
   c. On, in, and around your desk. Out of sight is out of mind, for you.
   d. Handled by someone else who maintains your reference files while you keep the active files in your office.

40. You are most happy working on a task when your boss:
   a. Gives you clear instructions and a deadline.
   b. Gives you permission to involve others and lets you discuss your progress with him/her any time of the day.
   c. Gives you an idea of what is needed and allows you to experiment with a variety of solutions. Oh yes, and leaves you alone to be creative!
   d. Gives you a specific goal and allows you to decide how best to accomplish it.

41. When you get a promotion, it is almost always because:
   a. You are right on target in terms of meeting deadlines and maintaining product quality.
   b. You have a big heart and a knack for creating a customer-friendly atmosphere.
   c. You have innovative, creative ideas that result in solutions.
   d. You help to achieve enormous financial gains.

42. When you need to lead a meeting, you generally:
   a. Present your company's policy and procedures and encourage members to follow them to the letter.
   b. Opt for a group discussion and hope everyone walks away in general agreement.
   c. Give them a vision of what is possible even if it's never been done before.
   d. Wow them with facts, figures, and graphs.

43. When facing a difficult decision, you are most likely to choose the solution that:
   a. Has a good track record from the past.
   b. Will make the most people happy.
   c. Goes with your feelings.
   d. Is the most logical.

44. When your boss calls you into the office and is displeased, you:
   a. Try desperately to work it out by e-mail but, if you can't, try to come up with an innovative solution that will avoid conflict.
   b. Try to collaborate on a solution that is a win-win for both of you.
   c. Hope you didn't break a rule. You certainly didn't mean to.
   d. Can hardly wait. You're going to win this one!

45. During your annual review, the HR director thinks that you:
   a. Have few interests or hobbies outside of work and worries about you not having fun.
   b. Spend too much time socializing with others on the job.
   c. Are somewhat of a daydreamer and a time waster.
   d. Are somewhat personally detached from those around you.

46. You like to go for lunch with the same people all the time because they:
   a. Are reliable and pleasant.
   b. Care about you and are so encouraging and nurturing.
   c. Always have something new to discuss.
   d. Are decisive and know where they're going.

47. When you prepare a report, you include:
   a. The facts in detail.
   b. Personal insights and feelings about the situation.
   c. A great deal about future possibilities.
   d. An analysis of the figures with suggestions for decisions.

48. The people outside of work that you are drawn to are:
    a. Dependable
    b. Sensitive
    c. Fun
    d. Decisive

49. It's time to give holiday gifts to your staff members, so you:
    a. Buy one present for each person and have it wrapped, tagged, and ready to go the night before.
    b. Go to the mall and purchase two gifts for each person. They deserve it!
    c. Call the nearest Blockbuster and order gift certificates for everyone. You are simply too busy to do this right now.
    d. Delegate the task to someone else.

50. On Saturday morning, you usually:
    a. Enjoy your time alone, reading the paper and having a cup of coffee.
    b. Meet your friends at the neighborhood hangout for breakfast, but not too early, okay?
    c. Look at your alarm clock, roll over, and dose off again—maybe you'll have a really great dream.
    d. Get up early and accomplish a goal or two before noon, if you're lucky.

Results

Write the total number of letters circled in the appropriate columns:

A's	B's	C's	D's

Explanation:
    A's: 20 or more = Maintaining Style
    B's: 20 or more = Harmonizing Style
    C's: 20 or more = Innovating Style
    D's: 20 or more = Prioritizing Style

A's: 20 or more = Maintaining Style

As you may have already guessed, your style enjoys being organized. You need organization like a fish needs water. Your life is most likely already well orchestrated, the result of conscientious planning and consistent implementation. Relying on self-discipline and often a love for maintaining order, you appreciate an environment that makes you feel grounded. Administrative duties come naturally to you and you like to do a job right, one time, every time. You truly enjoy being organized and feel safe and rejuvenated in a structured environment.

If you are already organized, how can this book help you? Perhaps you realize that your style is only getting you so far and you want more tools to help you go beyond where you are now. Perhaps you want to be able to work better with people who have few traditional organizing skills. Or maybe you secretly admit you have so little downtime or time for fun and you want to figure out how to schedule this into your to-do list. You also may be experiencing a lifestyle change or are tiring of being the constant crisis manager at home and work. You can always learn new ways of handling matters more efficiently, particularly in dealing with others who aren't quite like you. Modifying the way you get yourself and those around you organized so that you ultimately gain more self-assurance is what we're after.

B's: 20 or more = Harmonizing Style

Let's face it—you are a humanitarian. You are emotional, spiritual, communicative, empathetic, and your compassion affects others deeply. Since you learn through listening to and sharing ideas, you naturally harmonize with the feelings and experiences of others. You respond to sensory movement, music, discussions, group interaction, and expressions of all kinds of fellowship. Human values and personal growth are subjects that guide your life and lift your soul.

Since you enjoy maintaining things for you family or colleagues, your style falls between the loose and playful Innovating Style and the rigid and precise Maintaining Style. Chances are that you are more stimulated around people rather than possessions and get easily sidetracked when you are trying to get organized. Therefore, time management is a challenge for you. Purging is another skill you have to come to terms with. You can't keep everything—every recipe you ever read in a magazine or all of your ninety-nine Tupperware containers. And no, you don't need to read everything or clip every article to give to a friend. I understand that you need your environment to generate energy for you, but sometimes you get lost and have trouble getting work done. However, you must renegotiate how much stuff you keep and, using a little bit of logic, where you need to keep it. Working and spending time in a harmonious environment where your stuff doesn't rule your behavior but rather helps you stay connected to your surroundings is our goal for you. Together, we can do it!

★C's: 20 or more = Innovating Style

Let's face it, you are the master of innovation! You like to wear different hats, go different directions, think about things in the future tense, and explore endless new possibilities. You can easily get lost in thought, and may fail to notice that the traffic light has changed from red to green. But when you finally become focused, look out! You can easily conceptualize whatever lurks in your imagination and manifest those grand abstractions into a lively and original theory, conversation, or project that feeds your expansive soul.

Out of the four types, your particular style needs to be the loosest and most fun. Yes, you still have to keep your socks in one drawer but they don't have to be graded from light to dark, or from athletic to dress socks. Therefore, things will need to be loosely organized—for example, putting miscellaneous appointments into a planner—but not in the time-consuming ways you may have tried in the past. Traditionally, you have been taught that you need a filing system; well, I'm going to suggest that you don't. Throwing papers into a box labeled IMPORTANT PAPERS could be the only step you take. You are going to be opened up to organizing that is freeing and exhilarating, yet still enables you to be flexible while in control. The ultimate question for you is not where to keep it, but how much of it do you need to keep? You are in for an exciting ride.

D's: 20 or more = Prioritizing Style

You are the rational thinker of this organizing foursome. Where would we all be without you? You are the CEO of leadership, success, financial planning, and personal drive. Theoretical, fact-based, and certainly the most logical style out of the bunch, your technical, financial, competitive, and critical skills all support you as you tackle tough problems to determine rational and realistic solutions. You are also task-centered, action-oriented, efficient, and even ruthless with your daily planner, and you expect your personal goals and work output to be in perfect sync.

Even though you deeply value organization, you have trouble maintaining it or dealing with it. How then can you become organized without doing the work? Delegation is one answer. The amount of clarity you bring to this procedure will determine the level of freedom you will eventually have from basic day-to-day operations.

What if you have no one to delegate to? Then you must simply schedule organizing into your calendar around some activities that thrill you. You tend to have an all-or-nothing style and this book will help motivate you to deal with and maintain your environment in a relaxed yet effective manner. I'm sure you will have no problem committing to various organizing tasks, since you really don't keep a lot of stuff anyway. Remember that you have no problem with purging, but the little that you have to keep must be very well organized and accessible at the drop of a hat. What stresses you out the most is not being able to find something when you need it . . . *now.* You feel nurtured and thrive in an environment that is perfectly organized, even Spartan. In order to achieve a system that is energizing and easy for your style, you will have to learn how to delegate, what you need to keep, and where you need to keep it.

CONCLUSION

> Choose a job you love
> and you'll never work a day in your life.
> —**Confucius**

Studies by Dr. Richard Haier, a professor of psychology in the Department of Pediatrics and longtime researcher of human intelligence at UC Irvine, demonstrate that the brain works up to one hundred times harder when trying to perform activities utilizing functions that don't match our innate talents. This increased energy expenditure can lead to a variety of problems, including diminished success and health. Dr. Arlene Taylor (who wrote the Foreword to this book) suggests that the target for health and energy efficiency is matching 51 percent of your life's activities to what your brain does most easily. That's a doable goal overall, especially when it comes to organizing. Don't forget that it is easier to change how you get organized than to change your personality.

Keep in mind, however, that we tend to overlap slightly with other organizing styles. You may have a high score in another category. No surprise. Sometimes we modify our behavior to meet the expectations of others. Each organizing style can overlap and support another's function in a variety of ways. But if we pay attention and increase our awareness, we can identify the one mode where we tend to "hang out." We only have one area where we truly find our home. It is a challenge answering the questions in the quiz above and getting a total of twenty in any one category, especially when we may have disguised who we really are for the last twenty years. *Who are you? What comes naturally to you?* If you don't figure it out, the organizing system you put into place will not last. But you will notice that when you align your thinking preference with your mode of operation and your environment, your surroundings afford you comfort and stability.

Everyone has the ability to organize in their own style, their own way, their own time. We no longer have one definition of organizing, but four. There is now no excuse why you can't get organized. It is all about using your natural strengths and incorporating them into all organizing system. Believe me, *everyone has the ability to get organized.*

Introduction

How hard it is to hide the sparks of nature.
—William Shakespeare

I have created customized organizing systems for thousands of clients, ranging from individuals overwhelmed by clutter in their home to large-scale corporate offices needing streamlined systems. Across the board, they were embarrassed and even frustrated as they confessed how disorganized they were. I've discovered that almost all of my clients assume being organized means one thing, and one thing only—it's got to be neat, tidy, and put away. No piles. No random arrangements of items on your desk. The *Wall Street Journal* asked fifty-two top executives whom they would promote: (a) Someone with a clean working surface, or (b) someone with a disorganized working surface. What do you think they said? You guessed it. Fifty-one executives said they would promote the individual with the clutter-free desk. It seems the old adage, "A messy desk is the sign of a messy mind," continues to rule.

Most people are happier, healthier, and more productive when their goals are met; they function in accordance to who and what they are. Unfortunately, people can just become stuck, lacking the drive and desire to renegotiate their space, and this inevitably gets worse. It is very hard to work a full week, enjoy your children, have passions and hobbies, and remain successfully organized. I have heard countless cries for help from homemakers, managers, corporate leaders, students, executive secretaries, and even artists who tell me they want to "feel better" about their surroundings. With sincere intentions they read one organization book after another and yet lament that their environment is still a disaster. After taking multiple time management courses, they admit they have no time to implement the ideas presented!

Organizing is a lot like dieting. January 1 you are excited and raring to go. You buy all the right food, make the decision to change your attitude, and look forward to seeing the new you. But by January 15, it's over. Your willpower dwindles, you're hungry all the time and irritable too. The same thing happens with organizing. You buy all the labels, folders, and containers, go through your filing cabinet, and start to fizzle. Am I right? "Clutter," as defined on the Clutterers Anonymous Web site, is "anything we don't need, want, or use that takes our time, energy or space, and destroys our serenity." Clutter can insulate you from the world and make you feel lethargic, overwhelmed, and often depressed. According to Tim Kasser, author of *The High Price of Materialism*, ". . . materialistic values lead people into a style of life and way of experiencing that do a rather poor job satisfying their needs."

The truth is that learning techniques that don't match who you are and how you instinctively do things is a waste of time. Before I share solutions—and there are solutions, I promise you—let's look at some statistics that make managing your environment a necessity for today's lifestyle:

- ☐ Americans spend the equivalent of 4 days every year looking for things
- ☐ The average office employee may spend up to 1 ½ hours a day (6 weeks per year) looking for things
- ☐ Eighty percent of what you file you never look at again
- ☐ Three percent of all paper documents are filed incorrectly
- ☐ Eight percent of documents are eventually lost
- ☐ Most pieces of paper are moved 9 times before they are acted upon
- ☐ The use of office paper rose almost 15 percent in the U.S. between 1995 and 2000
- ☐ The use of office paper has tripled since the birth of the computer
- ☐ Americans receive close to 2 million tons of junk mail every year
- ☐ Each day the Internet superhighway carries over 5 billion e-mails
- ☐ Forty-three million Americans work at home
- ☐ Forty-six thousand American households relocate daily
- ☐ The average 3-bedroom home has 350,000 things in it
- ☐ Americans now sleep 90 minutes less per night than they did in the 1980s
- ☐ In 2003, nearly 10 million people were victims of identity theft

☐ There are 61,000 channel choices from your satellite dish or Direct TV
☐ EBay has 1,562,773 collectible categories
☐ Currently there are 31,000 self-storage facilities in the United States.

We are continually producing more and more clutter because of the transient and cumulative nature of our lives. Yet, while bombarded by more and more stuff, many of us maintain a profound, if not sentimental, connection to what we possess. Things make us feel good—for a little while at least. Then we get anxious about deciding what to keep and what to discard. It's no wonder that with too little time and too much stuff, many people describe themselves as disorganized. Remember, the more stuff you have, the more you have to deal with.

According to *Webster's New World Dictionary,* the verb "to organize" is defined as:

a. to provide with an organic structure;
b. to make into a whole with unified and coherent relationships;
c. to make plans or arrange for.

Interesting! Organic structure. *Organic* is the key word. A style that is natural, whole, and unadulterated. *Organizing for Your Brain Type* is just that, a system based on your own organic preference; a structure that comes from who you are, that allows you to create a comfortable space, to let go of excess, avoid mundane repetition, unleash your creativity, and spend more time on things that ultimately matter. The solutions in this book will allow you to design *your own version of organization,* reteach you what it means to be in control, and accomplish more in less time. Organizing made easy, so you can not only get caught up but keep it up. Your understanding of yourself will help you:

☐ Find things in 5 minutes or less
☐ Identify and respect your own style and direction
☐ Follow through on your commitments
☐ Exude confidence in yourself and your environment
☐ Create time to develop your true passion

☐ Live a style that reflects your personality
☐ Feel in control and more balanced
☐ Feel energized
☐ Thrive

Our goal is to examine the patterns that govern your actions and thoughts throughout the day, *from an organizing perspective*. Knowing your brain type will help you choose options that make you happy. Let's face it; we only have so much energy, and having to do things that aren't easy for you will make you less likely to do them repeatedly. Grounding you in your brain-preference needs renders organizing purposeful and successful. Remember that learning something new and evaluating your lifestyle—what you have done for decades day in and day out—is often disconcerting and can feel a bit strange; but if you want a life that finally gives you a sense of control over your environment, no more attics, basements, or storage units filled with forgotten objects or garages where you can't park your car, this book can help. Why wait?

NEUROSCIENCE HAS THE ANSWERS

I knew there was something I brought to my professional organizing work that was based on more than intuition or talent. I seemed to be successful at tuning into my clients' innate needs and desires to come up with systems that worked for them and they could easily maintain it by themselves. But I sensed that my techniques were about more than just a gut feeling. Over the course of six years, I recorded my thoughts about each and every new job—the original diagnosis of the organizing problem, the specific organizing challenges at hand, my client's behavior, and the eventual outcome. My spreadsheet grew and grew, and behavioral patterns emerged as I searched for answers.

It wasn't until I stumbled onto some applicable brain function research that things took a profound turn. What I learned about the way the brain works supported my own observations that some people do have an innate knack for traditional organizational solutions, while others struggle with convention and need something that reflects their own way of being. The *approach* to organizing was the problem for most people, not the individual's ability or inability to become organized. If the approach offered is not in tune with what truly matters to you, you will tend not to follow through, leaving you—at best—back where you started, feeling worse, and seeing no immediate end to the problem.

Motivation (something that is seldom discussed in most organizing books) is a fundamental component of the organizing game plan. As Jim Ryun, an Olympic medalist, claims: "Motivation is what gets you started. Habit is what keeps you going." When you understand what drives you, what truly motivates you, you are then able to create an environment that facilitates your goals. It frees up space so the new you can step in. There is purpose in how you live.

YOUR BRAIN KNOWS FOUR STYLES OF THINKING

Fortunately, in 2002 I was introduced to Arlene Taylor, a brain function specialist and internationally known speaker. I began to study how she helped people identify their thinking preferences, and how this helped them live in a way that matched their natural inclinations. I needed scientific validation to ensure that everyone can conquer the clutter in his or her own way. Dr. Taylor helped me understand that everyone can get and stay organized. She shared a wealth of information and introduced me to the work of other brain function researchers, including Dr. Katherine Benziger.

Dr. Benziger, creator of the "Benziger Thinking Styles Assessment," combines brain function research with the social/behavioral observations of Carl Jung and a variety of contemporary researchers. One of her findings is that our own innate preferences can either work for us or against us, depending on our awareness. If you are in tune with your natural preferences, you will generally lead a more peaceful, healthier, and less stressful existence. If you are not in tune with your natural preferences, then you may be at higher risk for making mistakes at work or succumbing to fatigue, depression, even disease. What energizes one brain can frustrate another.

Currently, through the use of PET (positron-emission tomography),

MRI (magnetic resonance imaging), and squid (the Superconducting Quantum Interference Device), researchers can now see into and study the living brain. The human brain is comprised of three subsystems: the reptilian core, the limbic system, and the cerebral cortex. The one that concerns us here is the cerebral cortex, which Dr. Benziger claims "is broken down into four essentially equal-sized areas by two intersecting fissures . . ."; she adds that "each of these four areas has its own specialized mode of accessing, as well as its own specialized mode of processing information, based on its unique structure, function and physiology." This sophisticated technology helps illustrate how the "thinking brain" possesses natural preferences. There are valuable quadrants in our thinking brain:

Prioritizing Style   Innovating Style

 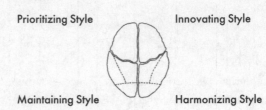

Maintaining Style   Harmonizing Style

1. **The three left posterior lobes** help us to develop and follow routines. People who find these tasks easier than most prefer structure and "traditional" styles of organizing. I call this brain preference the **Maintaining Style**
2. **The three right posterior lobes** help us to develop harmony and connectedness. People who find these tasks easier than most prefer organization that will enhance their relationships and keep the environment peaceful. I call this brain preference the **Harmonizing Style**
3. **The right frontal lobe** helps us to envision the future and make changes. People, who find these tasks easier than most have a unique "stacking" system for managing their environment. I call this brain preference the **Innovating Style**
4. **The left frontal lobe** helps us to set and achieve goals. People who find these tasks easier than most like order but prefer to delegate organizing and maintaining tasks to others. I call this brain preference the **Prioritizing Style**.

Let me introduce you to four individuals, each of whom exhibits a different brain type and thus a different style of managing his/her environment.

MAINTAINING STYLE

Marcy is an office manager for a very large commercial production company in Los Angeles. She keeps the company running in a variety of capacities—accounting, public relations, human resources, she does it all, and very well, I might add! When I met Marcy, I found that she was meticulous, detail-oriented, and loved the regularity of her routine. She began work at 9 a.m. and left right on the dot at 5 p.m. But even Marcy couldn't do *everything*. Since her organizing style was very nearly overkill, with everything addressed in such perfect detail, Marcy often felt exhausted. She wanted quick results and was eager to listen to my principles and put them to work. I helped her to standardize 50 percent of her daily procedures (since 83 percent of all business documents consists of forms), which gave her the time and confidence to handle her other tasks properly. Even though she usually didn't like change, Marcy immediately felt some relief and noticed she was more in control during her workday.

HARMONIZING STYLE

Cindy is a traditional stay-at-home mom who was finding it a challenge to keep things together, especially during the school year when her two sons brought back enormous amounts of homework every weekday. She called me in because she felt like a failure and didn't believe her environment was harmonious for her or her family. She confessed she enjoyed spending time with her family, shopping, and making dinner more than trying to figure out a system to keep track of things. When I came over, I suggested she make a pot of tea, gather all of the paperwork throughout their home, and bring it to the kitchen table. (Note: the atmosphere can greatly set the tone for getting organized.)

With music in the background and freshly baked scones on the table, we created two color-coded, vertical filing stands for each of her children—Jack's in green and Tyson's blue—and put them on the kitchen counter where the boys did their homework. They didn't even need to get off their chairs to file their own papers! (She later let them decorate their files with stickers and photos of their pets.) The boys were able to handle their own assignments with an easy, low-maintenance system, while their mom was in back preparing dinner and talking to them. Cindy was delighted. She felt relieved and happy that she was helping her family and creating a healthy, harmonious home.

INNOVATING STYLE

Monty, a movie studio executive who works on a multitude of projects with numerous producers, writers, and assistants, had his work cut out for him. He needed to have everything in front of him or he would forget about it and waste time recreating the same documents over and over again. A filing system was no solution, and an enormous Hollywood office still wasn't enough. Incidentally, for Monty, lack of office space was rarely the issue. He needed *surface* space for stacking his materials right in front of him, or he was doomed. Being extremely visual, he needed to see things or they would be forgotten.

In any case, Monty wanted better control of his paper. In short order, I brought in a carpenter who created enough shelf space to contain the movie scripts and all the other information needed to produce a motion picture. I suggested that we color code the shelves to help both him and his support staff remember where everything was. Now, when he meets with Jim Carrey, he shows up with the right script!

PRIORITIZING STYLE

Harry, a high-powered CEO, came to my attention through his assistant, Jane, who was experiencing anxiety as she was about to go on maternity leave. Because Jane was in charge of the incoming mail and all of the filing, she was worried that Harry needed to learn the classification system of his company's centralized files. Harry had always viewed filing as a clerical job, but there was no doubt he would need to be able to locate facts and figures while Jane was away. We scheduled a time to examine the situation, and Harry and I spent the afternoon creating a filing system in which he made all the decisions about names for the files that held his reference materials, along with the active files on his desk. Using subject rather than alpha filing categories, and working quickly and succinctly, Harry was able to discriminate what he did and didn't need and quickly learned to locate these documents by himself. By the time Jane left, two weeks later, Harry knew where things were and could do his job without relying on her. When Jane came back, she had the freedom to take on other duties that made her feel more needed and appreciated.

YOUR OWN SENSORY PREFERENCE

Knowing your brain type will allow you to get organized, but how do you really make it stick? To create a truly permanent organizing system, it is just as important to identify your sensory preference as it is to identify your brain type. Psychologists claim that procrastination occurs in rooms that are truly unmotivational. Knowing which of your senses gives you a better understanding of your world and lets you feel comfortable will make you want to work and be in that room. Sometimes, we need to call forth all of the "organizing gods" to get this show on the road. The better we understand every part of ourselves, the more we can be true to ourselves and really flourish. This book will also help you understand how you and others take in information from the outside world and what type of sensory stimuli gets your attention most quickly—be it auditory, visual, or kinesthetic (taste, touch, smell).

As infants, we tend to use all of our senses equally. By the time we enter kindergarten, however, our brain is beginning to identify more strongly with one of the sensory systems over the other two. This is how we develop a sensory preference. Over time we begin to feel most comfortable in environments that provide for and acknowledge this preference. After your brain type is determined and you have read your particular chapter, you can take a quick quiz to find out which sensory preference you use throughout your day.

For those with a visual preference, the brain relates to visual stimuli most quickly. Visuals crave attractive surroundings, often wear stylish clothing, and may enjoy *watching* everything, from television to animals at the zoo. They pick up information about the environment through the way things look and usually prefer face-to-face conversations rather than the phone. It goes without saying that books with lots of photos, graphics, and illustrations appeal to them.

An auditory preference, on the other hand, indicates that the brain relates to sound stimuli most quickly. Auditories tend to learn a lot about a situation by the tone of someone's voice or the sounds that catch their attention. They appreciate the joy of written communication and are often active, attentive listeners. Naturally, music and speech contribute to their self-expression. By the same token, they are often very sensitive to noise.

A kinesthetic preference occurs when the brain relates to touch, taste, and odor stimuli most quickly. Being sensitive to their environment, kinesthetics are very concerned with aspects of comfort—in furniture, clothing, even physical touch. They are often profoundly sensitive to odor, temperature, and texture, and pick up cues quickly from their surroundings. And since they relate to the world through touch, they may be very particular about whom they touch or who touches them!

When we create an environment that acknowledges and honors our sensory preference, we feel "together," validated, confident, and successful. Combined with the knowledge of our own particular thinking style, this enables us to interact with the world and those in it more effectively. Ultimately we can manage our environment in ways that make sense, feel good, and last.

HOW TO USE THIS BOOK

Organizing for Your Brain Type contains two quizzes (at pp. xxi and 154). You will be able to quickly ascertain "What brain type am I?" and "What sensory preference am I?" The answers to these questions will help you discover your natural preferences for managing your environment, so you can get organized right now *and* sustain the systems you develop with the least amount of stress. You will also learn how to identify other people's natural organizing tendencies and use this knowledge to create a more harmonious workplace and home environment.

Once you've identified your brain type, go to that chapter to discover specific strategies to organize your home and office quickly and effectively. You'll find that you can build on your natural preferences quite easily and then absolutely flourish in your surroundings. You'll also learn important time management tricks that can free up time for other passions and activities. In the last chapter, chapter 6, you will probably have a lot of laughs and learn a great deal about how you can deal with other people who think and function rather differently.

Remember that organizing can be a little bit of drudgery and some motivation is required. Thus, if you start with the things that really inspire you, matter to you, and motivate you throughout the course of the day, this task will be more meaningful and gain some depth. Creating an environment that supports your deepest goals and desires, you will enjoy the process of setting up organizing systems throughout the house. Finally, there is a real reason for these actions. You need to see the purpose behind what you are doing in order to want to remain organized. Don't forget to have fun in the process

ORGANIZING
FOR YOUR
BRAIN TYPE

Chapter One

Maintaining Style

The heavens themselves, the planets, and this center
Observe degree, priority, and place,
Insisture, course, proportion, season, form,
Office, and custom, in all line of order.
        —William Shakespeare, Ulysses in *Troilus and*
        Cressida, 1.3. 85–88

Let's start by stroking your ego. *You deserve it!* You see, your natural style matches societal expectations for the desirable organizational solution and the rest of us have been trying to emulate you throughout the ages. It's true, you are the epitome of efficiency, meticulous systematization, and clarity. Your work environment and home reflect a sense of reasonable order. No clutter. No piles. A place for everything and everything in its place. You are the technique specialist and like to keep yourself up to date with the latest approaches to ensure that you are doing your job well. So join me as you learn how to maximize your strengths and shed some light on new and proven ways to generate more energy, develop more skills, and increase your personal success.

Now, take a deep breath. For those of you who scored low in this section, you still use some of this type of methodical thinking for basic survival and efficiency. Although you may not feel comfortable using these skills for too long at a time, take solace in realizing that some of these techniques could give you a leg up, so it's a good idea to get to know this brain type. If a coworker, spouse, child, or friend is one of these amazing organizational types, reading this chapter will help you figure out what makes them tick and how you two can work better together.

Okay, Maintaining Style, you tend to prefer having specific steps you can follow, right down to the letter. I assure you, a custom-made methodology is coming! (Lots of bulleted points are right around the corner. You will be able to easily check them off, one by one, so you can incorporate them immediately into your daily routine.) However, let's first explore the way you do things, and see if we can better understand how you could manage your environment effectively.

Relinquish a bit of control and let me support you. I know that that isn't your style. You prefer to have the directions, your car all tuned up, your lunch beside you, a map open, and know exactly what is expected of you once you arrive. Here is your agenda for this chapter:

- How your brain type works
- Why do you need help?
- How to manage your environment in your own style
- The details
- The strengths and challenges of your brain
- Organizing your time
- Organizing your home
- Organizing your office
- Conclusion
- Overview of the Maintaining Style

I will help you set up a structure for organizing that will be easy for you to understand, maintain, and—most important—enjoy. Don't worry about how to implement any of these ideas right away. You are likely already a highly productive worker and you may only need to tweak a little of this and that. Ultimately, all of these insights and tools will strengthen your belief in your inherent talents.

Even though you like to work alone, we will work together in dissecting some of your daily actions. This will give us insight into how you can shift your perception of what you are doing in order to achieve more ease and calm. This new relaxation will actually enhance your ability to achieve even more in a way that makes you feel confident and powerful.

HOW YOUR BRAIN TYPE WORKS

> Order and simplification
> are the first steps toward the master of the subject.
> —Thomas Mann, *The Magic Mountain*

Your brain is blessed with the ability to understand work, activities, and life in general by following proven routines. With your linear, structured style, you focus on details and develop effective methods that allow you to manage tasks and complete assignments, checking them off one by one. Your work style isn't about speed, but reflects a methodical approach that usually requires uninterrupted time to get the job done. Being slow-paced, deliberate, and sequential, your brain type prefers doing things in a way that can appear to others as somewhat boring. But who cares, you do it right the first time and would rather take the time to be right than the first one done! Since you tend to be traditional and a somewhat conservative planner, you follow the rules. But that's your innate way, and it works just fine, combined with doing things in the same order, preferably at the same time of day. To you, routine is the proper and precise way to work. As you say, "If you are going to do it, do it right." Which way is right? Your way, of course!

You prefer to classify information in either chronological or alphabetical order. You may even have your own organizational system that you've developed and always use. (For example, A, B, C . . . 1, 2, 3 . . . I, II, III. . . .) You then typically store that information in a neat and conscientious way—since you are the "maintainer of info"—that still provides you with easy, stress-free retrieval when it is urgently requested for a meeting. Being the implementer of planned agendas and guidance, you don't like to just wing it. That would feel very uncomfortable and may even cause you to panic.

The tasks you need to perform on any given day are typically listed in your day planner. Being incredibly specific about your time commitments, even weekend time is included, and notes are structured in a step-by-step, timely fashion. You are able to schedule with accuracy, since you've done the same procedures a hundred times and know just how long they take.

Uniformity brings you consistency and accuracy—time and time again. Where you feel most comfortable many others feel stifled, or uninspired. By doing what has been previously done, your brain finds comfort and success as you continually use proven techniques. Others see you as productive because you don't waste time trying to reinvent the wheel. You tend to work methodically and are very thorough in all that you do. You find it easier to begin a project when you know how it was done in the past. And depending on your sensory preference, you would either prefer to see it done (visual), read or hear about it (auditory), or participate in a hands-on demonstration (kinesthetic).

The two biggest enemies to your comfort zone are interruption and surprise. As a result, change, in any shape or form, can cause stress and may even make you so confused that you find it difficult to get back on track. Your schedule may turn upside down if one thing gets out of place. In managing time, the crux of your dilemma is trying to complete tasks when things around you are hectic and present frequent interruptions. Take a deep breath. And then another. Remember, you are always willing to spend the time to get organized and that you are in control of your surroundings.

New things and new approaches can cause you discomfort. You overcome your fear of change when you see that a new procedure has proven effective. It takes a lot for you to move into unknown territory. Therefore, when you are asked to do something new, you may want to ask specific questions that you have written down first. You need first to understand why you are doing it that way, process it, and then do it. You think before you move. That way you are able to gather your wits, get the details straight, and plan a face-to-face meeting.

You receive recognition from your family or coworkers most often when you are able to integrate facts and figures with procedures that are already in place. By being able to report sequentially, in projects and correspondence, you can help your superiors "look good" at work. By maintaining and retrieving documents, you help them to make quick and accurate decisions. You offer good value wherever you go. You may not appear flashy, but you are the reliable behind-the-scenes person who systematizes routine tasks easily and effortlessly.

You also tend to be the quintessential keeper of all the paperwork, facts, figures, and policies in your organization. Thank God, someone knows the rules! When in doubt or need of something, your coworkers or family members always ask you, "Where is the . . . ?" And you always know! Your tax returns are filed on time; kids are picked up from school; and Christmas presents arrive before December 25. All of us owe a lot to you. Our world and families depend on you. When I lecture to various CEOs around the world, most of them crave working with someone like you, and other than their intimate partner, you may be the most important asset in their lives.

WHY DO YOU NEED HELP?

> Never before have we had so little time in which to do
> so much.
> —**Franklin D. Roosevelt**

During the past few years, 60 percent of my clients have been people like you—people who are very well organized but who are very stressed out keeping it all together. We work side by side and enjoy the process of discussing organizational skills. When I work with the rest of my client base, it's a different story. They normally disappear the moment I arrive. They want me to "take care of it" and are unnerved by the process of organizing, period.

Why do I work with your type the most? First, you are aware of the fact that so many people depend on you and you need to have everything in good order and easily accessible. Second, you, more than anyone, know the value of organizing, how beneficial it can be to your life, and are therefore willing to spend the time and the money to do it. Third, you are likely to stick to a new set of daily routines if they are explained to you and you see the value in them. You enjoy collecting the "right" supplies and ideas that make organizing work.

Learning to maximize your unique organizing talents is the name of the game. Once in a while you may fall into the "working harder and not smarter" category. It's rare, but it happens. Sometimes false deadlines can be a strong motivator for you. This may be due to one of two issues that go hand-in-hand. You are either up against your "perfectionism" or "trying to keep it all together 24/7." Let's briefly examine these two points.

First, perfection can be a wonderful motivational tool. But on the dark side it can kill you. Remember Marcy, the office manager at the production company in LA? She is one of the most cautious and deliberate people I have ever met. She knows details like no other—where every penny goes, where to find last year's launch campaign paraphernalia, and so on. She is the blood that runs through the company's veins. Her main organizing problem is that she must do things perfectly all of the time or she won't do them. If the label maker is broken, she won't even think about writing on a file folder tab with a marker (even though her handwriting was impeccable). She will wait until it is fixed and then work like a madwoman getting it all done. Since she doesn't trust anyone else to do the job and her standards are so over the top, she feels stressed most of the time. Even though she prefers to work her regular hours she will put in extra time, but preferably with advance notice, and will worry that it is all done correctly.

Second, let's face it, you do receive enormous pressure from most people, at work and at home to keep it all organized and easier *for them*. It is important for you not to lower your standards even if you have to pick up all the DVDs and put them in order after the kids go to bed. You have to find a balance where things are easy enough to let other people assist you in maintaining your own impeccable standards. This is one of the ways that you can allow other people to contribute without your having to be 100 percent involved all of the time.

HOW TO MANAGE YOUR ENVIRONMENT IN YOUR OWN STYLE

Let all things be done decently and in order.
—I Corinthians 14:4

Yes, you can improve your already well organized office, home, closet, and car. You appreciate that it requires a lot of work to manage all of the tasks in your life from scheduling a tetanus shot for your daughter to finding the folder that your boss needs *now*. You are probably methodical and somewhat rigid in how you define your space. Storage, therefore, is key: how much to keep and easy access to it. This should be easy for you since you pretty much know where things are at all times anyway. It is just the bulk that is at issue. Remember, *your task is to enjoy organizing*—something that you do easily and so well.

For you, the secret lies in maintenance. Below, you will find strategies you can modify depending on your lifestyle or what is expected of you in job-related tasks. Some things can be done weekly, monthly, or annually rather than daily. For example: daily—incoming mail; monthly—financial/bills; annually—reviewing personal files, bank statements, seasonal clothing, and so on. The process needs to be *practical* and uniform or you'll burn out in no time. Do what is easy for you, since you are probably going to be the only one maintaining a great deal of information. Some people may see you as a *neat freak*—everything lined up in order, linear and sequential. You prefer not to share equipment, files, etc., with other people if you can help it. At work it may be helpful to have a file card (an index card works well for this) for people to mark and put in the file drawer when they have removed a file. This can work well in situations that are very paper intensive, as at law firms or real estate offices. In a residential setting it may help to have specific rooms, cupboards, or drawers set up your way, even if that is different from your partner's. Just remember that for you, every object has a place and you may be the person who is expected to return things to their place at the end of the day. There is another important element that can support your unique organizing style: learning how to choose supplies and furniture that make your life easier. You need no-nonsense solutions. Objects such as computer equipment, various pieces of furniture, storage pieces, and boxes must be practical and stored neatly and in order. Aesthetics are not a huge issue for you. Colorful supplies or snazzy gadgets don't make that big of a difference for you. You can work almost anywhere and get the job done. What is crucial is that you must have easy access to the equipment and supplies you use every day.

Another crucial point in designing a lifestyle that really works for you is time management. By having time to plan and set up a productive yet reasonable schedule, you will be able to institute step-by-step procedures that help you feel good at the end of the day. Spending the appropriate time to plan out your day will be extremely beneficial. With your reliability and follow-through, you may find some extra free time and maybe even take a break.

THE DETAILS

> God is in the details.
> —**Ludwig Mies van der Rohe**

While the Innovating Style individual likes the big picture, you are all about the details. You tend to recall facts and figures easier than many others and as a result are able to cut through confusion and chaos time and time again. You look for errors all the time and prefer to give accurate and exact information. The more you approach your life in a detail-oriented fashion, the more likely you will feel that you can manage your surroundings effectively. People rely on you for specific answers, which you like to have at the drop of a hat. Labeling everything accurately, with no mistakes, is important so you can readily access those pieces of paper. Computer labeling or a label maker can help you. Marcy's labels are what most professional organizers want to see when they get to heaven. Perfect-looking: right font, right placement, uniform meaning, completely consistent.

THE STRENGTHS AND CHALLENGES
OF YOUR BRAIN

Quietness is indeed a sign of strength.
—Franz Kafka

Here are some typical traits I've observed in people with your brain type. This list will help you understand why some things happen the way they do and why you tend to respond one way or another.

Strengths
1. Organized—in the traditional sense of the word
2. Perfection-driven
3. Detailed-oriented
4. Accurate
5. Practical thinker
6. Sequential thinker
7. Reliable
8. Disciplined
9. Serious
10. Able to follow and maintain procedures and rules
11. Able to think ahead to the next step
12. Make decisions methodically based on proven techniques
13. Industrious
14. Predictable
15. Cautious
16. Sensible
17. Habitual
18. Respectful
19. Punctual
20. Consistent
21. Quality-centered
22. Responsible
23. Good speller
24. Able to write legibly

25. Loyal
26. A team player

Challenges

1. Unhappy with disorganization
2. Take a long time to make a decision
3. Dislike anything new, especially if unproven
4. Rigid about routines
5. Emotionally closed
6. Uncomfortable with unstructured time
7. Seen by others as boring or dull due to resistance to change
8. Prefer not to share
9. Obsessive
10. Uncomfortable being interrupted
11. Critical
12. Isolated
13. Narrow-minded
14. Unrelenting

ORGANIZING YOUR TIME

> Order is not pressure, which is imposed on society from without, but an equilibrium, which is set up from within.
> **—José Ortega y Gasset**

Ultimately, time isn't all that challenging for you; you're a natural planner. You rely on a daily calendar and are known to maintain long and very specific to-do lists. If you can spend adequate time preparing for your day in a way that is very specific, using a calendar that is easy to update and carry with you, you will create a successful road map that will garner much success and respect from those around you, especially when you present a detailed plan to manage a project or even record accurate minutes of a board meeting. Since you live by a daily routine, you need sufficient time to finish what you start and to wrap things up.

Your big time-related issue is how to combat interruptions. Anything that takes away from your schedule can cause enormous stress and lack of productivity. Remember that a half hour planned is four hours saved. Plan a little time into the schedule for interruptions or getting the most difficult task done when you have the most energy and more time to do it. This will make the interruptions less painful. When you have a plan of attack, you are able to be interrupted, but then you know where to return to. It becomes an important anchor in your day. Then at the end of your day you won't regret having spoken to this person or done something that wasn't on your list.

Time is such a tricky subject, but much easier for you than most. For the most part you make it work for, not against you. Below, I discuss some of your Maintaining Style strengths and challenges when it comes to time. Once aware of them, you are apt not only to make changes but also to improve upon my suggestions. That's your style. You'll schedule them into your week and make it happen. Remember, this isn't about giving you more tasks to complete. It is really about giving you the opportunity to do things in the correct fashion so you can feel comfortable throughout the day and enormously satisfied at the end of every day.

Strengths
- You get things done. Procrastination is not likely. You do it all, whether you like it or not.
- Steady, very productive work.
- You know your office supplies. The office supply store is a good friend and you take the time to find a PDA planner or wall calendar that works.
- Patience is your virtue.
- Checklists: Very important and easy for you—whether it's a grocery list or event planning. Use them. They save you lots of time.
- Forms—make them, use them, and enjoy them.
- You value the time of those around you. But do they value your time? Probably not equally. Think about this. Stick to your schedule rather than conforming to those around you.
- Time limits for any given task.

- To-do lists for every hour in the day, not just a-week-at-a-glance. Chances are you record these in a book or your electronic database, rather than trying to remember them off the top of your head.
- Mid-size, not long-term goals. Though you are very committed once a goal has been established.

Challenges

- Interruptions: If possible, laminate a sign of some sort—perhaps a hand motioning STOP—to be put up on either a corkboard or your office door. If you work in a cubicle, putting it on the back side of the computer monitor would work. You can even send an e-mail to those around you and let them know when you are working with deadlines. Obviously, at work you will be challenged, but there is always a way around this. Consolidate tasks, so if you are interrupted, you know exactly where to get back to. Here, your passion for punctuality will greatly benefit you.
- Telephone: An average incoming call takes 7–12 minutes and an average outgoing call 5–7 minutes. Try to make calls rather than receive them.
- Purchase a headset. If anyone can multitask, you can!
- Flexibility: Try to stick to your schedule the best you can—I know that makes you happiest—but if things come up, be willing to adapt. Since you always know where you're going, you will be able to return. This can be a difficult issue with colleagues or your family.
- Leave time in your life for emergencies. Don't take them personally.
- Doing things in a new way. Flexibility can be a good thing. By expanding concepts, skills, and anything else that shines new light on what you do well, you will develop skills that create a good working environment.
- Find estimates on how long things take, not just for you but for others. Unless you live and work by yourself, which you probably don't, realize that time for all of the other brain types is a bit of a challenge. It will serve you well in the long run.
- Delegation: You would much rather do something yourself without insisting and explaining over and over again and doubting the compe-

tence of the person you are delegating to. Still, you may want to see delegation as an option in the future.

- Schedule fun in your calendar. Just a little!

> Time is the most valuable thing a man can spend.
> —Theophrastus

You are the epitome of "on time, all the time." You usually know exactly what you are doing, 24/7. Ask yourself, "Can I improve my time management skills?" and "What is ultimately important to me?" You can learn a couple of quick time-saving techniques—ones that will feel comfortable structurally, but that will go beyond the obvious to align you with your deepest values and desires. It's important to have regular work hours, but it's also important to have regular hours for other kinds of activities. You can achieve 100 percent accuracy in repeating routines and can enjoy the repetition as though it is an art form, as long as you decide how it fits into the goals. You understand that practice does make perfect and can build accuracy and success. You are in good company. Franz Kafka worked his regular hours as a clerk for an insurance firm in Prague, and then every night after work he would write for a very specific amount of time. Year in, year out, nothing out of the ordinary. Always specific, exact, and with great attention to detail. Another great thinker, Immanuel Kant, the German philosopher, had a schedule that ran like clockwork. People always knew when it was noon because everyday at 12:00 he would walk in front of town hall, pause, and then continue on his way to the market. Kant was very productive, exhibiting no surprise behavior, but conforming to the rules in a way that worked remarkably well for him. He was very clear in his actions and had the capability to see and follow the necessary steps to get it all done. Let's get going. I know that you, more than any other brain type, can hear the clock ticking.

Your Calendar

Your ultimate perception of time derives from perceiving it as allotted for a task or project and then breaking it down into step-by-step increments. Obviously you desperately need a calendar that takes into account the whole picture.

For any project you are involved in, you must allow some time for unknown factors. You literally need to enter changes, setup time, cleanup time, and whatever else, leaving no stone unturned. It's all about feeling in sync with who you are and opening up to a united front. This is very empowering for you: to take your calendar seriously, sticking to it every day, and yet to remain free for the unexpected. Challenging—but you are tenacious enough to master it!

Recently, I helped organize a very talented, enormously dependable individual who is personal assistant to a famous Hollywood personality. (She hired me because she wanted her home office files to be A+. When I arrived, they were already A, but she wanted perfect.) She said that her desk at the office worked efficiently, but she needed to tweak her home files so they would correspond better with the work files. She felt out of control, worried, and ineffective because things were not consolidated when she got home. Scheduling this into her calendar made her uneasy because it was going to be a new process for her. With all of my clients, I let them know that we must work a minimum of four hours together to see any quality results. After the four hours we were almost done, and she had a little work to do on her own. Luckily, she had scheduled two hours of free time that afternoon and could complete her organizing homework without feeling out of sync with her schedule.

How Others Perceive Your Use of Time

Since you are pretty predictable, other brain types may view you as being a bit dull and boring. How dare they! But to them it seems like you leave very little room for spontaneity or fun, since almost every second is scheduled. Friends and family might feel a bit stifled and restricted. On a holiday they might perceive a lack of time to just hang out and "get lost." They may ask, "Why do you need to know what you're doing all the time?" Other brain types realize you don't like interruptions. But your love of structure and uniformity makes you a loyal, dependable, and very reliable friend, coworker, boss, or mate. This need not be interpreted as limiting. Since you usually know what you are doing and where you are going at all times, your mind is free to think about other things. If the other brain types could learn one thing from you, it would be that structure does allow for freedom. For you, time management is really stress management.

Your calendar—whether paper or electronic—must support your natural inclination to be punctual and efficient by avoiding ambiguity and unpredictability. Your love of detail and sequential order—not in subject categories but rather as alphabetized files, chronological order, and step-by-step procedures—needs to be addressed when searching out a workable calendar. Since you prefer more traditional systems, you thrive on respected approaches to organizing your time. You value consistency, accuracy, and predictability both at home and at the office. Therefore, time management is a crucial component in ensuring that you are satisfied. More than any other brain type, you aspire to get everything accomplished as assigned.

Let's take your natural inclination and make it work for you. I will provide you with a linear approach to how you organize your time that has been hugely successful for clients with your brain type, from executives and office managers to stay-at-home parents.

Scheduling

You will need to have a watch and clock available at all times. Knowing exactly what time of day it is all day long helps keep you calm and on target. Wear a watch and put several clocks in strategic locations. Uniformity works best for you. Nothing trendy or unproven; the more basic or traditional the better. Everything must be written down from your to-do list to schedules in your planner. Then nothing will be forgotten and you will feel thrilled when everything is completed. Another thing to keep in mind is that you need to lay out your schedule either last thing at night or first thing in the morning so you can get all your thoughts onto a piece of paper. Spending fifteen minutes to see that you are headed in the right direction could have numerous payoffs.

#1. Day Planner

A day planner is your best friend. No questions asked. Without it, you are lost. How well you schedule things in your calendar and how you keep track of various appointments can either sink or save you. This is the most important investment you can make. Compared to the other brain types, for whom exact minute-to-minute calculations are unnecessary, you perceive a calendar as a necessary appendage to your body. How you survive in this world, how you feel comfortable and nurtured every day, may depend on how you organize your day planner (having chosen the right one) and how you use it in the long run.

There are four generic calendar versions:

- The typical desk or wall calendar—that works well for general activities in the home or office.
- A paper calendar, which is great for those who are not computer-savvy or who prefer handwriting their appointments and contact information.
- Various computer programs such as **Outlook, Act, Lotus Notes**, etc.
- Handheld PDAs, which cater to those on the go and working in a corporate environment. You can even hot-sync this to your main computer database software and have one rather than two calendars.

Your day planner must include a generic appointment book, a database, and a to-do list. (Goal planning, special password, or ID may be included.)

You need to know what is happening 24/7, including weekends and holidays. You may even bring your day planner on holiday—off to Disneyland knowing that from 10:15 to 10:45, "It's a Small World After All," and from 10:46 to 11:30 you are on the Matterhorn Bobsleds, and so on. A client of mine enters everything she does every day of her life in her tiny monthly calendar and keeps it for future reference. She likes to look back and review where she ate, what movie she saw years ago. A bit extreme, but it worked for her. Your day planner should consist of:

- A daily page with specific times from when you awake to when you go to bed. Hours on the left-hand column, with a view of the day or week and even month to follow. (You need to decide what works best for you—and that depends on the demands your job places on you.) You need an hour-to-hour calendar, but whether your future follow-up is weekly, monthly, or annually is up to you.
- Adequate spacing for quarterly or 30-minute increments rather than hourly appointments, and a daily and weekly glance rather than a weekly and monthly one. The more you are able to pinpoint the exact time, the better. If you work from home, your day planner needs to correspond to the one in the office.
- If you travel a lot, a PDA would be more than adequate for all your needs. If you enjoy writing and aren't that technically savvy, a Franklin Covey Planner may be more than enough.
- Room to grow and change as the need arises. That may mean extra pages in the back for ideas or additional lists, a memo pad, etc.

Remember Marcy, in the Introduction, who ran the entire production company almost by herself? Her day planner was the most impressive I've ever seen. She had an enormous monthly desk calendar that she personally enlarged at Kinko's and filled in herself. She prioritized tasks by color coding them, using a highlighter, and crossing them off in red once completed. Her calendar looked like a piece of art, some colors assigned to different duties. She scheduled personal administrative time and creative administrative time for planning throughout the day. That is key for you, too. This way she felt safe and organized, knowing what was coming next. She continually put things in her calendar as they came up. If she happened, for example, to be taking notes at the company's monthly meeting or receiving a telephone call later that day, she jotted down scheduling information in a small notebook and transferred it to her main calendar later on. This approach allowed her to know what had to be accomplished tomorrow and the rest of the week. It was simple, easy to maintain, plus it provided a record of what she did and where she went. What an inspiration to us all.

#2. Your To-do List

This is your road map for action. With your calendar and this list in hand, you are on your way to record accomplishments. You will be able to jot down errands and other tasks as they occur to you and then add them to your to-do list, which puts the entire system into gear. Depending on your professional situation and whether you have numerous to-do's to accomplish, you can create a specific folder for them and go through them in your downtime. The more specific you are, the better you will be able to track tasks in a way that leaves you rejuvenated and motivated. When you start to feel stressed, chances are it is because you did not give yourself enough time to do the task. Normally, you are on track for getting it all done. But don't forget to breathe and smell the flowers. There is more to life than just checking off your to-do list.

A to-do list is the center from which your day unfolds. First, decide what duties you would like to get done, and schedule them in your calendar. The two work hand-in-hand and you can enjoy this process: what to do and when to do it. Try to match up your short-term tasks with your long-term plan. Focus on that particular day, and include everything on the to-do list. Then, you can begin the next day's list with a concrete plan that will encourage you for the rest of the day. Starting with our passion can give us enough energy to get it all done. This brings us to the next topic—prioritization.

Priorities are defined by Webster's as putting items in "preceding order of importance." Traditionally, you know what needs to be done, and most of the time you have the ability to accomplish everything. Sometimes you get stressed trying to do this on time. One client had over sixty things on his to-do list when I arrived. I didn't know if I should laugh or cry. He said he was stressed and needed to simplify his life. *Really?*

I encourage you to take your to-do list and rank each item in order of need-to-accomplish. This isn't anything new, but come at it from a place of passion, not from something inauthentic. The point is that once consolidated into the categories below, it is much easier for you to attack specific categories at specific times of the day. I have suggested to executive secretaries that they rank all their tasks as follows:

- **Must**—meaning now or today
- **Should**—meaning later today or this week
- **Could**—meaning whenever free time comes up (chances are this category is just a security blanket and most items never need get done that land in here)
- **Or, Hot, Warm, Cold . . . A, B, C . . . 1,2,3 . . . Today, Weekly, Monthly, Buffer . . . Focus, Free . . .** *whatever motivates you and lets you separate priorities into concrete, usable, easy-to-remember categories*

Set up three baskets or file folders to put all of those various pieces of paper where you can deal with them later, or a vertical file stand that lets you see them easier. (Vertical stands that have ascending steps work great for this. Having a tickler file, something on your desk that "tickles" your memory may change your life!) However, you tend to work better with horizontal in-trays than the other brain preferences. Sometimes, this means doing the difficult thing first and then working down the list. I prefer to tackle some of the more challenging items first thing in the morning and then do a "Could" list of the easy ones so that by noon I've done four to six of the things on my list. Sometimes, it's a case of alternating complex and simple tasks. I strongly advise that you allow no more than fifteen items on your to-do list; ten is more reasonable and reassuring. Everything you do should inspire you to move on, complete something else, and feel rejuvenated.

#3. Electronic Organizing
- Preferred communication style in the modern world.
- You most definitely prefer to communicate with people electronically rather than face-to-face.
- Database system for your calendar and all of your contacts. **Outlook** is easier and more universally used, but **ACT** is more specific and elaborate. **Palm** software should not be used—it is not specific and simply not as good for your brain preference.
- Get to know your computer software systems. I have witnessed several clients not using these to their full ability and unaware of the elaborate features they have to offer, e.g., you can color certain ac-

tions in **Outlook** that help you know what is important and what isn't. Contact your company's IT person for further clarification.

- Print hard copy as backup. This doesn't mean you have to use it, especially if you enjoy your computer, but it can be filed away. On more than one occasion I've seen clients lose important data due to computer failure. Back up your data regularly.
- PDAs are a must if you work outside the home and have a family. Don't forget that your calendar is important to you and you need to have it with you—at all times.
- A Rolodex for business cards? *No way!* Get rid of them (you could donate them to your church). They tend to get too bulky and make you work to find a specific business card. Purchase a business card binder for those contacts that are just professional and for names of contacts that you don't use regularly.

#4. Paper
- **Franklin Covey** traditional planner, or **Avery, Filofax, Day Runner,** or **Eldon**. Any spiral-bound book that is commonly used.
- Think of the size above all else before purchasing. Bigger isn't necessarily better. Ask yourself which one fits your purse or briefcase. But keep in mind that smaller isn't better either, because you are overly detailed yet need to carry it around with you.
- Quarterly to half hour increments preferred.
- Daily and weekly viewing.
- Monthly and annually viewing in back.
- Desktop calendar is a good idea but hard to take with you.
- Binder with business card pockets to be sectioned by category and purged annually.

ORGANIZING YOUR HOME

> Strength of a nation is derived from the integrity of its
> homes.
> —**Confucius**

Your home is traditionally seen as being very well organized. As you
are reading this section, you probably occasionally look up and glance
around at your surroundings—which are in great shape—and smile.
You enjoy putting things in their place, filing, (even making labels for
anyone who needs them), and using the various containers you store belongings in. Typical books on organizing that stress a similar formula
such as "Eliminate, Organize, Containerize, and Strategize" work for
you and really no one else! You think systematically. That is a great at-
tribute in setting up a traditional organizing system.

Some of your favorite tasks appear very routine, nothing fancy: paying bills, buying groceries, folding your clothes, organizing, cooking,
and so on. Your traditional routines, like paying bills on Thursday night,
shopping for groceries on Sunday afternoon, and folding your clothes
immediately out of the dryer, ensure that your home is well organized
from top to bottom. Your version of creativity is being organized.

Your main fundamental questions on the home front are: "How much
to keep?" and "Where to keep it?" Storage is a key element. Since you
are likely to maintain all of your family's needs, not just for today but
also what they may need for tomorrow, such as memorabilia, off-season
items, and so on, you have to remember where you put them. That is
why having a master list for storage, or even a record of where you can
locate a certain piece of paper, just as they have in a library, can be
beneficial. When someone in your home needs something, you are the
person they likely come looking for. If you are not home, things are so
well laid out that they will hopefully have no trouble finding it.

Try to maintain a system that can be effective for several years—
perhaps indefinitely, depending on the different things that happen in
your life, such as moving, having a child, and so on. Life changes can

challenge your well-crafted organizing system. If you are planning any major changes, such as relocating or having a baby, keep them in mind before setting up your organizing system and reserve additional space in your garage, dresser drawers, or filing cabinets.

Purging—eliminating things—can be a challenge for you. Don't keep everything; be discriminating as this will be easier on you in the long run. Set up perimeters of how long you need something before you start to purge that area. Most often, you keep things you perceive as useful. However, try to donate unnecessary residential goods to various charities or recycling centers; in most states you can receive tax deductions. It is a win-win situation.

Allan kept every tax return he had ever filed, along with the relevant paperwork, in cardboard banker's boxes. He was in his late sixties and moving to be closer to his grandkids in Florida. For many years he paid the price of a storage unit, over $200 a month, to store more than fifty boxes that could have been shredded years earlier. I suggested he consult with an accountant. It turned out that he found out he only needed to keep information for a certain number of years. Once he knew that, he had no problem disposing of past paper. His money could now be spent on his grandchildren instead of a storage unit!

Your ability to manage your environment may appear to the other brain types as overly neat, anal, perfect—even stifling. But for you it is just right. Since you don't do well under stress, you cope better when you are master of your surroundings. You can become frustrated when you have to find things (scrambling through the house to find the theater tickets for that evening's performance), since it isn't planned in your schedule to have to look for something.

Another key factor in keeping things organized at home and in the office is to spend the time *labeling* things nicely, neatly, so that they are easy for you to retrieve even if they are on a high shelf or at the back of a filing cabinet. You are a master at legibility—a black marker may do the trick. Or you might prefer to purchase a label maker. Computer labels work, too, and you are probably really good at that. But they work better for creating an entire filing system than when used to label just one box. Labeling has to be done in order for you to finish the process.

For you, this aesthetic dimension is just as important as what you are putting away for easy retrieval. You're the only brain type that thrives on this. One client told me that when she died, in her coffin would be her dog's ashes and her label maker!

You need little time to relax. You like to make things perfect—to work, tidy up, put things away. The risk is that you may do and do and do until you fall into bed exhausted, just sinking down after a hard day keeping it all together. Organizing in a way that builds on your strengths will prevent you from burning out. When a system works for you for years, you are less likely to try to change things and implement something new and original. But there are engaging time-saving techniques. Keep an open mind. Here are a few specific ideas.

#1. Design

> Set thine house in order.
> —II Kings 20:1

Design is better known as "space planning" to a professional organizer. Utilitarianism is your prime concern, with extra space for storage items where aesthetics come in second: purpose and function over style and pattern. If you feel comfortable in a room, you will stay and get the necessary things done. Being conscious of this will make organizing easier. But the simpler the better. For example, metal filing cabinets may look more industrial than wicker basket filing boxes, but they will neatly contain your files and make you happier in the long run. You store a lot of information, and having a design structure will prove enormously beneficial in your daily routine.

Use subdued tones—maybe two-toned as you don't like anything too flashy. Muted colors are good so that you are able to concentrate on a particular task and not be distracted. When going through a store, look for objects that are brown, dark gray, or black, solid and square. Think angular, not round or cushiony. Function rather than flare dictates your design preferences, and you are not anxious to rearrange. An example of this could be purchasing a coffee table. Choosing one with enclosed storage—where you can't see what's in the drawers—would be a plus for you. Think about function over design and you will come out a winner.

Your furniture and the flow of your living space must be properly set up at the beginning because what you keep can be challenging to move when the volume increases over time. So, you first must examine what the task or activity is, then design your space with the appropriate gadgets. Assess the situation at hand *before* the carpenters arrive. Knowing how much you have and how much you really need to store is pivotal when purchasing new accessories for the home. You not only have things to store but need to get things done in the most efficient, timely manner possible.

When you purchase electronic gadgets, you need to understand them clearly to max out their benefit. Spend time to get familiar with how things work (i.e., what cycle your delicate clothes should be subjected to, what temperature will wash your Tupperware). Again, this will make you feel comfortable in your surroundings.

#2. Storage

Storage can be a problem. One of the many organizing rules is, "One in and one out." But you already know this! The problem you encounter will be how long you need to keep things and what kind of storage is appropriate for the size of the items.

Purging can pose difficulties for the best of us, but you tend to have little emotional attachment to things. Having predetermined criteria and familiarizing yourself with them makes the task more logical and you will be more sure of yourself and what you are doing. Check your policy and procedure manuals, or ask someone like your accountant about what it is required that you keep— say for tax-related issues.

Once you have determined on what you wish to keep, built-in, closed, and fixed storage will benefit your style the most. You are likely to measure things to a T, knowing how much of this and that you have and where you want to put it.

- **Built-ins**—may cost a little more money, but last a very long time. Normally they can easily be added onto and look fantastic!

- **Closed**—like a closet door, or a curtain. Here you don't have to see what you have, since normally you have a pretty great idea where things are.
- **Fixed storage**—storage that is created for one purpose—e.g., a shelf that pops up for your blender or ironing board.

Most drawers work best with divided storage. Use the hooking drawer dividers that come in a multitude of sizes; or the drawer dividers that you actually measure to fit your drawers, made for every type of item. The various drawers in the kitchen may take time to set up but will be more accurate for those unusual-sized corkscrews, baking paraphernalia, and other seldom-used items. It is very easy to work. You could also purchase plastic strips that can be cut to fit any drawer. They come in different heights from ½ to 1½ inches and you only have to cut the length to make it work. Stackable baskets work quite nicely for drawers as well as cupboard storage and can be labeled on the side. If money is an issue, try to use an old shoe box for larger items and an old check box for little things. There are many ways to get organized without having to spend an enormous amount of money.

Plastic boxes are my absolute favorite. Cardboard storage is on its way out. They are of clear, lightweight plastic that prevents mold and mildew. They come in a variety of sizes:

- **6 qt**—Shoes, crayons
- **16 qt**—Dishes
- **32 qt**—Linens, records
- **66 qt**—Seasonal decorations.
- **90 qt**—Ski clothing

These boxes are amazing for many reasons. They can store an enormous amount of family items without being burdensome to move around. They have snapping handles that open easily. They come in many sizes and can be stacked one on top of another. A must for long-term storage of any kind. They are great for you and your Innovative Style friend, who likes to stack all of his belongings. Remember, it is great to stick to one brandname—never buy organizing paraphernalia on a whim. Think before you buy!

Depending on your space, clothing may either have to be rotated after every season or stored in perfect order, light to dark, short to long, and so on. This requires a lot of maintenance but looks great. Clothing that needs to be hung can be stored in plastic or cloth with a cedar block.

I have yet to be in a home where memorabilia wasn't a huge issue. Again, store items, such as your college jacket or a box that once held something meaningful, in plastic boxes. They are relatively inexpensive, lightweight, and can hold high school yearbooks in a container as big as a banker's box. Also, it is ideal to keep negatives in a safety deposit box. You probably already have a box where you put the photos and the negatives together. One company, University Products, has created archival storage that is just superb: they have fantastic boxes to store photos in and you could easily fit a year of family photos into one box, rather than multiple boxes that could get lost. Family members can each have their own box or sort chronologically. You can create archives that are easy to maintain. Take charge in this area ASAP, otherwise it takes a very long time to catch up. Perhaps you could with the current items and work your way back, in case you already are behind!

It is crucial that these boxes are labeled in the same corner on both sides. There is nothing more annoying then taking the time to get organized, labeling a box to store someplace, and then realizing it can only be stored one way—the side the label isn't on! Go figure! Sure, many labels are removable. I simply would rather label both sides and be ready for action. Remember, consolidation at this stage comes in handy. Labeling storage boxes, cupboards, and shelves can help every family member, regardless of their brain type.

#3. Paper

"The little things are infinitely the most important."
—Sherlock Holmes

Paper is a challenge for most of us. You may already have systems in place such as accordion files for seasonal papers—taxes and memorabilia—regular file folders with matching hanging files prepared with matching tabs to ensure easily classification and upkeep. Can I move in with you? Just kidding! Since you are so adept at this, more than likely you also have extra systems in the back for future use. Labeling, again, is an important step for you and creating a centralized filing system at home can be rewarding and validating. To be honest, it is an essential component in your happiness. (I would recommend that you create a similar filing system to the one you have at work—same colors, tabs, sizes, etc. The more uniformity the better.) But if you can, try to go letter, not legal; you will save so much more space. If your file cabinet is legal-sized. Switch the brackets to fit lettersize. Avoid using legal hanging files with letter interior files. A few quick and important points for you:

- Since you tend to store a lot of things, use binder clips rather than paperclips for paper in a file folder. Paperclips tend to get caught and if you refer to your papers a lot, they can be bothersome.
- Two-inch for files. If larger, they are too thick; you must subdivide.
- Two-inch bottom hanging files for larger items. Rather than opening a file drawer to find different heights that make it difficult to see what is behind, this is a great solution.
- Accordion hanging files are very appropriate for you as they easily contain various paper sizes.
- Either use 2- or 3-inch tabs.
- Tabs should be located at the front of the hanging folder. Otherwise, when a document gets bulky, you will be unable to see the tab that is in back.
- Spending time zigzagging title tabs would be great for you. There's nothing like looking at a beautiful filing system, and you would have no trouble maintaining it. (*Other brain types—don't even think about it!*)
- Schedule regular maintenance appointments for paper documents— biannually would be sufficient. And once you've gotten things in control, annually would be fine.
- Get to know your local office supply store and what works for you. Time well spent.

A desk is essential. A filing cabinet either in your home office or in the garage would also reflect the order you crave, especially when it comes to paper. You must ascertain what size filing you prefer. Since you keep a multitude of documents, it is best to have a lateral filing cabinet where files can be easily stored. I'm a fan of letter file folders because they are easier to handle, but in your particular case legal files could be preferable. At home, a letter filing cabinet is preferable.

Color coding may or may not work for you. It could serve just as well to use the army green hanging file with the manila file folders. It is less overall maintenance in the long run, and normally every filing cabinet drawer will be subject specific enough for you to retrieve a certain document. Remember, finding documents isn't an issue for you. Many professional organizers suggest that if there is one piece of paper in each hanging file, your system isn't working. However, you can handle this and wouldn't find it at all frustrating. But you will eventually need more filing cabinet space then the other brain types, since you are apt to use each hanging file for each item and they take up more room. That's fine if you have the space for it.

It is very convenient to specify a place to drop off incoming mail and parcels at home—an actual location with a recycling bin and a shredder close at hand, too. You tend to try to file paper in your home office or your tickler filing system immediately; however, a basket may be more efficient. This could seem strange at first, but in time you may like the feeling of being relaxed and not having to file things the moment you come home. You naturally enjoy organizing; but creating a specific place and time for those activities in your calendar can give you more room to enjoy your passions in life. Avoid being a slave to the organizing component of maintenance. You will never feel caught up completely. This is all about feeling better about yourself, not worse.

Identifying which papers to keep is part of effective maintenance. Be careful about purging when it comes to catalogues, magazines, or paperwork in general. This may sound strange, especially coming from a professional organizer, but I've met people who have thrown something out and needed it moments later. If you have qualms about throwing something out, keep it for a few days or weeks, write the date on the front and then purge. It can be frustrating trying to recreate something or spending the time to go online or to the library to find some information you just tossed out. Purging is a good thing, but only when performed with a plan, as you know.

The storing of various papers depends on how you use them daily. Obviously, on your desk is a place for "active" files. Your storage files, or "archival" files, can either be stored in a filing cabinet or a banker's box by your desk. Storage is pretty simple. But it must be gone through periodically to determine if what you are storing is still important to you.

Lastly, you do well with written lists, which truly maximize your efficiency. You keep things moving forward by having lists that you can quickly check off—tracking what you did and what must still be done to ensure you won't forget anything. Periodically, you must update these lists, including database, calendar, and any other directories you use.

ORGANIZING YOUR OFFICE

Not long ago when I walked into the *Napa Valley Register* office, I noticed part of it was organized one way and the rest another way. Some cubicles were exceptionally neat, and I just knew that they managed reference material effectively. A typical desk boasted matched containers, staples, pens, pencils, paperclips. Everything was in its place: calendar on one side, timer in front, a to-do list placed on the arm of the computer, and traditional music playing in the background.

For you, an office is a place to work. And work with few interruptions. Let's review your work style and then create an organizing system that supports that. You:

- Prefer written forms of communication and are more likely to focus on policies and procedures for mediating a conflict than personal feelings.
- Need time to review important documents.
- Are likely to read instructions slowly before operating any new equipment or beginning a new assignment.
- Need more time in staff meetings to digest the information and then put it to use.

- Need specifics in doing a new task that you haven't performed before.
- Like to think and have a plan before you jump.
- Think rules are important and define undertakings at work.
- Are notorious for completing assignments on time.
- Thrive on routines and need an organizing system that supports them.
- Prefer regular hours, similar jobs, day in day out.
- Need machines that are productive and efficient.
- Enjoy compiling, recording, and maintaining papers and documents.
- Like to work with things rather than ideas.
- Achieve enormous satisfaction when your skills match the tasks to be accomplished.

Your own office needs to have all the amenities for getting the job done, minimizing clutter so that you are able to create reports, keep the minutes of meetings, mistake-free. You are less concerned with appearance and more with performance. Staying simple yet practical is the best organizing style for you. Having technological gadgets at your fingertips and extra office supplies in your office rather than the supply room can help create an environment of efficiency and control. Having extra filing folders in the back of your file drawer, ready to go, would be one of the solutions.

Review your daily schedule throughout the day or at least at the end of each day. You excel at getting things done on time. Just take time to smell the roses, and be jubilant about your talents.

#1. Electronic Organizing

Computer organizing can match your talents and be something you really enjoy doing. Your methodical reasoning and ability to organize in a sequential manner give you the capacity to master a variety of databases, from something like Outlook to more complex entry systems such as Act to financial and spreadsheet software such as QuickBooks and Excel. Name it and you can do it! Backing up daily, you are also willing to spend time learning the steps required for a specific program. Your computer can become an appendage, a friend, something you rely on, that gives you immediate support when you need to find an item pronto. More than likely, you also interact with your computer quickly. For example, if you receive an e-mail, it's quite probable you will either respond or relocate it to an electronic file folder immediately. You are not the type that prints stuff out unnecessarily.

Whether it is researching an item on the Web, shopping online, or communicating with friends and coworkers, you enjoy staying on top of things. Which approaches can best optimize your electronic organizing strategies? Since you are ultimately the one who maintains the electronic files (you are probably the residential office Excel expert), computer proficiency is a given. The more you can finesse how you store and retrieve documents, the better. E-mail communication was made for you. You thrive and actually are more relaxed using this method than most.

Clear-cut classification systems, as in your paper filing systems, must be created first or printed out as a reminder of exactly where to find things. It is more difficult finding a document that is lost electronically than a hard copy. Since you tend to keep the most and your colleagues tend to come to you when they need something, be very careful how you categorize your electronic files. Since you tend to be discriminating when it comes to what you do and don't need, you probably devote scheduled time to selecting what software is best for each organizational challenge. Receiving so many e-mails and documents daily, it is necessary not only to file well but also to purge well. Give yourself the gift of a monthly purge of electronic documents. By scheduling this into your calendar, you will save time down the line, guaranteed, especially when one of your superiors needs something important at the drop of a hat. With less stuff, what's important will be easier to access.

CONCLUSION

> All things are not only in a constant state of change,
> but they are the cause of constant and infinite change
> in other things.
> —Marcus Aurelius

Overall, the strengths of your natural talents cannot be underestimated. You offer a service that helps others to connect with ideas, people, or make big financial decisions. Traditional organizing skills are greatly needed for our business to expand and our home life to be enjoyable. Ultimately you provide services that the other brain preferences all require. Organizing for you isn't a huge challenge—you are wired with the right equipment to find it easy and beneficial. But the amount of documents, books, and so on that you need to feel comfortable and confident can get out of hand. Nonetheless, you enjoy organizing and are more than happy to keep it up and spend the time necessary to do just that.

Be very clear on what you need to keep, for how long, and where it should be located before you spend the necessary time to do this well. Appropriate labeling and containers will serve you nicely if you plan for them carefully.

Change is uncomfortable for you, but you probably won't have to do much of it. Tweak little things here and there, and notice how doing things a little differently can improve your life. Remember that 75 percent of other people likely approach organizing in a different way. This isn't good or bad. It's just different. It's all about different strokes for different folks. Go with what works for you naturally.

Getting Started:
For Example—
Household Paper Clutter
1. Plan on setting aside a certain day and goal. A minimum 4 hours of uninterrupted time is preferred.
2. Have all supplies ready to go—labeler, files, etc.

3. Gather all the paper in the entire house.
4. Go to your office and presort into thematic piles, e.g.: "Bills to pay," "Action."
5. Deal with each presorted pile on its own terms. All of the "Bills to pay," then all of the "Actions."
6. Toss out and recycle old articles, magazines, or manuals where you no longer own the product.
7. File the remaining documents in your filing cabinet.
8. Purge remaining files. Quickly review.
9. Create a linear structure for all remaining desktop supplies to store incoming paper and magazines.
10. Install a maintenance program in your calendar either to continue what you started or to begin a new project.

OVERVIEW OF THE MAINTAINING STYLE

Purpose: To produce and provide services dependently.

Organization of Space: Structured and rigid about this. "A place for everything and everything in its place" is your motto.

Strengths: You maintain the status quo by labeling, filing, and retrieving data with detail and accuracy. Prefer that labels, styles, and linear products match.

Challenges: To handle being interrupted, being asked to think outside the box, or to be artistically creative.

Time
Calendar: Prefers one calendar where daily/weekly viewing is shown and to keep specific schedules in fifteen-minute increments (even weekends). The more specific, the better.

To-do List: Utilizes checklists, plans in advance. Every action has a plan behind it.

Goals: To complete assignments accurately and on time, paying attention to detail.

Contacts: Maintained in one master location or place.

Paper
Incoming Mail: Put it in a horizontal tray and sort at a designated time. There is usually an in and out box.

Desktop: Everything earns its space, and items that are used daily are lined up in linear fashion.

Filing System: Use filing cabinets (in desk drawers—weekly use; in credenza—monthly use). Files are alpha filed, often using a specific kind of labeling system. Periodically purge on a predetermined schedule.

Closets
Closets: You keep like with like in order of type, size, style, length, use, etc.

Drawers: Each drawer contains specific items in exact order for size, style, or use.

Storage: Utilitarian containers—do not have to be visible. May keep master list of what is stored.

Purging: Based on predetermined criteria of what your accountant or company demands.

Memorabilia: You like to take photos, to record the date, and store them with the negatives. You label the box appropriately and will keep it indefinitely.

Chapter Two

Harmonizing Style

> Simplify your life. Don't waste the years struggling for things that are unimportant. Don't burden yourself with possessions. Keep your needs and wants simple and enjoy what you have. . . . Don't destroy your peace of mind by looking back, worrying about the past. Live in the present; enjoy the present. Simplify!
> —**Henry David Thoreau,** *Walden*

Your top priority is maintaining an effective environment where others feel welcome and appreciated. Your home is inviting, with music playing and candles burning. At work your office is warm and friendly, filled with lots of light, with tea brewing, and comfortable chairs. You love to make a nest and surround yourself with deeply personal things, each imbued with special meaning. A stark Spartan workspace with one lone pen and an open file folder would not match your spirit and could prevent you from feeling satisfied and complete. That type of empty space just isn't for you.

Since you prefer a less "traditional" organizing style, the mantra "a place for everything and everything in its place" works less well for you. I officially give you permission to forget about that saying forever. Instead, I encourage you to tackle managing your environment in a new way. You are no doubt playing "catch-up" rather than "keep-up." Initially it can be tough, but chances are you won't be in this situation again, and with the right tools, you can emerge triumphant. I call it the "one clutter pocket at a time" approach. Once you understand the concept, you can really flourish.

Traditional organizing styles can be drudgery for you. Being relationship-oriented, you may maximize your energy by inviting a friend or colleague over to help. Try, if you can, to invite someone who not only gives you encouragement and focus but also is impartial about your belongings. This "organizing buddy" can help you set realistic goals and deadlines and install systems that last. The process of clearing the clutter needs to be fun. However, be discriminate in who you choose to assist you.

It is sometimes a challenge for you to request help in getting organized because you don't like to inconvenience anyone. You are definitely more people-centered than task-centered. For example, Priscilla tends to run here and there, nonstop. She dedicates everything she does to ensuring the happiness of her children, husband, and friends. She may stay up until two in the morning doing paperwork and getting her three children's lunches ready for school. But being so sensitive to others' needs—and ignoring your own—can be dangerous. She will let her personal tasks go to spend time with her immediate family. Values are her top priority. An unselfish person, who is generously helpful, she easily works behind the scenes without public recognition. Where the Maintaining Style has to learn to schedule fun in, you must learn to schedule *yourself* in . . . at least sometimes. As Michelle Passoff, the author of *Lighten Up!*, puts it: "The time that you designate . . . should be considered sacred, and honoring it is to honor yourself."

You may even worry that spending time clearing the decks takes away from time spent with others. That's part of the reason you feel organizationally challenged. Since you are a peacemaker, you suppress your own feelings so that others aren't hurt. However, people tend to take advantage of your good nature since you extend yourself to meet their needs at your own expense. You need to treat yourself to this same type of TLC. This trip down the organizing road has to be concerned with your needs first. I give you 100 percent permission for this to be all about you. When we go through this process, you aren't going to dispose of something and think, "Why toss it when I can give it to a friend?" *No!* Choose to toss, recycle, or have one donation pickup.

The energy you spend on examining and improving your own day-to-day organizing style will make your life less hectic, more tranquil, and can eventually give you far more time to spend with those you love. Your loved ones, in turn, will have more of your undivided attention—which of course makes you even happier. Your preference for connecting with others is crucial to understanding what makes you tick. It speaks volumes about why you need to have so much stuff around you—even though you probably have no idea what is stored in your attic or basement as you read this. Since your fundamental desire is to care for and be in the company of others, you also love to care for and be in the company of stuff that people may need to want. These supplies make you feel good, and it's okay to keep them. Wow, what a radical statement, something that is truly shunned by almost all organizing methodologies!

Let's face it. *You love your nest!* Does this sound familiar? At home and in the office, you have photos of friends and family, pretty cut flowers or exotic plants, a special one-of-a-kind china mug your best friend made, and so on. Both home and office have personality and come alive with little touches, the special objects you've collected from places here and there. All of this gives you a sense of well-being and identity. It stimulates you. It reminds you who you are. But you still need to manage your environment in your own way so that you can find things but not worry about the overall appearance. Rather than "a place for everything and everything in its place," Michelle Passoff, who is a professional organizer, suggests: "a path for everything and everything on its path." This can help you find more peace and harmony.

Let's start with setting ten immediate rules that will make you feel rejuvenated:

1. "To clip or not to clip, that is the question." I give you permission to stop clipping. Even though it is fun for you, you normally don't know where to put such items, and your close friends or family don't want them.
2. Say no to coupons—unless you see one and immediately realize you are out of that product. Coupons require a lot of upkeep; you don't have proper storage space; and more important, you will end up buying things you probably don't need.
3. Try not to save every greeting card. Review them each year and keep the ones that really mean something to you. You can also recycle the picture, cut it with special scrapbook scissors, and use it as a gift tag.

4. If something is broken and isn't that meaningful or valuable; toss or recycle it. Chances are you won't ever fix it.

5. Magazines: I only allow you 5 subscriptions. No questions asked. I give you one for every week of the month and one extra one because I like you. If you receive the new one and haven't gone through the old one, *out it goes!* I mean it.

6. Catalogs: If possible, look online. If you, like so many of my clients, receive a bazillion catalogs, go through them immediately and either toss them or, if you are serious about ordering something, do it immediately.

7. Don't take the hotel toiletries or be a matchbox collector. Don't hoard 100 shopping bags that become unruly and a nuisance.

8. Recipes: Are people still eating that orange Jell-O coleslaw salad? Probably not. Sure it's easy to glance over the page and think it sounds good—even though you don't even have half the ingredients, chances are you won't ever make it, and you will have many reminders of how inefficient you are as a parent. I think not!

9. Don't keep things you have had forever and never used. If you haven't used something in 10 years, such as a big bag of old elastic bands, toss it out.

10. Last, try not to shop in bulk—unless you have a large family. Extra paper products are necessary, but not eighteen bottles of Spray 'n Wash. I allow you to keep one for backup and that's it! Who has the room or the time to keep this all together?

Every person's organizing style is just as unique as his/her brain. To you, organizing means *I put things where I know I can find them easily.* Good for you! It's a fun approach to a somewhat dry topic. But it doesn't always optimize how you run your day, and it doesn't always help you take care of business. Remember that all belongings are a symbol of the past. Chronic lateness or chronic busyness may drive you, but at the end of the day, it depletes you. You have trouble saying no to anyone, even when you are already overbooked. Chances are that you work more out of necessity than pleasure. By choosing to take care of some of the unnecessary clutter now and making some simple, colorful changes, you will create a more harmonious life and can make a huge contribution to your family at home or at work. Yes, even you can find some elements of joy in getting and staying organized. If the Web site www.flylady.net works for you, great. But don't be a slave to reading those daily affirmations and get absorbed in this Web site. Your connections to people can really be deepened and improved.

A big piece of the organizing puzzle for you is renegotiating what you have and where you need to keep it. We are going to do this together. My theory is that 75 percent of the population would rather do anything than get organized. For you, it must be simple and fun. The end result should be to give you more time to spend with people rather than continually maintaining stuff. People are your number one priority. Your house or office needs to give you a feeling of collegiality, harmony, and joy. Together, we can create a comfortable environment for you and develop a style that is warm *and* effective.

HOW YOUR BRAIN TYPE WORKS

> Stop choosing between chaos and order, and live at the boundary between them, where rest and action move together.
> —Rainer Maria Rilke

Your brain likes to manage your environment harmoniously to achieve a sense of unity, togetherness, and reliability. You thrive in the realm of the concrete here and now. You don't hear just one note; rather, you hear the melody created by all the notes. No wonder you are known for your moves on the dance floor and enjoy singing in the shower!

You bring a concept of unity to all the various parts until they are in harmony—in your own way and your own style. Your number one talent is your ability to build goodwill wherever you go. You may make special efforts to celebrate a coworker's birthday, or know when someone is hurting and needs a shoulder to cry on. You can absorb information to help you assess how someone feels by how they look or sound, not just by what they say. Picking up nonverbal cues is how you sense subtle differences. Your highly expressive nature instinctually reaches out to comfort, encourage, and relate through gestures, actions, and words. This can enhance your own feelings of safety and comfort. The C words are what it is all about for you—caring, consensus, cooperation, community, connection, communication, and contacts. Your personality gives you a direction for the reasons why you need to stay organized.

Since you tend to believe in spirit, you are able to read the body language of nonverbals better than any other brain type and you can pick up a great deal in a conversation. You use e-mail, but prefer talking to someone or hearing their voice on the phone so you can decipher the conversation by reading body language and the subtleties of human expression. For you, the spoken word is about much more than passing on information.

Some people use communication as a tool to check off something on a to-do list. You talk and use your computer or fax machine as ways to connect with those around you. You like to transmit ideas, but also to relay your feelings and emotions. You tend to reach out and connect with a greeting card or a phone message. You follow your hunch as the determining factor when making a decision such as hiring someone; past work experiences or credentials are not the only criteria. Margret, a Canadian CEO who was a genius in her work, continually engaged her employees on a very appropriate yet personal level. People came first, over profits; she never forgot someone's birthday or their anniversary with the company. It is interesting to note that her first corporate job was running a human resources department, where people's concerns were the bottom line.

Spirituality and human connection nurture you above all else. You are often engaged in some form of spiritual practice, whatever allows you to connect with your higher power, whether it be prayer, dance, even gazing in awe at a waterfall. Connection with your environment, which gives you a feeling of harmony and wholeness, is what helps you to thrive. Your holistic lifestyle, environment, and attitude give you divergent ideas about life and love.

The way your brain thinks and feels leads us to a number of conclusions. You:

- Thrive in open spaces
- Need to be comfortable
- Have an "in the moment" attitude to time management
- Love nature
- Tend to enjoy music
- Skip around from this to that
- Have an ability to empower others
- Enjoy people over things
- Would drop anything in order to help someone
- Inspire loyalty

These are all qualities that we are not going to change or eliminate. Rather, we are going to celebrate them in designing a more organized lifestyle, one that is going to be easier for you.

WHY DO YOU NEED HELP?

> It is much easier to keep up than to catch up.
> —Toni Ahlgren, *Organize Your Stuff:*
> *The Lazy Way*

Getting organized can be a challenge and may feel overwhelming since you don't naturally possess some of the traditional organizing skills. "Who needs them?" you say. "I just didn't come out that way." It's true; you are often bored by detail, precision, logic, long-range thinking, and repetition. When you set up organizing goals, you tend to run into problems because you find it difficult to set time limits to get it all done. To top it off, you don't really like change one single bit unless it makes it easier to connect to others. But wait. You picked up this book, didn't you? Just take a moment to reflect on the main reasons more organization could benefit your life. Really feel out the answers. Consider the skills and talents you possess that will help you manage your environment in your own way. Ready?

Since you are driven by your mood, not your calendar, feelings can trample schedule. You like to go with the flow. That works and is fun, but not all the time. For example, if you needed to pick someone up at a specific time and forgot because you were talking to your sister who was really upset, your whole schedule could be thrown off. You can't please everyone in your life every minute; but you can develop a more conscientious approach to streamlining. The goal is to figure out how to keep you on track in a way that is harmonious.

You need permission to be kind to yourself while working through this. Take frequent breaks to connect with people and chat about this and that during the organizing session. Relationship-building breaks can give you the energy to do less favorite tasks. Also, since you do thrive when people appreciate what you do for them, ask for feedback so that you get recognition for your contributions. Setting up minimeetings that support people by expressing appreciation for another can brighten everyone's week. Feeling connected in any capacity makes you feel more sure of yourself, more at ease, and therefore better able to focus on the task at hand.

Your style way be a challenge to getting things done on time. This is no surprise, but it can hurt to see it spelled out. You are not a clock-watcher and you may not be accustomed to sequencing daily or weekly tasks. Setting up regular hours to get things done (and that includes organizing) can and does work. The secret is to weave these tasks into your day between other meaningful events. "Sandwiching" can work if you dislike a task, e.g., filing, that doesn't match your brain preference. Your deep motivation of connection must be present to feel driven. In order to be successful in organizing, it is imperative that you develop a plan to do the things that you really would rather not do. Therefore, it is especially important for you to be aware of your highest and lowest energy levels in order to complete duties you dislike. Yes, it sounds like you are tricking yourself into getting things done. In a way you are. Putting the most difficult task first on your list—during prime time—may work. If it feels comfortable, you are more likely to complete the task.

Fortunately, the number one thing you have going for you is a love and devotion to personal growth. You are always taking classes in this and that. You may also sense that the organizing bug bit you and you really need to do something about it. Alleluia! And you realize that understanding why and how you do things, even when it comes to organizing, can help you learn more about your deepest self, which in your case means helping others, too.

You don't need to purchase *anything* before you get organized. I was recently in a home where a woman had lost weight, gained weight, and then lost even more weight, and she had over forty pairs of jeans. With limited closet space, she purchased the type of hangers where one can add ten attached additional hangers below to store her pants vertically rather than horizontally. But this was enormously challenging for her to use, and three-quarters of her jeans could be stored in the garage. My suggestion was to hang the pants that she was choosing to wear on one easy clip hanger for each garment and store the rest.

I know you enjoy to shop and be around people, but I can save you money that you can hopefully spend elsewhere. In the meantime, you can use:

* Grocery bags
* Trash bags
* Recycling paper bags
* Ziploc bags—especially the 2-gallon ones. Plus they are great when moving
* Envelopes
* Suitcases
* Shoe boxes
* Stapled filer folders to put tiny pieces of paper in
* Elastic bands, binder clips, paperclips

It's interesting that when people want to get organized, they rush out and buy everything they think they need. They tend to buy the wrong things and too many of them. Ironically, they then end up having even more stuff to deal with. Organizing isn't an excuse to go shopping. Yet when I arrive at their home or office, they usually have more than enough files, boxes, and labels.

Okay, you can do it! Let's begin with the process of paper for now— *everyone's nightmare*. A ton of undigested paper can be too difficult to handle and even provoke irritability. Working without being judgmental—no in-depth inquiry of every piece of paper you pick up—

quickly gather all of the paper in your home/office in fifteen minutes or less. Putting it into a couple of generic piles, the space feels immediately better. Then you can presort all the tiny scraps of paper into big, easy categories. Use a stapled file folder to collect pieces with miscellaneous information on, or toss these papers into old shoe boxes. Yes, I know they aren't that pretty, but for now they will work. This is all very temporary.

Go through the pieces one at a time. Organizing has to reflect an aesthetic preference or you won't want to be in that room one minute longer. During this initial process, just keeping things together is what it's all about. At the end of our dance together, it will not only be easy for you to maintain a new way of being organized, it will appeal to your aesthetic sense.

HOW TO MANAGE YOUR ENVIRONMENT IN YOUR OWN STYLE

> We tend to spend the most time at the things we prefer. We are much more likely to repeat a lesser preferred behavior if we follow it immediately by a greater preferred behavior.
> —Ann McGee-Cooper, *Time Management for the Unmangeable People*

Neat doesn't necessarily mean efficient. I have witnessed people who thought they were totally organized, who didn't have one piece of paper on their desk, but they couldn't even find their checkbook to pay me after a session. The ability to find something in a couple minutes or less is part of what all this is about. You will discover the many methods that can give you access to everything you need in your own way.

You do need an environment that sets the tone of comfort and joy. Feng Shui, the art of placement, can connect with the natural forces to enhance energy flow in your overall environment and create more productivity all told. Sally Fretwell, who is the author of *Feng Shui*, claims that purging can create an enormous change in your overall well-being.

"Also your subconscious feels lighter because it no longer reacts to the overwhelming number of objects. Your body, spirit and emotions respond to unarticulated impressions from your environment. In other words, every object holds a vibration with which you interact." Remember that your turnoffs are feeling isolated, hurried, and overloaded by work. Motivation is key for all of us when conquering drudgery.

Remember your "organizing buddy?" It is wise to have this person come back, perhaps biannually, to join you in keeping things up to speed. You need this kind of human contact, love, and support. It can be anyone—a sister, neighbor, professional organizer, dear friend— anybody willing to give energy and good cheer as you tackle pockets of clutter. One area at a time is the clue. A couple of my clients—one a pediatrician and the other an actor—call me their Personal Trainer, with capital letters. They are so relieved to have me cheer them on as we get things done that they admit they couldn't do as well by themselves. If there isn't anyone around (and maybe you are too embarassed to have someone over), try to talk this up positively to yourself. Also use a kitchen timer to keep you on track and focused on a given task. Or you can work with the TV on or music in the background.

You need to consider and embrace certain concepts so that you don't lose sight of your own style. Try to make your environment reflect who you are. Try to have the following qualities present in your life:

* Harmony between people and their environment
* A sense of fun
* Connecting with others
* Love of nature
* Enjoyment of color, especially pastel or rich earth tones
* Interesting textures
* Collegiality

Before we go any further, consider the first word: harmony. What does that mean to you? According to Webster's, *harmony* is "a combination of parts into a pleasing or orderly whole; agreement in feeling, action, ideas, interests, peaceable or friendly relations; a state of agreement or orderly arrangement according to color, size, shape, etc." Ask yourself, Is there a feeling of harmony in my home and office? Is it missing? Continue with: Does this work for me? And last, How can I increase the harmony in my environment? Move things around, move them out, and experiment until you actually feel in harmony with your surroundings. Keep in mind that even though it looks terrifying to have a countertop with nothing on it, this can promote a sense of peace.

Using essential oils or candles can create a nurturing environment for you while working away. Experiment with aromatherapy or certain candles to stimulate you and nurture your actions:

* Basil—clarifying thought process, uplifting
* Bergamot—uplifting
* Eucalyptus—invigorating
* Geranium—harmonizing
* Juniper—stimulating
* Lemon/lemongrass—refreshing
* Orange—refreshing
* Spearmint—energizing
* Cedar wood—reduces stress
* Chamomile—calming
* Fennel—relaxing, calming
* Frankincense—calming, reduces fear
* Lavender—soothing
* Sage—cleansing
* Sandalwood—stress-reducing

Certain colors can stimulate various moods as well:

* Red—strength, passion, courage, determination, zeal
* Orange—joy, enthusiasm, optimism, self-expression, freedom
* Yellow—mindfulness, focus, insight, communication
* Green—healing, abundance, renewed energy, vigor
* Blue—inner truth, peace, spirit, serenity
* Purple—dreams, psychic awareness
* White—spiritual awakening, divine insight, realization

Again, we are not talking about the traditional organizing routine, but *harmony,* which imparts a real sense of purpose and meaning for you.

Let me give you one example. A client of mind had an enormous home. Her office was in her bathroom. (Yes, I know, I almost died when I passed the shower and saw a vertical filing cabinet there.) It took her over two hours to get ready in the morning, and meanwhile she was making calls, preparing her to-do list, and getting ready to leave. Perfect. Her actions matched her style. She had candles lit every morning, sprayed perfume on, and felt very comfortable and relaxed in the environment she had created to make her sales calls and run her business. She even scheduled conference calls in that enormous bathroom. (If she had wanted to put a conference table in there, I would have had to put my foot down!) She had amazing energy in the morning, drawn from the soothing colors in her bathroom; the candles were always lit and jazz was playing in the background. She told me later that it took her years to figure out how to situate herself to do work she didn't want to do. Now, that is a success story!

It may seem that some people have no idea what lurks behind your organizing strategy. Just a quick reminder: It takes twenty-one days to develop a habit. So don't get discouraged if you're still trying to find your way in a couple of weeks. It took me a little time to get all my personal financial papers in order so they would be easier for me to understand and monitor. (By the way, I hired a bookkeeper to reconcile my accounts. It saves me time and energy plus I know it's being done right!)

THE STRENGTHS AND CHALLENGES OF YOUR BRAIN

Your main concern is, and always will be, people. I strongly suggest that whatever organizing system you put in place, it has to be people driven and people motivated. You are driven by a deep desire to create harmony among all living creatures. This is your gift, and it must be emphasized, expressed, and celebrated in any organizing system you put into place.

Strengths

> The more freedom in self-organization, the more order!
> —Erich Jantsch

1. Empathetic
2. Visceral
3. Emotional
4. Usually combine styles and colors effectively
5. Harmonious
6. Sensitive
7. Spiritual
8. Soothing
9. Perceptive
10. Encouraging
11. Caring
12. Fun to be with
13. Instructive
14. Concerned
15. Nonlineal
16. Holistic
17. Deep feeling
18. Trusting
19. Nurturing
20. Humanistic
21. Expressive
22. Devoted
23. Interested in personal growth
24. Welcoming
25. Warmhearted
26. Can read nonverbals

Challenges

> Life shrinks or expands in proportion to one's courage.
> —Anaïs Nin

Here are some of your challenging qualities. As Dr. Phil states in *Self Matters*, "You cannot change what you don't acknowledge." Think of this as a way to learn more about yourself and obtain insight into your behavior.

1. Trying to stay on top of everything in your environment
2. Weak at managing time
3. Easily lost in the present moment
4. Dependent
5. Sentimental
6. Lacking focus and structure
7. Touchy-feely
8. A chatterbox
9. Fearful of being alone
10. Easily hurt and intimidated
11. Bored with detail
12. Procrastination
13. Nonassertive
14. Nonanalytical
15. Overly sensitive
16. A nonconformist
17. Not good at setting limits

ORGANIZING YOUR TIME

> Those who make the worse use of their time are the first
> to complain of its shortness.
> —Jean De La Bruyère

You may be challenged when it comes to getting assignments done on time, being punctual for staff meetings, or even showing up for the start of the family dinner. You tend to be seen rushing around, pressed for time, all of the time. You get there, but barely. You pump adrenaline and feel somewhat "juiced" from this kind of panic, but there are more effective ways to work, for you and those you care about. You will work best when you are not rushed, when you have plenty of lead time to meet all your deadlines. Even though you are more concerned with the person than the clock, you need to be in a relaxed environment, one with a slower pace, where you can give requests rather than orders, and create low-stress surroundings.

Let's face it: *you forget about time.* The other brain preferences see your friendliness as a time waster and a roadblock to speedy achievement. However, setting up "rigid" schedules just won't work for you. You don't like to do the identical thing day in and day out at the exact same time. But there are practical ways to maintain your playfulness while retaining reasonable control over the mundane aspects of your life. Since you are the type who likes to have fun while working, devising rigid minute-to-minute calendars isn't going to work. Instead, use your natural preferences to build an organizational lifestyle that is more suitable. Just think how all that hurrying around, juiced-up energy could be put to better use.

I once worked with a very successful winemaker in Napa Valley. As she discussed what needed to be done every day, she broke down and started to cry. She was the mother of two grown sons, but due to the nature of their business, they entertained five nights out of seven. She was just too overwhelmed to deal with everything at once. Going down her list of action items, I had to ask her what would be the consequences of not getting something accomplished. It was clear that she needed to ask this of herself every time she thought she had to do something. She needed to slow down and wait for her feelings to tell her what the next step should be. Hard to do when you feel rushed 24/7. Many people struggle with this one. You can get lost in the present and then rush to overdo and overcompensate. Interpersonal activities rule over impersonal tasks and you readily interrupt whatever you are doing to deal with people. You tend to do tasks only when you perceive them in relation to others. Therefore, you prefer to work regular hours so you can have time to be home with your family and friends.

For you, fulfillment is all about being with people so *you need to create a workday that satisfies you on an emotional level.* Pay attention to when you need a break to connect with someone, and then go back to your task with the energy and inspiration that comes from human contact. But let's also find ways to keep you on task and enthusiastic by developing a day planner that works for you, as well as a basic to-do list that will make mundane life easier.

#1. Day Planner

> Life must be measured by thought and action, not by time.
> —Sir John Lubbock

Ask yourself these questions:

1. What is the time of day when you feel the most energized?
2. What are the current issues, tasks, problems that need to be resolved for today?
3. Which ones matter the most?

David Allen, an organizing business guru, gently insists that if you think something will take less than two minutes, do it right then and there. That may not quite work for you if you initiate a phone call and could talk for two hours. I knew of a professional organizer who wanted to invent a little buzzer for talking on the phone and trying to end a conversation. The buzzer takes responsibility! Try to use a nice spiral-bound book, which can assist you in prioritizing. Don't forget that you must find a pleasant one that jumps out at you. I have a beautiful baby pink leather journal that warms my heart every time I use it. Keep in mind that sometimes for you, the bigger the better!

The first question recognizes that getting organized is not something you long to do. Period. But, if you can identify the best time of day for you, it will help ensure that the job gets done. For me, early morning is the best time to do things I don't want to do. In the afternoon, from about three to five, I find myself fading, less able to focus. You need to know this in order to maximize your time and energy levels, not work against them.

Second, what needs to get done today? You don't need a fancy list timed out hour by hour; big, chunky, two-hour blocks of time should work for you. If it's not on a piece of paper or in your head, you will either forget it or run in the same direction ten times a day. Writing it down may seem like an unnecessary chore; but at the end of the day it is such a terrific feeling to look back and see how many things you've accomplished, as well as knowing that your day is filled with purpose.

Third, create a checklist for recurring activities. Your Maintaining Style friends need to keep lists as well, but where they need them for control, you need them for survival! Travel supplies, contact lists, grocery lists, babysitter info, a list of computer cartridges and a list of the various batteries you need for certain electronic stuff, even house-cleaning duties. You can store this information in your car, on the fridge, but especially in your day planner.

Last, keep all your contacts, business cards, and resources in one place. I was recently with a client who had a computer database, an antique Rolodex, a business card binder, and a stack of business cards with an elastic band around them. When I asked him, "Peter, where would you put my business card?" he replied, "I thought I was paying you to tell me!" If you need all of your various contacts and don't want to lose anyone's number, try to keep it centrally located. Here are two recommendations. First, get a traditional business card book (I bet you already have one because you get to see all of the pretty cards there, with a business card holder in back of your planner). It will get a little full, so purge it annually and have additional paper and card holders in the back. Second, if you have an electronic database, chances are all your contacts are in one place, so that business cards can be entered and thrown away. If you want hard copy available for members of your family or office, print out the database and put it next to every phone. It will be handy without having to turn on your computer.

Your Calendar

You need a playful, enjoyable calendar that really encourages you to move concretely into the future and unite with the people and things in your life. What excites you may not necessarily be an electronic and contemporary version like a PDA. You may prefer stickers or colorful pens, cartoons or fun paper. One of my clients uses two dry erase boards behind her desk, where she can color code the things she needs to do first, and erase the tasks she has completed. The larger the better; the more strategic the location the better. If you can, try to keep *one cal-endar* rather than several.

I suggest a big desktop calendar that could be hung on the wall or placed on your working desk. This can help you "containerize" all those various family activities, yet supply the family with a visual clue of what is happening and where (kitchen, laundry room, mudroom). One plus for this calendar is that anyone can add to it and feel part of the family. You probably may need to use two calendars if you have a family—but maximum two only! If you prefer the electronic way, try getting a screen in color. If you enjoy both worlds, you can easily print out your calendar, and add the color and fun stuff to it to motivate you. Place it in a strategic position. You can also print out the database and have your directory easily on hand rather than rebooting your computer every time you need someone's number. Try to keep to one source, one place where your basic plans (current and future) and contacts come from.

A colleague of mine preferred both ways. She had her colored Palm in a nice yellow, leather zip storage case, and a three-ring binder to the right of it with another monthly calendar where she could write things down. She liked the quickness of inserting someone's contact info and then would later put it in her Palm via her desktop computer keyboard. It worked for her.

Scheduling

You don't need to be too rigid about scheduling. For example, suppose you've written down that tomorrow morning you want to go through a stack of paper. So you sit down and start to sort through it. Then the phone rings, you pick it up, and it's your brother, who needs some advice. You talk to him—probably giving him your full attention—and an hour later you get to that pile again. You resume going through it, then realize you need to get a glass of water because you're so thirsty. And so on. Chances are you probably never got the mail opened for the day, never mind going through the pile you had so adamantly intended to deal with.

It is important to have some freedom in our day and to also play around a bit. When you catch yourself starting and stopping the same task, you're in trouble. You must achieve the balance of focusing on one thing, and if you find that you are distracted, going off, then coming back to complete it. Remember that you need to get up and stretch your legs while connecting with people via e-mail or on the phone. But such breaks need not detract from what has to get done. Be good to yourself; but also be aware how much better you will feel when you have accomplished something you didn't want to do in the first place.

#1. Your To-do List

Write things down in order to remember them. Use a chalkboard, a corkboard, or a nice book from a museum gift shop. Just no loose scraps! The aim is to feel good at the end of the day, and nothing makes you feel as happy as having accomplished tasks. I prefer to have an ongoing list. Rather than recreating what I need to do the next day, I simply cross off what I've completed in an appropriate color and then quickly scan to see what needs to get placed on tomorrow's list. Be creative and you will have fun in the process.

Jane, a client, had no ambition getting anything accomplished prior to her deadlines. It wasn't unusual for her to pull numerous all-nighters to get a report ready or plan for a party. She could do that in her twenties, but by her late forties she found she would forget things and not do them as well as she had hoped. After talking to her, I discovered that she had difficulty simply structuring her day. She responded to everything right then and there, and as a result had no control over her schedule or her life. I suggested that she cut strips of paper and put her to-do's on each one. (Sometimes her younger son helps her color the pieces of paper.) She could then put them into a fishbowl and "fish" every morning for her next activity. Sure, this is an untraditional approach to time management; she isn't doing the urgent or immediate thing. Nonetheless, she is getting things done, enjoying her day, and feeling good about herself. Jane can now say, "I went fishing and caught seven fish today!"

When you have random thoughts, try to use Post-its. The color can help you remember things, for example, baby pink for personal things and purple for things that are top priority (use whatever works best for quick and accurate recall). Then just stick them onto a blank, stiff piece of cardboard or a vertical standing clipboard. You can put them in rows and set closest to the top the one that needs to be done today. You'll have fun moving them around and tossing them when completed. Not only does this allow you to be unburdened by details of what does and doesn't need to be done but you can also easily be reminded. The board is open and the vertical stand awaits your gaze. It *never* gets buried with all of your other stuff. And the colorful collection of Post-its will make you smile. This is how you make parts of your life work without restricting your natural flow.

#2. Clocks

Time management can be somewhat challenging for you. You may miss the teeth-cleaning appointment you made six months ago if you notice someone in the parking lot is in need of cheering up. Taking this to another level, you may have avoided wearing a watch. But this doesn't always work, does it? You need to master time. How about thinking of making friends with it instead? Get the word "tardiness" out of your vocabulary. Help everyone to feel more comfortable by taking steps together to be on schedule.

Try to set your clocks ten minutes ahead. If you are always running late, that change can help make you prompter. Try hanging amusing clocks all over the house, strategically placed so you notice them. Your eyes never really see what time it is on that tiny computer clock. You may find it useful to have an alarm with music to remind you of your next appointment. I actually prefer the good old reliable kitchen timer, which recalls the time in a less abrupt way than someone honking outside the door to let me know the ballet starts in thirty minutes!

Time can so easily get away from you. I worked for a large company once where staff members confessed they had no idea where their time went. I asked them to track the hours as they went about their business for one full day. The results were surprising: It seemed a good deal of their time (almost 50 percent) was spent on returning e-mails. Most of us don't know where our time really goes, even though we talk about time management so freely. Just becoming more aware can be very helpful.

If you spend a lot of time on the phone, you may want to purchase a telephone headset. It leaves your hands free to do something else while talking. I'm not a huge fan of multitasking. I don't recommend speeding up in a world that is already time-fanatic. But it may stimulate you while doing certain tasks you would rather not do. In fact, we need to slow down and get the most out of a single moment.

ORGANIZING YOUR HOME

> The house is more than a box within which to live. It is
> a soul activity to be retrieved from the numbness of the
> world of modern objects.
> —Robert Sardello, *Facing the World with Soul*

Your home is your castle! Warm and cozy—that sums up how you want your personal space to be. You like to have your things around you, and creating a sense of abundance (what some might call the "cluttered effect") stimulates you. You were probably fluffing up your nest just before you sat down to read this. You feel so alive and happy when people are around, and that is why you want your surroundings inviting, to encourage people to stick around and feel good. As Denise Linn, the author of *Sacred Space,* suggests: "You are not separate from the home that you live in any more than you are separate from the air you breathe. Your home is not just an extension of your thoughts and feelings. . . . Both are outer manifestations of your inner energy fields." A sensitive, nurturing environment works really well for you.

Since your home is your haven, organizing it can be a challenge for a number of reasons. First, people tend to interrupt you. Whatever you are currently doing, you happily put it down for a conversation or just to help someone out. Second, you rarely finish something or put it away when completed. You prefer things left wherever they are; you figure you will put them away once everyone has gone. Sometimes your art projects stay on the dining-room table for a long time.

Third, you like to keep everything out for friends to view, and to display your children's artwork, or any accomplishments—not to brag, but because you're excited to share your personal life with others. Purging can be really difficult for you. You keep everything because you find it all so precious and hard to part with. It is tough, but we are going to come up with some easy and motivating solutions.

Fourth, you prefer a very comfortable environment. Stacks of paper, magazines, or catalogues around where you can view them while sitting on the sofa, or at the kitchen island, make life pleasanter for you. So, what can you do to make all this work a little bit better without giving up your identity and personal style?

#1. Design

> Space and light and order. Those are things that men
> [and women] need just as much as they need bread or
> a place to sleep.
> **—Le Corbusier**

For you, it's all about comfort and function. I recently worked with one of the most successful businesswomen I have ever met. Talented in a hundred different areas, and a lovely person to boot! When I walked into her home and saw her dining-room buffet full of souvenirs, and a bazillion photos on her refrigerator (I couldn't even tell what color the refrigerator was), I knew I had my work cut out for me. As a former artist, Anna had each room decorated with a specific theme, and it was amazing. There was such an enormous amount of vibrant energy present. The colors she choose were bright red, yellow, blue, and green. There were objects in every nook and cranny—plants, seashells, and so on. She was able to store much of what she collected in containers, but this had become a bit of a challenge because there were so many little containers, all filled with things. Each room had comfortable chairs, ethnic art, and mementos from every period of her life. She had enough stuff to fill five museums!

Anna hired me to get her paperwork in order—and every flat surface had a stack of paper. Piles sat everywhere. If you entertain, or live with someone else, this can pose serious problems. Anna admitted that her clutter was starting to crowd her, and I applauded her for hiring me to suggest space planning. It takes courage to ask for help, especially in our society, which tells you that you should be able to deal with this stuff—*on your own*. But she simply had too much. Since she traveled extensively for her job, shopped on all her magnificent trips, and was an avid collector, she was literally spilling out of a large three-bedroom home.

The first tip is "Organizing begins at the store." Do you need it or do you just *want* it? Think about it, then again, and again. Otherwise, you'll end up with too much. And renting a storage facility is not the answer.

Organization is about keeping things together in a way that isn't exhausting. I can only stress the importance of creating an environment that nurtures who you truly are. This is vital in setting up any process. Feng Shui could be important for you to investigate. Anna's design was nurturing for her: memories of friends were displayed in every corner of her home. But once we were able to examine what made her feel good about herself, we could plan her home space seasonally and store things that she could take out at different times of the year. This didn't require getting rid of stuff, just recycling collections that could be stored in her garage (one or two boxes) for every season, to be on display for different times of the year.

Anna made it easier on herself too, as she had designed the house to be very comforting and fun for her two boys, aged ten and twelve. She encouraged the kids to manage their own environment, using different-colored hangers and even laundry baskets for easy maintenance. Buy big, lightweight, transparent containers, to which you or your children can easily return things and remember where they are. Always keep children in mind when getting organized. Letting go of some of the domestic duties and making them responsible for their environment will be a win-win situation. When designing a space where little ones may be involved, try to encourage them by making it attractive, fun, and easy. It will free up your day and make all of you happier.

You want to keep your home interesting but uncluttered *to a degree*, inspired and soothing. Choosing more relaxing color tones, comfortable furniture, and easily maintened systems can help. Having things that remind you of your life—such as photos of your friends, things you've done, art, a fountain, anything that encourages your concern for interrelatedness—should come into play here. Living things like plants or pets can also ground you while in a particular room, whether you are working on a project or doing some pleasurable activity. Decorating your home so that there is much to enjoy and to comfort you will provide a pleasing environment where real work can get done. Use beautiful, attractive things, yes, but *not too many of them*. The more you can choose items that make you feel connected and happy, the more you will enjoy staying in that space to file, fill a scrapbook, or arrange a closet. The trick is to place all your stuff so that you are able to feel nurtured but not overwhelmed. A difficult road to walk. But once you know the benefits, you can be easily encouraged to keep it up.

#2. Purging

> Learn to let go, that is the key to happiness.
> —Buddha

Once the stuff is in your home—*it tends to be there for good.* Asking yourself at the store, again and again, "Do I need it or do I just want it?" is a step in the right direction. Once it is in . . . it is in. Even putting your recycle bin by the garage door is helpful, so you can go through your mail right then and there and bring less into the office or basket. Your belongings become so personal that you hate to depart with them. I have worked with some clients who actually shed tears when trying to purge. But I always wonder what those tears are really about.

For you, the cluttered effect creates a sense of abundance. You think everything is valuable and worry that you may offend somebody if you throw out something they gave you a hundred years ago. Sure, things have meaning. But the problem comes when you feel bombarded with so much stuff that you can't move forward in your life and are fearful of taking the next step. So, *toss mindfully*. Remember the term "clutter pockets"? You can toss items about which you are ambivalent from one clutter pocket at a time, so you don't have to reel from the emotions of letting everything go at once. Aim small, and try to stay focused on one room, one cupboard, or one file drawer. Such laser focusing in a predetermined space can make the task seem a whole lot smaller and even manageable, and less painful for you when trying to let go of things. Eventually, you will get better in time.

I should warn you that in this process things tend to look worse before they look better. Give yourself two to four hours *minimum* to do any organizing job. Making the area look better, not worse, when done, takes about half a day. When you want to purge a closet, you have to take everything out in order to see what you have going on. That's why an organizing buddy is so crucial because between you you can get this job done in half of the time and have some laughs along the way. Half of the way through, things start to look better. And when you're done you'll feel very happy, energized by your newfound space.

You tend to see everything in your vicinity as potentially useful, either now or in the future. Releasing some of these things to other homes, donating them to religious organizations, garage sales, outreach programs, and so on, can be good for you and your community. Anna had difficulty deciding what she needed to keep. She would read each single piece of paper, for hours on end, because someday she thought she was going to do this or show that to someone. This just keeps you stuck in more clutter. As Odette Pollar, author of *Organizing Your Workspace*, claims, "Clutter also makes the amount of work you have to do appear greater than it actually is." How true.

Decide *why* you need to keep something—and for how long. If keeping it, define where you are going to store it, *prior to the actual process of purging!* For catalogues, six months; newspapers, weekly; clothing, seasonal; personal finances, seven years; and so on. A structure has to be in place, parameters as to how long you need to keep something, otherwise your emotions will take over the decision-making process. It's as simple as that.

Focus on things that you can do for yourself, or with the help of others, to create more space in a room, closet, or day planner—space that can allow for something new and unexpected in your life. The Jains, an unorthodox Indian religion, believe that divinity dwells within every one of us. They also believe every inanimate object has energy. If a room is filled to the brim with objects, many of which have no meaning or are broken or not chosen with care, the room is awarh with disconnected energy, or the energy is so confusing it simply seems to freeze. When I walk into a client's room or look at their desk at work, I immediately try to sense what's going on with the client's psyche. The person's spirit very often resembles their environment. (Your surroundings are a deep reflection of what is happening inside.) According to the Buddha, "Just as pictures are drawn by an artist, surroundings are created by the mind."

Look around your room right now. I bet you are holding onto some things that don't enhance who you are; objects that don't make you feel good; items that block you and reinforce beliefs that are not in fact true about you. Your environment is a spiritual house. Conversations about clutter can be a blessing. They can force us to examine what we have in our lives, in our drawers, and in our electronic files, and determine what works and what doesn't. This allows us to find ways to simplify and put meaning back into our lives. It is a challenge, but you can emerge triumphant.

When you decide to purge your closet, you end up with a bagful of old clothing waiting for the Salvation Army. Unfortunately, most of it walks right back into your bedroom. Does this sound familiar? To make it easy on yourself:

* When shopping, ask yourself, "Do I need this or do I just want this?" Go primarily with *need*. This principle has saved me hundreds of dollars.
* In with the new, out with the old.
* Use or lose!
* When in doubt, throw out.

* Don't bulk shop—things get old and you end up wasting more money even though you think you got a deal. This becomes apparent when you start to purge medicines and bathroom toiletries.
* Have only one backup for stuff like detergent, shampoo, tape. (Obviously paper products are a bit different.)
* Date-stamp or write down the date of all paper that comes across your desk or use a highlighter to see when you received it. Write at the top of an article what it is about so when you decide to purge you can remember rather than having to reread the article.
* Store only records that you may need, and only for a requisite length of time.
* Keep clothes that make you feel good.
* Keep things that make you feel positive and happy; not a wedding frame from your first marriage if you're on your third. (Yes, this was a true story.)
* If you receive a gift you don't need or like, recycle it. However, keep in mind who you received it from so there are no embarrassing moments!
* Review greetings cards, Christmas cards, letters, and pictures on a day when you have some quality time to yourself and try to whittle them down. Keep what warms your soul and recycle the rest.
* Purge clothing after every season.
* Purge your filing system every January and July.
* Purge bad photos at the checkout before you take them home.
* If a new *Glamour* magazine arrives and you still haven't read the old one, *throw out the old one or donate it.* (Doctors' offices, hospitals, libraries, coffee shops are often glad to receive them.)
* Children's artwork: Keep one portfolio or one 66-quart plastic box for each couple of years, say. Then at the end of elementary school let the children assist you by keeping one box only from that period.
* Try not to do extensive purging when children are home.
* When purging, don't set things aside for this or that person. Just release it into one pile and let one designated charity such as the Salvation Army, receive it. You mean well, but this is about getting you caught up, not farther behind. They will forgive you!

* Here are some organizations that can help you speed this process along. Check out Appendix 2 as well:

  - Goodwill
  - Purple Heart Veterans
  - Salvation Army
  - American Waste System
  - Bulky trash pickup

Since I know how much you enjoy hearing about other people, let me share two stories that show the creative possibilities that can come about from purging. I recently worked with a woman whose husband and child had died in a tragic accident. When I went to her home, it was as if they were still living there. Their clothes were in order, all of their stuff in place, and it was very painful for a vibrant woman to live so closely with all those painful memories. She wanted me to help her dispose of their belongings. Luckily, she was an accomplished quiltmaker, so I suggested that we cut up some of the clothing for quilt patches. She could make one that reminded her of her daughter and another of her husband. That way she was able to let go of the bulk of the stuff and still keep the memories alive.

Another client of mine was an award-wining fisherman. He had Marlins up to the ceiling. It was driving his housekeeper and his wife crazy, since they were the ones dusting them. I suggested that we place all the awards in order and hire a professional photographer to take a photo. He could frame the picture with the plaques from the trophies to create a beautiful, original frame. My client was able to keep the memories rather than the stuff, and even received a tax deduction for donating the trophies.

Ask your organizing buddy or a dear friend to help you get organized. They can offer encouragement and may walk away with something fabulous. It's hard work. But having a team not only makes this terrifying process go faster; it also provides a laugh or two. Some affirmations that may help you:

* "I gladly release and bless all unnecessary objects in my life. My life is full, complete, and great."
* "My number one daily to-do is to take care of me."
* "I ask for help when I feel overwhelmed."
* "I wish to create space in order to allow something new and good to enter my life."
* "I take care of myself during this process. When I'm hungry, I eat; when I'm thirsty, I drink; when I'm tired, I rest."
* "I am gentle with myself and know that I'm a beginner in this process."
* "I create beautiful surroundings where I'm connected to my spirit and higher purpose."
* "Simplifying is a good thing. It allows me to see what is truly important in my life."
* "I deserve surroundings that are filled with harmony, light, and inspiration."
* "Organizing is fun. It makes me feel great."
* "I can succeed at organizing. I can accomplish what I put my mind to. I am a success."
* "I deserve to live with dignity and ease."
* "My life works."

#3. Storage

> The answer is not to acquire more, but rather to seek more meaning in what we require.
> —The Hospice Center

Since you tend to keep a lot, you need to have one easy storage system in place. You like to have things at your fingertips, "just in case Aunt Betty comes over and I want to show her the latest holiday photos." This challenge can be conquered by a number of small and easy tasks. The key thing here is, "Don't go overboard and don't go crazy." Sure, things need to be contained, but once in the container, not overly organized. Get it? Things need to be put back—that is a given, or any organizing system will fall apart—but not to the specific degree that you've been led to believe is necessary. You have better things to do with your time.

It is nice if the spices are all in alphabetical order, but how long are they going to remain like that and how much time do you want to devote to organizing your spice drawer? Remember, your priority is connecting to *people*, not necessarily things. Don't forget that the more you buy, the more you have to store. Let's consider:

* A pedestal sink isn't going to work for you! You need *storage*
* Hanging is better than folding. Why torture yourself?
* Your socks don't need to be folded. A drawer for the socks, loosely put together, will do
* Store scarves hung, not perfectly folded
* Try not to store things under the bed
* Store as much as you can on walls
* Open storage—e.g., baskets on a simple shelf—works great
* Use hang-ups for storage: pegboard, high-tech grid, suspending pot rack, hooks for utensils or pot and pans, magnetic knife bar, glasses that hang, storage shelf under table, etc.
* When you buy furniture, storage is just as important as comfort and looks
* Clear plastic long-term storage boxes. Try to purchase one size or one brand. *Avoid cardboard at all costs*
* Use portable storage such as a handle box for papers, rather than a difficult banker's box
* A curtain works if you don't have a door available
* Open shelving can be your new best friend!
* Bubble wrap is the best shock absorber for fragile long-term storage
* For seasonal or long-term storage, use acid-free tissue and cedar blocks to keep moths at bay. Plastic rather than cloth will prevent moisture from getting in
* Label boxes; with a black marker, metal-rimmed hang tags, or whatever makes it easily apparent to you what is in the box.

Your containers are just as important as the belongings that you are storing. However, you first must come to a realization as to what you are storing and when you are storing it. Spend money on nice, attractive things that you will enjoy using time and time again. Aesthetics should come before utility. Use wicker or leather baskets for everyday storage, something that doesn't have an industrial look. Place them in strategic positions throughout the house. The bigger the storage basket, the better, within reason. Also, consolidate a bunch of things like antique bottles rather than spreading them out on an end table. By limiting the space of your collection you can create a harmonious feeling without the clutter.

Let me reiterate that you don't have to do what other brain types do. Sure, a specific type of hanger for certain garments may be nice, but you don't need to be that specific. They may appeal to the eye, but the upkeep will just be too much for what truly matters in your life.

Memorabilia can be every home's nightmare, but especially yours, where it is so profoundly important and the volume gets out of control. For you this can be a huge headache. My theory about memorabilia is that it should be *used* as much as possible. Some things need to be stored, for example, your report cards from primary school, if you choose to even keep them. Scrap booking is a fun and effective way to let your family see their accomplishments. However, scrap booking can become a full-time job, so be careful. When I went through my photo books at one time and got rid of the magnetic, sticky old-fashioned ones (eight in total), I ended up putting the contents into one beautiful "Creative Memories" album. I have two additional books that are sheet protected and good to review on my coffee table where friends and family can see them easily. For bulkier things, like your grandmother's cuckoo clock, store them in a lightweight, labeled plastic box. I gently suggested to my last client that when her children get older she should keep one plastic banker's box of her children's artwork per grade. Simple, structured room for growth is a huge advantage, especially if you ever decide to move.

Collectible: It may be only salt and pepper shakers or antique dollies, but everything you own has to be accounted for—it must have a home. Sure, it's nice to have things around you that you like to collect. For me, it's purses and books. But I limit myself as to how many I want to collect and even how many I need. Try not to have too many hobbies such as sewing or needlepoint projects to begin with.

Use counter space and any other conceivable work surface to store belongings. Wall space may be an option, especially in the kitchen and family room. Wall pockets for incoming mail, or children's homework, will get it off the floor and give it a new home. Keeping it out in the open without becoming an eyesore is the goal here.

I encourage you to honor all the organizing tasks, especially purging tasks, entered on your calendar. If you don't do this, all of your hard work playing catch-up will fall by the wayside. The more often you do it, while you can remember what you have and where it is, the less work it will be in the long run. Organizing the children's artwork, for example, could be done seasonally, and with your children's help you can discriminate between what you want to keep and what to toss. You can evaluate every room in your house biannually.

#4. Paper

> I like work; it fascinates me. I can sit and look at it for
>   hours.
> I love to keep it by me: the idea of getting rid of it
>   nearly breaks my heart.
> **—Jerome K. Jerome**

Purging paper . . . two of your least favorite words in the entire dictionary! This may prove one of the most challenging parts of managing your environment. You can avoid triggering frustration (e.g., urgently needing something you just had but now can't find, or missing plane tickets when about to go on a trip) by transforming piles into files that are loose and easy to maintain. Remember, it is easier to look in a couple of larger hanging files than twenty little ones. And since you have a lot going on, it is easier to look in just one place. You need to structure how you go about organizing paper and to create various homes for it in your space. Don't feel that *you* are the problem. We get more mail in a month than our grandparents got in a lifetime. The problem is you never had to be so ruthless about it and cultivate a genuine solution to deal with it.

First, a really solid step is to prevent stuff from even coming into your home. There are a couple of ways you can immediately eliminate it. To stop the problem *before* it gets inside:

* Write to Stop the Mail—PO Box 9008, Farmingdale, NY 11735-9008, and request that your name be removed from all general lists
* Telephone solicitations: Write to Preference Service, PO Box 9014, Farmingdale, NY 11735
* When you order anything through a catalogue, let the person know you don't want your name sold or added to another list. It is a legal right that they must grant
* Remember, filling out a warranty card just puts you on another list! If you have saved the receipt that is more than sufficient.

(More solutions in Appendix 2.) That wasn't too painful now, was it?

Second, you need to deal with all paper—incoming mail, newspapers, catalogues, children's report cards—at specific times of the day or week. Some things are challenging since they may be seasonal, but encourage yourself to deal with these when you are ready. For example, if you have a PO box, you don't have to check it every day. Consolidate your activities and go once or twice a week when you are ready to cope in a systematic way. Try not to deal with this daily as it causes unnecessary stress.

Third, try not to pick up a piece of paper and put it down again in the same place because you can't decide where it should go. Paper needs a home, just like your coat or dishes do, otherwise it lands wherever. Let me put an end to the myth, "A piece of paper should be dealt with only once." What planet was somebody on when they suggested that one? Sometimes, it needs to be handled maybe two or three times, once in your in-basket, once on your desk or in a vertical filing stand, and then in a reference filing cabinet, especially if you are getting overwhelmed. My suggestion is that papers should take fewer steps to process in the future and be easier for you to remember.

You need a filing cabinet, a plastic box, a banker's box, or even a traveling file box with a handle on it. It doesn't have to be a serious-looking lateral filing cabinet such as the Maintaining Style needs. This is for long-term storage—passport, travel documents, ID, medical records, tax returns, and manuals. If you pay your family's bills on the kitchen table, not in your office, create a traveling office in your pantry where you can store a filing box with all your supplies, checks, and previous financial receipts. A beautiful wicker or fabric filing box works well. Keep it simple and together. You don't have to know the Dewey Decimal System to get everything in order. Henry David Thoreau said that "our life is frittered away by detail . . . simplify, simplify." Last, always ask yourself not Where should I put it? but *Where will I find it?* That is the winning ticket for today!

* Purchase vertical rather than lateral filing cabinets. You save space on the outside and have more room on the inside. A four-drawer filing cabinet will do.
* Try to classify each drawer and store in the 2-inch drop bottom hanging files that are fantastic for long-term storage.
* Make sure that your thinking isn't too detailed.
* It can be made easier if (a) you loosen up the traditional filing approach with big, broad, generic categories—not one piece of paper for every hanging file; and (b) include photos to look at, or music in the background, that generate warm feelings as you do the task.
* Label the hanging file and not necessarily the interior file. One less step will make you a happy camper.
* Use 3-inch rather than 2-inch tabs. You will need to buy them separately from the box of hanging files. Longer tabs, all of the same color if you prefer, make it easier to keep up and to create the labels. (Longer words, printed in one font, can fit on one line and look much nicer.)
* Try to purchase a filing cabinet that either locks or is fire-resistant. Privacy and preventing damage to your papers are very important factors.
* Store important papers, stock certificates, old letters, and wedding negatives off-site—perhaps in a safety security box at your bank.
* Use staples or binder clips rather than paperclips for storing documents. Paperclips that clip to the file folders become annoying after a while.

As for memorabilia, this should be *stored*—whether in a closet, garage, or file. However, if your children like to see their old stuff around, keep it in their bedroom on the top shelf of a closet, and open it up for special occasions. For long-term storage of papers, use plastic rather than cardboard as cardboard tends to discolor and attract moisture and insects that may destroy something precious.

For short-term storage, information that you need to refer to either daily or weekly—bills to pay, action, pending, to file, to read, a monthly tickler file—use a corkboard or a magazine holder for events or school homework that can be stored on a counter in horizontal trays or even in a rolling filing cart that stands easily in the pantry or a closet. Store paper in the room where you spend the most time. Your home office on the second floor in the room farthest from the staircase may not work. If you use the kitchen table, setting that filing stand in the corner by the refrigerator will be a big help. Even though you may spend a lot of time in the bedroom, I strongly discourage you from setting up a home office or paying bills there. That's the place for you to relax and rejuvenate; so put the files elsewhere.

Color coding can help, but don't get carried away and create a rainbow filing system. Happy medium is where we are going. Colored dots, stickers, even coloring a desktop accordion file works nicely. Pay attention to color when purchasing file folders, binders, or even paper. There is an ancient understanding of color. For example:

- #1 Red—a hot color that represents our life energy, our physical strength and vitality. It sends warmth.
- #2 Orange—a warm color that energizes, invigorates, and nourishes. It can also bring out self-confidence.
- #3 Yellow—a warm color that stimulates the nervous system and affects the mind and emotions. Yellow can help with mood elevation and alleviates exhaustion and burnout.
- #4 Green—a cool color and a great balancer. Green can help soothe and bring harmony.
- #5 Blue—a cool color that brings lightness, peace, and calm, and helps with sleep.
- #6 Indigo—another cool color that helps to build a positive outlook and bring inner strength.
- #7 Violet—a regal color and the color of inner power. Violet can bring higher understanding and calm.

Once you have picked the color, consider using binders, as it is a nice alternative from a filing system. Assign one each for directories, takeout menus, directions/maps, financial investments, recipes, and so. Sure, you have to hole-punch the pages and may even prefer to have some of them in sheet protectors; but all in all you will have easier access to the materials that you use daily and can immediately see what you have. You feel in control and are ready to move forward.

Labeling can be a challenge. Think bigger, broader—the 2-inch drop bottom hanging files rather than the little traditional hanging ones. For example, create one single insurance file—not one for medical, another for auto, and a third for home. When you need to find something related to insurance, it should be in that file. There, we just got rid of two file folders and paired three down to one! Consider a labeler. You may want to spend about $50 getting a Brother labeler, since they are excellent and fun to use. You also may want to use a colorful Sharpie as well and label your interior files or the corner of a document. Highlighting would work well for you. Just as long as you are able quickly to identify which color you use for certain things.

Accordion storage is another helpful option. Great thing. This is a fantastic idea for filing financial papers—one accordion file can hold a year's worth, or greetings cards, your children's report cards, or cartoons from the paper. I recently used it for a client's cartoon humor clippings. Some of this can easily be contained in a box with a handle for easier carrying. Labeling on the outside of the accordion file makes it simple for you to know what is in there in the first place.

Consider wall space again—a corkboard, or even the inside of a kitchen cupboard. When you want something, you want it now. And traditional styles focus on out-of-sight, out-of-mind. Place the paper in a box underneath your desk or in a closet—it is better to have one place rather than several to have to look for it. You can easily throw it in there; chances are, you need never retrieve it again. When it is full, you can quickly scan it and chances are that you can purge the entire box. This is also a great technique for your innovating style friend, too!

For newspapers, magazines, catalogues, and the rest, big, large wicker baskets are ideal. Depending on how many subscriptions you receive, it is imperative that you go through each basket every month.

During the holidays you may even need to do this more than once. If these baskets are strategically placed throughout your house,—for example, an in-basket at the front door and a magazine basket by the sofa—you will be in charge of all the incoming paper that comes your way!

You may want to limit subscriptions—say four magazines a month, one for each week or go to the library a couple of times a month. Maybe you suffer from "information urgency" syndrome and like to have a hundred magazines around to give you the illusion of keeping up with things. Few readers actually read each issue; meanwhile, there are eleven *Architectural Digests*, nine *Yoga Journals,* and twelve *Cooking Light* cluttering your house. Use proactive therapy: "One comes in and one goes out." It is that simple. If, in your profession, you need to keep specific issues, place them in acrylic holders that can store up to two years' issues for one magazine. Once it is full, look through to see which ones you need to keep and purge the rest.

Stop clipping, ripping, or tearing. Nobody really wants that stuff. The piles you create never get moved and the people you want to give things to likely don't want them. Just look at the article, read it, and move on. Your friends will thank me in the end. Guaranteed!

ORGANIZING YOUR OFFICE

> If a cluttered desk is the sign of cluttered mind, what is
> the significance of a clean desk?
> —**Laurence Peter**

The office can be a very challenging place. First, you typically have too little space for your personal mementos, and yet, ironically, this is where you need them the most. They remind you of who you are in an environment where you may get little validation.

Second, you tend to care more about your coworkers' feelings than about your monthly reports. You are much more prone to socialize than to schedule or monitor tasks that can be frustrating and unsatisfying. It would be great for you to locate your desk out of the traffic zone. You would probably get more done and still see people when you go for a break and take a stretch. It is hard for you to defend yourself and your work style, since you typically don't want to upset colleagues or superiors. You are terrific at creating a team atmosphere and getting to feel grounded and at ease. As a conscientious person, you prefer to avoid conflict and controversy at all costs.

Your number one career goal isn't a raise or a promotion but rather approval and knowing that people like you and the work you do. Your "country club" approach to work-related tasks, frequent breaks, and pace of work is driven by your mood. (Others may perceive this as rather inefficient.) Last, your space must be a warm and a friendly one. Since comfort and connectedness are of prime importance, you tend to prefer to perform unpleasant tasks with memories around you of what you really love and care about. You are profoundly aware of disharmony and unhappiness, and this can affect your overall performance, partly because you may be more worried about other people's feelings than your own.

What sort of organizing dilemmas does this cause? First and foremost, a working environment needs to be pleasurable. There are numerous ways of spicing up your environment without going overboard. Selecting objects that ground you—your own coffee mug, for example; or plants, prints, memories from a trip, or last year's Christmas photo—can help make you feel less lonely. But don't import them into the office by the hundreds. One or two will do.

Indulge in some colorful file folders or handouts. Desktop tickler files are appropriate for organizing the day-to-day routine. Rather than going metal or black with supplies, try to purposely pick something that motivates you and is a pleasure to look at. Develop a rational sequence in storing things, and you will have fewer problems when retrieving important documents. Spend some time putting things away at the end of the day. Perhaps limit calls during the last ten minutes of your day—to make room to work tomorrow.

Since you like to talk with coworkers and discuss things, you may want to develop a traveling file folder for the offices you visit. You could use portable functioning tools such as a laptop, or even your Franklin

Covey Day Planner. Such tools should reflect your need to connect. Since you thrive on face-to-face meetings, having the appropriate supplies handy will let your superiors know that you are not only competent but have a personality, too. Something that can easily get lost in most organizations.

#1. Electronic Organizing

If you turn on your computer and see a picture of your dog on the desktop, you're more prone to use the computer day in, day out. Technology for you tends to be a way to communicate your feelings rather than a way to share information. Taking a computer class could help you decide which programs best support connecting with friends and family. Be careful with e-mail communication. e-mail eats up your time. Before you know it, two hours have gone by and you wonder what happened! It is vital that *you monitor just how long you spend returning and sending e-mails.* I suggest you put a kitchen timer on your desk and set it for a specific time. When the bell rings, move on to something else!

You have the ability to learn computer programs that can help you generate terrific documents that inspire people to do their job better. Tweak your computer skills if you know this will serve everyone around you. Remember, acknowledging and scheduling organizing tasks is paramount. When you include service to others as a top priority, you can achieve a more rewarding work life.

CONCLUSION

Sally Fretwell, writing about Feng Shui, points out that "everything around you is alive and interacts with your energy."

Managing your environment should incorporate your driving need for interdependence; it should be encouraged by simplicity, aesthetics, and functionality. Stay ahead of the game by keeping equipment comfortable and user-friendly. Include family members, friends, even coworkers in the process. Keep things people oriented and unstructured. For example, if one day you want to organize the master bedroom closet, invite a friend or two, and give yourself a time limit. Once completed, have a celebratory lunch or dinner. Your main concern should be to get your environment manageable, but not at the expense of spending less time with your family and friends. Use your calendar. Schedule specific activities to do weekly or monthly. Again, reward yourself when completed. The quality of your life should dramatically improve.

The real issue is retaining a balance between the external and the internal. If you spend every waking hour thinking about shopping and spending money, or if all your time is spent organizing videotapes and forty-five boxes of Christmas decorations, you are not really living. Janet Luhrs, author of *The Simple Living Guide*, maintains: "Most of us never consider that we are devoting the precious hours of our lives to the pursuit of not happiness but junk." Live your life with greater ease. Less really is more. Organizing is about saving time, not creating more work. I can't imagine meeting the Dalai Lama and seeing him not being able to get off his meditation cushion for fear of falling over religious books and paraphernalia! Remind yourself that a garden is never finished. The older you get, the more challenging it can become.

You may be tempted to ignore organizing since you would prefer to play, have fun, and just be with those you love. That is why it is imperative to put your things in reasonable order in a way that helps you *keep* them in reasonable order so that you can spend quality time with the important people in your life. You do need to manage your environment effectively, but not in the way you supposed it had to be in the past. Gentle, easy, enjoyable, and manageable systems are called for. If you observe piles starting to accumulate, you are moving into troubled waters.

One of the keys to feeling more whole, especially in this day and age, involves learning how to clean up the clutter in your life. I don't believe Gandhi or Mother Teresa ever buried themselves beneath books, or shuffled papers that took time away from deeper spiritual pursuits. I encourage you carefully to evaluate your day-to-day surroundings. In order to create the peace and space you yearn for, rearrange and organize so that you can feel the power of the spirit in your life. I have seen this happen to numerous people from different walks of life, each with a specific challenge.

My goal is to encourage people to live with *dignity* and *ease*. According to Karen Kingston, of *Clear Your Clutter with Feng Shui*, "Real wealth is measured by the fewness of your wants." The way you live moment to moment is what real living is all about. As a result of this process, you can begin to create more space in your chest of drawers and on your calendar. You will no longer hide behind clutter and busyness. Undoing the clutter gives you the freedom to see what is lurking beneath the actions you take in your life. This can be liberating for some, but for others it may be a terrifying proposition. Seeing emptiness can create an empty feeling. Ernest Holmes, the founder of Religious Science, once said, "Nature demands change in order that we may advance. When the change comes, we should welcome it with a smile on the lips and a song in the heart." Changing your attitude is the first step in living a clutter-free life. Eventually you can learn how to experience a basic axiom: *Space equals Peace.* The more reasonable space you have, the more peace there will be in your heart, and the more room you'll find for the spirit to dwell there.

Happiness means being content—not continually desiring every material thing you see around you. It means feeling whole, complete, and blessed with what is in your life already. When you have less, you can see more. A quote from Salvador Dalí sums it up nicely: "There are some days when I think I'm going to die from an overdose of satisfaction." I doubt he would have found that shopping at Wal-Mart!

Getting Started:
For Example—
Household Paper Clutter
When you're in the organizing mood and there is a good chance your friend is home, give them a call and tell them you need their help and that you will take them out for lunch when done. If a friend is unavailable, put some music on or work with the TV on.

1. Start in one room that is less intimidating and makes you feel good. Depending on the condition of the room, start there and remain there. If done early, great! Slowly build up your stamina.
2. Start in one corner, gather the miscellaneous items, and put into two piles: toss or keep. Have a paper-recycling bag next to you.
3. Recycle old magazines that you will never get to and catalogues. Create parameters for how long you need to keep them.

4. Examine what you have kept, but don't spend much time reread-ing an article or going through things in detail. Put into large, generic piles.
5. Purge each pile again. You will notice some things you keep and some you don't.
6. Put the ones remaining in a hanging file in the filing cabinet.
7. If you need to create a new file, put in a file folder and a 2-inch drop bottom labeled hanging file.
8. Place a catch basket in strategic places in that room and eventu-ally as you work through the house, room by room, do the same thing. Promise yourself that you will go through them bimonthly.
9. Now reward yourself. Go have a great lunch with your friend . . . or take a hot bath!

OVERVIEW OF THE HARMONIZING STYLE

Purpose: To achieve harmony in all aspects of life. Your surroundings need to be personal and comfortable.

Organizing Space: Everything must be in harmony.

Strengths: You tend to be sensitive and desire to create a soothing, nur-turing environment wherever possible.

Challenges: Managing time can be an issue where you tend to make subjective rather than objective decisions. Nesting and lack of purging are other concerns.

Time
Calendar: You need a fun, bright, colorful calendar, using markers or stickers; this can either be a big desk calendar, or mounted on a wall or the refrigerator. Any convenient place where you won't miss it.

To-do List: Use one attractive, large spiral-bound book. The bigger the better, so you don't misplace it.

Goals: You tend to act in relation to other people and their comfort levels. So you may need to set up generic appointments with *yourself* to get things accomplished.

Contacts: Either a business card binder or an address book is preferred. An electronic database will work, if you print the entire thing out and are able to have it at your fingertips

Paper
Incoming Mail: Use a big, colorful wicker or decorative basket, placed in a strategic area near the door.

Desktop: Use personal mementos to remind you of relationships. A vertical filing stand with colorful labeled file folders works well.

Filing System: Use a filing cabinet, with as much color as possible, and file drawers for various subjects with either alpha or subject filing. May have large, more generic file categories. A labeler or simple handwritten labels with markers could be helpful.

Closets
Closets: You tend to sort by color.

Drawers: Different drawers for different items by color and category.

Storage: Boxes may be colored and labeled with the name of item, color coded or with a picture on box.

Purging: You need to set boundaries on how long things should be kept *before* purging. Think "need" vs. "want." Purging can be challenging since you become emotionally attached to memorabilia.

Memorabilia: You tend to retain items much longer than other brain types in order to keep the memories alive—greetings cards, high school yearbooks, etc.

Chapter Three

Innovating Style

> I will be organized. To that end I will take stock and see what organization I really need. I will not stop at straightening my desk, but will better organize my thoughts and more clearly envision the great work I mean to do. I will risk reorganizing the pieces that comprise the puzzle of my life.
>
> —Eric Maisel, *Affirmations for Artists*

If you scored strongest in this category, you tend to approach life with the most adventurous, artistic, and nonconformist part of the brain. You can do a hundred different things at once without blinking an eye. You tend to be a spontaneous, passionate, and imaginative soul. You enjoy an aerial view of reality, using your creativity to introduce new and exciting ways of doing things, and are easily bored by repetitive tasks. Your thinking is complex, so you may find it challenging to articulate many of your deeper thoughts and ideas. Don't worry; you are the philosopher of the universe, always inspired to try to make sense of the world in your own unique and humorous fashion.

Basically, your brain has the ability to process the big picture and you have your finger on the pulse of change, always guessing future trends. Your free-spirited and natural risk-taking approach makes for a lot of fun. Remember, that is why people enjoy working and being around you—if it is only for five minutes. If you're introverted, you may be a visionary thinker, and if you're extroverted, you may be a visionary leader.

You tend to be somewhat disinterested in left-brained "traditional organizing" details. You are normally not embarrassed by your own lack of organization, the fact that you frequently lose things, hand in brilliant but error-prone reports, and have little concern for appearances. Even though deep down you believe that some rudimentary organizing systems could be of benefit, it is hard to find the time and even harder to know how to do it—*your unique way.*

You prefer originality, thrive on variety, and typically get bored maintaining any type of rigorous or conventional organizing system. You work best when given a ton of freedom and flexibility. Face it, you thrive on taking risks. This can cause a multitude of problems and those around you may continually misunderstand you. You are the type who answers questions with questions in order to gather more information. For example, you're probably scanning this chapter rather than reading each line carefully. (Is it possible you didn't even read that last sentence?) Therefore, organizing is way more challenging for you than for any other type. It's just how your mind works. But let's try to use your strengths and make them work to get you organized.

Here is a typical organizing session with you, the Innovating Style. First, you can't even imagine all of the necessary steps it takes to get anything organized, but you just blast ahead in any way, shape, or form when you want to do so. You are energetic, a fast worker, a natural risk taker, and will try anything once. Your organizing style is an all or nothing approach. When you purge you are a maniac. But you may only do it when you have to or are inspired to do so. For you, juggling a hundred tasks is easier than juggling two. For example, at home, if you want to keep all your paperwork together, you might purchase file folders and actually drop important pieces of paper inside in two seconds. Then you take a break, check your e-mail, and make a cup of coffee. You watch the bird out the window, then go back to the pile of folders. You don't label them or put them in a drawer. They, along with the rest of your piles of paper, remain right on the table where you began. At this point you feel spent and discouraged, and now your motivation and creativity are squelched. Sound familiar? The root of this particular cycle of futile organizing is your brain. It processes information so quickly and gets bored almost instantly with routine and detail. You have a lot of thoughts going in many directions at once. This, as you can imagine, can be a problem when trying to get and stay organized.

Think of it as a unique, problem-solving challenge. Your new motivational concept needs to be: *managing my environment effectively can be enormously creative and fun!* Not only is this doable; more important, it will enhance original thinking, imagination, and your ability to convey ideas. Remember, you are naturally innovative. You thrive on the new and like to explore the potential of what might be. You are a master at resolving spatial dilemmas as well and are usually willing to take a crack at solving almost any problem.

So, how do you go about managing your environment? First, I know the word "organizing" isn't one of your favorites, and that "time management" certainly follows as a close second. However, like other kindred right-brainers, like your Harmonizing Style friends, you bought this book knowing that something wasn't quite working in your life. Perhaps stress was impeding your progress. You may have grasped that your surroundings were not stimulating you, supporting your passion, or helping you realize your goals, and you may have been getting frustrated at the little insignificant things. Or maybe you were having increasing difficulty dealing with negative comments from your partner or boss about issues you tend to consider insignificant or trivial (e.g., being late for dinner, missing a meeting, stacks of paper everywhere). Now you are ready to solve these dilemmas. But first, understand that for you organizing is not what you think it is. Hooray for that!

Organizing must fit your needs, especially your creative needs. Let me revolutionize the profession and suggest something that suits you completely: *You don't need a traditional filing system!* You will have to custom-make one that either sits on your desk in horizontal trays, or on a credenza or bookshelf; better yet, you can just dump it into a cardboard banker's box and leave it under your desk, something the Harmonizer might do. But you keep it there for much longer. If you date a lot of the material, by writing or even using a date stamp on the top right corner, you can just toss old documents in the box. Periodically, you can purge, at the end of each month, say, or biannually, and if you only give yourself one or two boxes, you will have fun tossing a lot of stuff out. Important documents need to be kept in a regular drawer file or even desk drawer. Remember that your ultimate solution is: store less paper—store things.

So, for the ever-increasing amounts of paper in your life, you don't need to buy a label maker, use 2- or 3-inch cut tabs, or get heavily invested with hanging files, interior files, and everything else. Traditional filing cabinets certainly aren't the solution because for you, "Out of sight is out of mind." "Simple" is the answer. You need to see as much as possible—right in front of your eyes. For those few important documents or files that you must have easy access to, store them in a 2-inch drop bottom hanging file. Then store that hanging file in an open desktop file folder. Big, easy categories are just the ticket. I will give you a plethora of ideas in all basic categories that are creative, and most important, easy. You are in control and you will be able to pick and choose what works for you. Remember your own way is the right way.

Let's use your high energy, determination, and vision to create an organizing system that empowers you into an initial weekly, then eventually monthly, maintenance schedule. You're impressed by the innovative skills and procedures all around you. Use them to your benefit and see how things can be controlled. That is part of our agreement. What I offer will stimulate and balance your personal needs in a world that unfairly rewards left-brain functions.

HOW YOUR BRAIN TYPE WORKS

> A mind too active is no mind at all.
> **—Theodore Roethke**

Your brain basically views the world in abstract and intangible patterns. You have a talent for putting these in some order. You can be quite agile in moving pieces of information around, as with a huge puzzle, assembling and reassembling, interpreting and reinterpreting, trying to make sense of the big picture. This ability helps to make you an excellent problem solver and innovative thinker. Your brain can often generate intuitive solutions to virtually impossible problems. When absorbed in a problem, you like to be left alone. People, possessions, paper, and time all take a backseat to figuring out what needs to be done. You may not come up for air for hours because you are so involved. Albert Einstein was almost thrown out of college for daydreaming too much and being unable to focus on what was discussed. Does that sound familiar?

An ability to absorb a ton of information about a given subject, see future trends, and brainstorm new processes is a great organizing talent because you see where you are headed and formulate concrete solutions to a particular issue. Your drive and passion is a beacon to those who enter your surroundings. Now that you want to get organized, you can enjoy the challenge and welcome the change that lies ahead. Since you excel at new beginnings and love the risk of doing anything new, your challenge could be the follow-through.

As a voracious reader of biographies about artists and scientists, I have come to realize that most of these people appear to use features in the right frontal lobe of the brain most easily. Perhaps the nineteenth-century notion of the "crazy artist," with characters like van Gogh leading the pack, still looms in your head. Some people actually deny their talents because they want so much to fit into the left-brained world. In the end they can lose themselves in the process. This inhibits rather than stimulates their natural talents, such as creativity and brainstorming. It can be even more of a challenge for those in the corporate world, where creative talent tends to be put on the back burner, as insignificant to the bottom line. However, some organizations are slowly changing this perspective and fostering an environment that not only supports their staff but will enhance the company's profits.

It can be difficult to be *creative* and *artistic* and still make things work smoothly in your environment. I think being more conscientious in your space will help. Eric Maisel's book *Affirmations for Artists* has a section on the value of organization and how to integrate that concept into your daily practice. Think of Mondrian or Matisse. They were conscientious about what they created and how they functioned. They met deadlines and produced their work on time for art dealers. Thomas Edison came up with over one thousand different patents and worked twenty hours a day into his late eighties. Michelangelo finished the Sistine Chapel in four years—*by himself!*

I suggest that once we devise an organizing system that supports your brain's inclinations, you can produce more work in a way that is ultimately less draining for you. Did you know that on his death Leonardo da Vinci left more incomplete assignments than completed ones? Let's take your natural strengths and use them for even greater success. Save your energy for creating a final draft of your book, tweaking a project, or gearing up for a presentation . . . instead of having to hunt for the car keys or search for a piece of paper with a client's number on it! Wouldn't this make your life easier?

WHY DO YOU NEED HELP?

> There is no such thing as pure pleasure; some anxiety
> always goes with it.
> —Ovid

Managing your environment successfully and efficiently is often related to good time management. Time management is defined as *doing the right (BEST?) thing at the right (BEST?) time.* I think a lot of organizing has to do with this. And keep in mind that you don't live in this world alone. You have family, friends, coworkers, and casual acquaintances who think differently than you do. You need a schedule that not only takes into consideration your goals and time restraints but also, perhaps more importantly, your need for flexibility and the desire to accomodate and be sensitive to those around you.

At all costs you need to avoid repetition and routine. When the fun is taken out, you are no longer around. Think of a schedule as being like a compass—something that keeps you heading in the right direction throughout the day. Sometimes you get the "I've got to get organized" bug, only to realize two weeks later you're in precisely the same situation you were before. In these cases, most people give up. Because you are spontaneous and willing to take risks, allow these strengths to work for you. If you are in the position to ask for help, anyone's help—your partner, assistant, or the gardener—take it. They can encourage you to stay on track and to emerge victorious. When I work with many of you, I feel that I just have to hover over you for you actually to be forced to make the decisions you don't want to.

Recently, I was working with a famous businessperson in Southern

California. An avid world traveler, with a plush white robe from every famous hotel and spa he had visited, he had little time or patience to get organized, although he understood and valued organization. With the encouragement of his wife, herself a business executive, I noticed a couple of salient features common to your brain type. (You don't have to be an artist; people in the business world can have similar traits.) He was exhilarated about getting organized and couldn't wait until I arrived. But ten minutes into it, I found him in the garden having a cup of tea. Cajoling him back, and letting him think that he was working ahead of me, we were able to purge specific items while I devised a game plan for our next plan of attack. I had to monitor his every move. Being positive and encouraging wasn't going to cut it! He needed direction at every juncture as he was beginning to lose his focus in the process. (His wife later said that I'm an organizing "interventionist," since he preferred to work alone but was having difficulty accomplishing it by himself.) He purged, I organized, and what would have taken him a weekend took us six hours to complete. He was pleased with the outcome and could now get on to something else. It would have killed him if I'd shown up twice a week for an entire month.

Again, let me stress that it was hard for this successful person to ask for help. But in the end it was a win-win situation. Work with someone—as I suggested for your Harmonizing Style friend—who is more than willing to help you. Don't be embarrassed. Who knows—there may even be something in it for them.

I applaud your originality and your desire to simplify your life and reduce stress by envisioning nontraditional organizing systems that can serve you better. Your desire to improve and your freewheeling style are assets to getting organized, *not* detriments. You already have the talents and skills to fine-tune your lifestyle, even though you realize that patience and dealing with detail aren't your strongest virtues. Let your originality shine, while you inspire and lead those around you. Isn't that ultimately what you want? To be influential and make life better?

HOW TO MANAGE YOUR ENVIRONMENT IN YOUR OWN STYLE

> I've found that every time I've made a radical change,
> it's helped me feel buoyant as an artist.
> —**David Bowie**

You, too, can feel buoyant while managing your environment. Many organizing books specify one particular approach to conquer clutter. I don't believe that's effective for 75 percent of the population. It's up to you to decide what you really need and what your own solutions might be. Don't do what others wish you would do. Don't jump at the chance to change without a follow-through system in place. Don't expect to get every point, every detail, and every nuance in place, or to accomplish everything I suggest. This is about **living your uniqueness.** You have the smarts to transfer your skills to managing your environment effectively. Being aware of why you behave in certain ways will help. What some call "clutter" may simply be the result of not taking the time to consider where something should have gone in the first place. Your clutter areas tend to be places where you want to just relax.

Remember the movie executive, Monty, mentioned in the Introduction? Monty felt he had no time to think about where things should go in his office because the demands of his job were enormous. I have never seen anyone work so hard and endure such pressure 24/7. He just allowed paper to accumulate in stacks and thought he'd get to it later. This is wishful thinking. The very notion of "later" contributes to frustration. It never happens. The paper continues to pile up; when you experience a crisis, you work feverishly for a day playing catch-up, but don't have the time to do it right. Ironically, I hear time and time again that you know what is in every stack. But does your secretary or partner? A sustainable system to help you manage your environment must require very little maintenance—but must try to be friendly to all. You of all people don't want to spend every waking moment staying organized, and neither does your spouse or office worker.

Our movie executive needed to examine honestly what worked for

him and what didn't, then buy the organizing gadgets that he needed—
not the other way around. So let's take what you like and have fun with
it, and design an organizing system that matches the real you. It won't
take long. You're a quick study.

I want to add a final point in clarifying why it is so crucial to manage
your life in your own way. The best example I can give is the paper issue. Sorry to keep bringing this up, but let's get it out in the open. It is
your worst issue. No one understands your relationship with paper but
you. However, after reading this paragraph, you may feel much better
about sticking to your innate qualities and making them work for you.
The fact is, your piles of paper make sense to you and represent ongoing, intellectual, active thoughts. They provide many proofs that electronic viewing simply doesn't work as well. At work or even when
reading an article at home, very seldom do you go through it
sequentially—from beginning to end or start to finish. You need it
around because paper enables your specialized thinking to work. I bet
if I went into your office or saw your kitchen counter, you would know
where everything is. Am I right? Malcolm Gladwell, who wrote an article in *The New Yorker* on "The Social Dysfunction of People" (March
2003), says of people like you, "They can't file because you haven't yet
sorted and filed the ideas in their head. It isn't a sign of disorganization,
but rather a sign of complexity." Did you know that Edison, Winston
Churchill, and Auguste Rodin all were viewed as failures by their teach-
ers for not obeying traditional styles of thinking?

Just tweaking your style into using easier, simpler locations on the
desk—the left side for pending documents and the right side for active
ones—could be an easy solution for your partner or colleague to help
you. Even moving your telephone or writing tablet two inches closer can
make your life easier. The solution to your paper problem, like most organizing problems, is *to store less*. But more on that later. Let's take a
break from paper and talk about something we know you enjoy.

THE BIG PICTURE

> What answer to the meaning of existence should one
> require beyond the right to exercise one's gifts?
> —W. H. Auden

Generally, your brain excels at viewing *the big picture*, as well as being
able to trend data and envision the future. You are able to perceive the
whole and see how all the parts fit together. People and organizations
that need this kind of problem solving often seek you out because you
enjoy devising strategies that match your love of innovation. How liberating and enriching that can be! And how much fun! Other brain types
may view your type as belonging to dreamers who are off in their own
world. They may even perceive your sense of humor as off the wall. You
can keep them chuckling when no one else can. That sense of humor
can be a definite asset in any challenge that lies ahead.

Your brain enjoys intuition and vision and you can usually tolerate a
great deal of variety and spontaneous "chaos." However, you prefer to
spend as little time as possible in dealing with details and objects. You
can become energized as you straighten things up, consolidate information, and purge the unnecessary. You tend to do this in spurts. After
reading this chapter, though, you'll "organize" more often, committing
to a schedule for one hour a week or several hours a month. Don't look
the other way. You don't have a traditional organizing bone in your
body—no big deal. You still can establish a schedule that works for
you. Since you often have great hunches about how to make things
work for others, call on your innate creative and innovative abilities for
your own environment. Listen to your inner voice—it usually comes in
loud and clear.

THE STRENGTHS AND CHALLENGES OF YOUR BRAIN

In order to be a good writer, self-discipline and stamina
are the two major arms in a writer's arsenal.
—Leon Uris

Let's take a closer look at your talents and the challenges that might get
in your way. You may laugh or you may cry. However, at the end, you
will know more about yourself, and the "problems" may not seem like
such a big deal.

Strengths

I'm in the world only for the purpose of composing.
—Franz Schubert

1. Entrepreneurial
2. Artistically creative
3. Innovative, inspirational, intuitive
4. Enjoys change and variety
5. Expanding limits
6. Can envision the "total" picture
7. Can often accomplish the "impossible"
8. Can take in large amounts of data second by second
9. Thinks in pictures, symbols, and metaphors
10. Can come up with intuitive solutions
11. Enjoys new beginnings, reinventing, start-ups, or turning a project around
12. Imaginative—ability to visualize and daydream
13. Space planning
14. Motivational
15. Adventurous
16. Adaptable
17. Problem solver

18. Sense of humor
19. Visionary leader/thinker
20. Independent
21. Enthusiastic
22. Energetic
23. Willing to take risks
24. Passionate
25. Expressive
26. Multitalented
27. Can completely focus on a project
28. Good at improvising
29. Good at juggling 100 different tasks

Challenges

> When the individuality of the artist begins to express it-
> self, what the artist gains in the way of liberty he loses
> in the way of order.
> **—Pablo Picasso**

1. Easily sidetracked
2. Can become too absorbed in one thing
3. Dislikes rules of any kind
4. Short-term interests
5. Often late, inaccurate, and error prone
6. Can become drained when dealing with details, structure, sched-ules, repetition, etc.
7. Works in "fits and starts"
8. Has difficulty completing a given task when details are involved
9. Impulsive
10. Maintenance of systems is a challenge
11. Dislikes conflict
12. Dislikes slow-paced work
13. Dislikes routines
14. Can delegate well, but has a hard time with follow-up

Now let's focus on techniques for managing your environment with ease and success!

ORGANIZING YOUR TIME

> In my relativity theory, I set up one clock at every point
> in space, but in reality I find it difficult to provide even
> one clock in my room.
> —Albert Einstein

Time management for you requires a *major attitude adjustment*. It is the key in ensuring that organization happens. This can be a challenge for people who prefer to work alone or in their own style. You may even lose track of time while wearing a watch. Spontaneity is where you rule supreme! Missing appointments or showing up late could be your nemesis. Deadlines make your eyes glaze over, or prompt you to bury your head in yet another report. It's not that you don't value being on time or time in general. But your brain values daydreaming, envisioning, innovating, and creating more.

It can get absorbed in one activity and forget that time exists. You live for the present, which is great when meditating, but not really practical in day-to-day situations. Consequently, you tend to follow a timetable that others may never truly understand. You march to your own drummer, oftentimes noticing very little of what's going on around you while visualizing and creating, blithely unaware that the clock is ticking loudly next door or even on your desk. The real crux of this problem is how to be reliable and still remain true to who you really are.

Setting limits for your own energy often poses difficulties and you fail to pace yourself. You find spontaneity so invigorating. The good news is you can handle a large to-do list. The bad news is that sometimes it feels more like a sugar high than a solid steady "up." How do you view time? As linear, along a set path of appointments from one to the next? Or as a pie shape, in which there is a finite amount that is sliced thinner and thinner to fit everything? Are you happy with how you spend your time?

Do you get everything done on your list and still have time for extracurricular activities with friends and family? Or perhaps I should ask if you even have a to-do list. Anyway, take five minutes and close your eyes. Visualize today. Did you feel stressed out about something you could have done differently—something that cluttered up your mind—something that could have gone smoother, but didn't?

In theory, organization is very similar to what we perceive as order. Obviously, some structure has to be put in place, but it must fit your needs. Having an honest relationship with time is no simple task. First, you have to open up to the possibility that time is your friend, there to help you, and that recording future plans in whatever way you see fit isn't a burden but rather something that strengthens your pursuit of your dreams. When scheduling things into your planner, keep it simple. You understand that it is counterintuitive for you to work methodically. Come up with a simple way to tackle this. Ask yourself one question throughout the day: "What is the best use of my time *right now*?" You normally don't know what that answer is because you rarely take the time to notice, never mind drawing a road map for your day. Don't get stuck in the Maintaining Style of managing time; that approach is too rigid and structured for you. Learning to write things down is the first step, but an a.m. or p.m. calendar would be more than enough for you—a calendar would be a start in the right direction.

It can be fun and challenging to do several things at once. And it is fine to have a diversion or two along the way. They can inspire you. But when you ask yourself, "What is the best use of my time *right now*?" and listen, you will be amazed at how quickly you discover the answer and how easy the plan is to follow. You just need a way to record this, a process by which to achieve it.

Lena, a former client of mine, sat at her desk, head in hands. She was due at the Board of Supervisors' chambers in exactly eleven minutes and she could not find the latest budget analysis. *If only pages could talk,* she said to herself, *I'd be able to hear them and know exactly where the analysis was located.* Lena was very sensitive to sound and had 20/20 vision, though she often joked that her eyes were primarily for decoration. When she looked around the office, all the papers and folders seemed to blur, and she found it energy intensive to locate anything by sight. Getting to her feet in despair, she heard the crackle of paper hitting the floor. There it was. She'd been sitting on it! "There has to be a way to manage my papers more efficiently," she murmured to herself.

When you become bored, you tend to lose your zest and creative edge. So your system has to work without getting in the way. Many of my clients like to concentrate vigorously on one thing, and then take a break to do something else, such as going through their office supply drawer or some computer entry. Forget that you are the social specialist for a moment. You thrive on excitement, spontaneity, using your gut reactions to determine the next step. As long as you know what your goals are for that particular day, although you may get offtrack temporarily, you can still finish what you started. Diversions can be like a treat, rewarding you by doing something completely different for a couple of hours. You need it or you will go berserk! Don't. There are so many ways to tweak the system to avoid boredom.

So, how do you get away from the stress of feeling like you never have enough time for the day? Where do you start? First, come to terms with where your time goes. Examine what you do and how you normally get it done. Are there better ways? Most certainly. Organizing isn't about being able to do more—that's a total misconception! Rather, it is about being able to focus and concentrate on one job, and avoid worrying that you missed something else. To set up the system, you have to begin by understanding where your time goes. Then you can devise a simple road map to refer to throughout the day, which ensures you stay on track.

You work well when you have something tangible—a weight or deadline—to help remind you what you need to do at any given time. This may be the real conundrum for you: how to quantify an action that stems from creative roots. Suppose you give yourself three hours to brainstorm new ideas for an ad campaign. Perhaps you're able to accomplish it in two or two and a half hours. If you stick to a loose, basic simple time frame, you can at least feel more at ease, aware that you are doing something that has to be done.

#1. Making Space for Time

> We work not only to produce but also to give value to
> time.
>
> —Eugène Delacroix

Space! This is your number one priority. Space that is both tangible and intangible. Your environment must have room to let your ideas grow, especially when you are working on something new. Without room to move around within the calendar, you will eventually feel stifled and perform poorly. A calendar that is full of a thousand tiny commitments will suffocate you, encouraging you to retreat rather than rise to meet those deadlines.

People around you may truly try to help you but may unintentionally hinder the creative process. Sarah, a lawyer in a very impressive large firm, just couldn't seem to use her company's day-planning system. When her new assistant came on board, she filled an empty calendar in hopes to keep her boss productive. This was kind of her, but appointment-to-appointment, minute-to-minute, it didn't work for Sarah at all. She was chronically late, stressed, and out of control. Forget being made partner; she was just hoping to get through the day.

I encouraged Sarah to keep an appointment book, where certain kinds of appointments, such as meetings, client visits, and so on, were all consolidated into one chunk of the day—morning, afternoon, or even a complete day. This left time open to review client documents or brainstorm strategies. To paraphrase Julie Morgenstern, who wrote *Time Management from the Inside Out*, given tasks need to be envisaged in compartments of your day planner, just as sweaters need to be on a shelf. You require a clear road map for daily activities, but one that also permits play and flexibility. Not only will you know where you are going but this can reduce frustration for you and for others around you.

You do need a planner of some sort. In today's world, it is really a necessity. You have to track where you need to be on any given day in relating to the broader picture. Time/space dedicated to brainstorming, envisioning, and innovating are important. If you are booked back-to-back with appointments, make certain to give yourself enough time to finish one task and gather your thoughts before you have to move on to the next. Rushing around may pump adrenaline for the moment, but it can result in uncompleted assignments and the desire to start something new rather than complete what was previously started.

Managing your time can keep other factors in your life together. Try to see organization as invigorating. If you notice that you're more concerned with time than with ideas, you may have a problem. Time should not be your number one focus—but a basic awareness can help everyone. This system is meant to aid you, not to hinder what you already do so capably. Here are some basic principles for time management, broken down into four topics.

1: Keep It Simple

1. Figure out the time of day when you have the most energy to tackle the hardest task.
2. Make your calendar memorable so that you notice it and like to use it.
3. Write down *all* of the steps needed in order to complete any given task. Then make time for each one. Initially give yourself more time than usual and have a clock to alert you when you need to finish that particular step.
4. Create deadlines or dates to motivate you.
5. Record time-sensitive actions in pen rather than pencil to make the commitment stronger.
6. Have one to-do list.
7. Say no to any added job or commitment until you've spent a couple of minutes just asking yourself if you wanted to do it anyway.
8. Have one contact list or address book. If this is too much of a pain to keep up continuously, try keeping the little Post-its all taped to one book.
9. Go vertical and visual ASAP.

2: Keep It Up to Date

1. Keep your calendar in clear view at all times.
2. Enlarge your current electronic daily calendar, print it out, and put it next to your computer monitor, corkboard, or even on your fridge at home.
3. Have a daily calendar simply divided into a.m. and p.m. sections, and either a monthly or yearly calendar at your fingertips. Play with it. You won't use it if it isn't enjoyable. Use stickers, markers, a chalkboard, whatever works for you. You must have fun!
4. Keep track of changes in your schedule. Don't try to keep all those reminders in your head.
5. Avoid scraps of paper. Use a book, and date it at the opening.
6. Purchase a see-through plastic desk mat to keep important names/ events or papers beneath. You can change these continually.

3: Allow Time for Work *and* Play

1. Give yourself some creative administrative time (CAT). Review your to-do list and decide what can be transferred to the next day. Put on some great music and bop around! Just 10 minutes a day, morning or evening, is great.
2. Even though you tend to go wild when trying to get organized, focus on one project at a time, such as the paper in your office or the mess in the garage.
3. Give yourself extra time around appointments.
4. Allow extra time to do the things that crop up unexpectedly.
5. Plan and schedule rewards for a job that you consider well done.

4: Protect Yourself

1. Hang up signs: WORKING ON A PROJECT or UNAVAILABLE 1–5p.m.
2. Schedule a chunk of time (e.g., a 2-hour period) to let your brain innovate.
3. Discuss with assistant or significant others ways they can help you be productive.
4. *Pace yourself.*

Your Calendar

> The triumph of anything is a matter of organization.
> —Kurt Vonnegut

A set designer in Hollywood, who had been speeding at 100 miles an hour, was still late for our first appointment. He told me that many people reported to him on this particular feature film, which was being shot on several locations and continually rewritten. Not uncommon for a Hollywood film, he said. His challenge, using a revolving staff, was to keep all the pieces together in a coherent way from Morocco to the Mojave Desert. The crux was his need to write everything down, color-code it for priorities—he was a very visual person indeed—and then be able to change it throughout the day. My suggestion was that he use an electronic day planner since his travels took him around the world. (A basic Microsoft Outlook database that lets you color-code or prioritize tasks could easily travel with him and be printed at the drop of a hat.) One that has a colored screen and a snazy case will be beneficial.

This solved his problem by (a) giving him just what he needed to see; (b) maintaining awarenesss of the people in various areas of the production; (c) allowing him to edit and make changes whenever they were needed; and (d) enabling his support staff to know his every move. If you are not that electronically savvy, try a large desk calendar. Place it in a strategic position—*vertically*! It can't be lying on the desk amidst all of your other work. You also need a simple portable planner. Paper planners can drive you berserk. Tiny spaces for tiny thoughts is simply not your style. Try a month-at-a-glance pocket calendar (unless you absolutely must record more than three to four appointments per day). This gives you the big picture and still allows you to track key appointments easily.

You may prefer to make your own planner and have fun doing so. Use colorful markers, large sheets of paper, even your children's sticker collection—anything that inspires you to keep track of the days of the week. Even using different colors for flagging daily to-do's can be fun. If you go this route, try hanging the planner in front of you on the wall. Location is important. A planner works better when it can be seen from a distance. Putting it behind your computer monitor could be enormously helpful. Ultimately, envisaging what lies ahead can help you to relax and enjoy the day. Make sure the calendar stays *in exactly the same place* over time. This helps you to keep tabs on it more successfully.

If you love gadgets, an electronic organizer may be an option as long as you can keep track of it. Losing them gets expensive! Some people like these at the outset because they get involved learning something new and the challenge is stimulating. Be aware, however, that electronic organizers may not be ideal for you over time, especially if they require small, step-by-step actions to record and retrieve information. If you do stick with them, I would recommend a PDA with a color monitor. If you use a database (e.g., Outlook, Act), try making a printed copy at the beginning of every month. Then color code the days or appointments and hang it right next to your computer. If things change, you can just reprint it. Another plus is that everyone who comes into the office knows exactly where you are (assuming you want them to!). Some right-brain thinkers find computer gadgets daunting and impractical. You may prefer the Mac to a PC and find that it is easier and more enjoyable to use.

Other systems you can try are chalkboard or dry erase boards, placed in a prominent position in your office or home. Again, color coding the months or themes that are important to you and writing appointment times for each day in different colors can help. The office manager I worked with always hung the current month and the next month side by side so everyone knew what was happening now and what was coming up. This saved her from being continually interrupted. She also had an 8 by 10 calendar on her desk as well, just in case she was on the phone and couldn't see the big calendar on the wall. Maybe a couple of calendars could work better for you, giving you the numerous reminders you need to get everything accomplished. Don't go overboard here. But it worked for her.

#1. Use a Clock

> It is difficult to stop in time because one gets carried away. But I have that strength; it is the only strength I have.
>   —Claude Monet

You may not be able to find your clock. You may suggest that someone else knows the time or you can just step outside your office and look at the clock at work. This won't do. *You need to have a clock where you spend most of your time.* And not just any clock. Buy a very large one and hang it in a prominent position in your home. Get another for the office and car. Time is going to become a very good friend. You might enjoy a radio-controlled clock that automatically adjusts itself for Daylight Savings Time. That way you won't have to deal with that detail twice a year. You may also make use of your computer's reminder function. If you record appointments in an electronic calendar like Outlook, hot sync the computer with your PDA. The PDA will have an alarm alerting you of that appointment five minutes before it's due. This can be an enormous help.

When you glance up from your notes or computer, the clock alerts you to your next appointment. Do the same thing at home. The microwave clock just won't do—you need to be able to see a clock when you're at the dining-room table, or coming in the back door, and at various other strategic places in your space. Spend a little extra money here and you can't go wrong. Whenever you start to wander off into an inner world, that huge clock reminds you to get a project in the mail, make the ballgame that night, or better yet, show up for a date!

You may lose track of time when dealing with your own ideas. I suggest an alarm of some sort—even a kitchen egg one. A system that lets you know when it is time to stop and begin something else enables you to stay on a loose yet meaningful schedule. Don't think of this as smothering; it's actually liberating. It enables you to get the right things done and still affords you the freedom to pick and choose. Think of it as an asset, not a hindrance. The right frame of mind is very important if you are to absorb and put these new skills to use. This becomes especially useful when checking e-mails. So now you know where those two hours went!

#2. Buy a Wristwatch

> Once you concentrate on organizing, ideas fall into place with an almost audible click.
> —Jane Harrigan

You may never have had a watch that worked. Rather, you rely on others to remind you what time it is. This can be annoying to your assistant or mate. Become responsible. Wear a watch! It can be a Mickey Mouse watch (they tell time, too) but just make sure it's exciting, innovative, and colorful. Or, try buying a very inexpensive model, like a Swatch; get one every few months, or buy several and rotate them so you don't tire of seeing the same one. You can also buy one watch with a lot of different faces. A watch with an alarm could serve you well. They are mainly sports watches but they can be attractive, too. Experiment with a waterproof watch—you never have to take it off. Many stores now sell beautiful watchcases that allow you to change the look with ease. Above all, purchase a watch that requires very little maintenance. Your grandfather's antique pocketwatch may not do. Think easy, not nostalgic.

#3. Ask for Help

> We do things, but we do not know why we do them.
> —Albert Einstein

Use someone else's talent to your benefit—your coworkers and family may be delighted because you are not only improving your life but theirs as well! Understanding your own methods is important, but understanding others' is crucial. Encourage your assistant or partner to remind you of upcoming appointments, say thirty minutes in advance, so you have time to wrap up your thoughts and make an entrance! When scheduling an appointment (hairdresser, dentist, mechanic), ask the assistant or person on the front desk to call the day before and confirm the date. If you've missed the last few, they may suggest this themselves. Collaborate with others. You may be the leader and expect others to bend to your rules; nevertheless, you have to help each other. At home, collaborate with family members. They can often accomplish specific tasks more easily than you can. In turn, you can concentrate on the tasks that are easier for your brain type.

The clock is continually ticking. It is important to create a daily schedule that allows you to get things done but isn't so complicated that you get discouraged. If, for example, you are on the road a lot, you will find that a chalkboard to-do list isn't all that practical. Ask someone at work, if possible, to roll your calls for you or perform data entry. If you notice that you are not actually using what you've set up and are again running late for appointments, feeling stressed out, making mistakes, and feeling defeated at the end of the day, you must try to spend some time examining what we've talked about. Nothing is set in stone. Time is so mercurial that it is a challenge for the best of us. You can ask for help and, if it doesn't feel right, brainstorm for a different solution. That is what makes organizing invigorating: you always have the freedom to change it.

ORGANIZING YOUR HOME

> We turn clay to make a vessel, but it is on the space where there is nothing that usefulness of the vessel depends.
> —Lao-Tzu

For all brain types, their home is their haven. You want to create an environment that is comfortable where you can relax, or even crash after an exhausting, brain-intensive day. This poses some challenges in getting your home organized. Try to do it when you have the time, on a weekend, say, and not directly after work. Do it when your energy is at its peak.

Even though the same principles apply for residential organizing and corporate organizing, residential organizing can be a little trickier.

There are a lot more distractions at home than at the office! Give yourself time to do this well the first time or you'll feel like you are never done. Don't go overboard: the more steps you take, the less likely you are willing to maintain a new system. That's the truth. However, once you have done one area well, apply similar approaches to all the rooms in your home. Since your schedule probably varies from day to day, give yourself at least two to three hours; but I have known many with your brain preference work until midnight because you're so inspired and ready to rock 'n' roll! Make a conscious effort to eliminate distractions prior to getting organized—get the kids a play date, your partner out the door, etc.

You tend not to find conventional categories for the information you collect. Instead, you tend to organize your home by visual or spatial cues. You usually find it fairly easier to manage and rearrange your furniture to work in the available space both at home and in the office. Actually, you are more talented at this than the majority of people. The placement of furniture is key for a room to function properly. Karen Kingston stresses the importance of energy being able to move about freely in a room. She would probably call you a master at space planning. You can usually take pieces in a variety of sizes and shapes and space plan them to satisfaction. Typically, you like your furniture to be arranged in an innovative yet functional layout. The pieces you gravitate toward are often expressive, eclectic, futuristic, unusual. If your environment reflects your natural preference, you will be able to manage it for years to come with minimal effort.

You have the talent to set up the initial plan, but follow-through can be a little taxing. Easy, easy, and easy are your watchwords. People tend to get a good sense of you by the styles, patterns, and colors that you choose. You can design or combine things in ways that are truly striking. Your challenge isn't with the big stuff but the small stuff. When little things become disorganized, it can make your entire environment appear cluttered. Acknowledging your accomplishments here will encourage future success.

You tend to like clothes and have a whole lot of them. Examine what you want to keep and what you want to discard. This is the first step and the most enjoyable. You will have it done in no time flat. Put the discarded items in the garage for a donation pickup. Arrange your clothing in such a way that when you get up in the morning, you go to one area of the closet for the basics and another for accessories. Things don't have to be in perfect order in your drawers. As long as when you open your sock drawer, both socks are there and matched up! Simple, very basic, and low maintenance will make you successful here.

I had a client who liked to hang a beautiful scarf from Africa at the entrance to her closet. It made her feel the warmth and comfort of her journey back to her homeland, and she liked being in that closet to re-arrange and put things away. Whatever works for you. Another client had an enormous closet that contained a stereo system. Music got him in the mood and made organizing fun. Think motivation.

A Number of Simple Solutions

1. Entrance to your home: whether you come in from the garage or the front door, have a catchall—a large storage container to drop off your daily stuff.
2. Try large generic containers that are nicely decorated (for incoming mail, toiletries). Keep things simple so they stay in place. Lids are just another problem for you. I would advise putting them under the containers or into the garage in storage.
3. Easy retrieval is paramount. It's no good putting something away if it's hard to get out again.
4. Focus on one area, one flat surface at a time. When completed, move on to the next. Stay in the pantry. Work shelf-by-shelf, cupboard-by-cupboard.
5. Write down your first assignment—for example, "kitchen pantry," on your calendar.
6. Give yourself a minimum of 4 to 8 *uninterrupted* hours on that specific job. It may take double that but you can work intensely. Max that out to get you staying organized.
7. Have supplies ready, such as trash bags, empty storage boxes, a black Sharpie marker, and masking tape.
8. Set the kitchen timer to go off at an allotted time.
9. After every organizing job, give yourself a reward. You deserve it!

10. Once things are in place, go the extra mile and try to keep them where they belong.

#1. Design Elements

> When I am working on a problem, I never think about
> beauty. I only think about how to solve the problem.
> But when I have finished, if the solution is not beautiful,
> I know it is wrong.
> —Buckminster Fuller

We all need to feel motivated and nurtured by our surroundings. How can you possibly accomplish any real work in a room if it doesn't make you feel good? Inspiration must come from inside. Your type of brain preference used more open space than any other. If possible, you prefer a room that allows your ideas to roam. If you have the option to remodel, consider high ceilings, modern colors, natural lighting, mirrors, and anything else that helps your thoughts expand. Tiny accent tables are one thing. Large flat surfaces on which to work, eat, stack, and play are another. Keep the space tamed. You need space, but sometimes that comes at the cost of cluttered surfaces. Brainstorm ways to store your materials or belongings vertically. A vertical or wall hanging basket that allows you access but leaves a flat surface space for work is ideal. Or use a bench or catchall on a long wall surface to store reading materials. Keep in mind ease of movement for you and your belongings when structuring a space. Additionally, you will enjoy a clean, large workspace—provided that you put things away after you're done.

A designer I worked with in Los Angeles had one of the most beautiful homes I've ever seen. It was spacious and had more flat surfaces than she needed—especially in her home office. She called me because she wanted to put some order into the piles of miscellaneous paper that were starting to accumulate at home. She needed to see things around her to make that room work. The first thing we did was to examine what she was keeping and then purchase open vertical filing boxes to put on her various desks for the active paper she needed to work on. Her brain type has to see things in order to remember them, return to them, and enjoy them—when we developed a system to cover these purposes, she became an organizing superstar!

Aim for an unstructured look in your environment. Loose pillows thrown on the floor can provide areas for reading, relaxing, or entertaining. Abstract patterns and geometric shapes can provide you with mental stimulation plus variety. Magazines and books on different topics, and innovative/unusual music, can be good friends. A balance between stimulation and relaxation is what you're after. Creating an atmosphere that combines options for both can enhance your success as long as everything is in reasonable order and you are not continually having to look for things. Keep in mind that your place isn't going to be perfect—and who cares? If it works for you and there are some basic systems in place—what more could you ask for?

#2. Storage

> To enjoy freedom, we have to control ourselves.
> —Virginia Wolf

How things are stored can be the most important point. Time management comes a close second. Remember: Out of sight, out of mind. You tend to stack things and want everything in plain sight. Pay attention to how you can accomplish this and still be organized. Otherwise, your environment will not be enjoyable. Some storage solutions:

1. Stackable see-through storage boxes
2. Window boxes
3. Elfa baskets—see-through wire baskets
4. Closet shelves rather than drawers
5. Curtain rods
6. Rolling blind for any open wall space: roll up when working, roll down when done. A great time-saving technique as you can be in a room and not have see the clutter. If you have closets, try to keep the door closed as much as possible.
7. Employ as many hooks as possible

8. Labels can be fun and custom-made if you affix the item, such as a piece of film negative, colored labels, kids' drawings, on the outside

9. Hampers must be kept in a strategic position

Use large, attractive containers (wire, woven baskets, Plexiglas, see-through plastic, or glass) to stack the items and objects that you use frequently. Try to keep them in the same room and if possible right where you would normally use them. When you come home with a stack of mail, dump it in a basket near the entrance. Don't even think of having that basket down the hall, up the stairs, or around the corner. Get my drift? When you purchase office supplies, dump them in a container in your office. Get rid of the enormous amount of packaging that each item comes with and minimize all storage pieces.

Each room in your home needs its very own in-basket to contain traffic for that area. Photos or anything labeled "Memorabilia" need to be containerized immediately. If not, these items can bury you, and they are far more difficult to deal with when they have reached mountain status. Make it easy at the outset. Train yourself to become aware of items that can quickly become burdens. Create a system to deal with them *before* your energy is zapped. For easy access and visibility use open containers or ones with lids that open and close easily, or forget the lids completely. You may not need to spend time with a labeler. Simply write the contents on a piece of paper and put it on the outside of the box. Think "minimal upkeep" and you will emerge victorious.

#3. Paper

> Putting off an easy thing makes it hard, and putting off
> a hard one makes it impossible.
> **—George Lorimer**

As we've already discussed, paper can be a nightmare for everyone, but it can be lethal for you. Paper is your pet peeve, especially in today's world where you continually need to print hard copy. I know you already feel better about how we are going to solve this with the ideas mentioned earlier in this chapter. As you are well aware, once a piece of paper has been filed, it may be gone forever ("What label did I file that under anyway?" "Did I ever have it?"). One way to make this easier is to continually purge paper. **The solution is not to use less paper, but to store less paper.** If you can't bear to part with something yet, or aren't sure it really is ready for purging, stick it up on the wall on an attractive corkboard. Use unusual magnets, colorful glass tacks, or interesting clips. Try a "Design Within Reach" corkboard in rooms where paper tends to accumulate and even multiply. Be creative: use the inside of cupboards, or place a binder on the counter to create a way of seeing what you have and locating it easily without the area looking too cluttered. Use any highlighter you can find to point up important info, such as dates, money amounts, or names on the top of an article, so you don't have to reread something over and over before you decide to toss it. Spiral notebooks for journals, random thoughts, to-do's, etc., are the answer. I allow you to have *several* journal books that are big, bright, and colorful for the different areas in your life.

Remember, you are probably not in love with detail and shouldn't waste your time with it. Whenever possible, create an open filing system where you can easily see what is inside (wire containers, stacking bins, even a decorative milk crate). A portable filing system is a great idea and a desktop vertical tickler system a must. You need to make a huge distinction between *active* files and *reference* files. Active files mean files you refer to daily. Reference files mean you hold things that you refer to infrequently, such as an ice cream maker manual that could even be stored with the actual item, so you never lose it.

Color coding your active and reference files may be helpful. Be judicious: avoid a rainbow filing system that doesn't make any sense at all. Two simple colors should be sufficient. Use what is at your fingertips. Do you need to put *all* of your files in your filing cabinet? No! A hanging file on a desk or tabletop works just as well, and you avoid putting things into drawers—one less thing for you to do.

For the active files, if you have the wall or surface space at home, you should go *vertical*. Horizontally stored documents are goners. They may work well for some people but can be a disaster for you. Any incoming papers, magazines, or bills only get acted upon if you can see them. A wall pocket or vertical cardboard stand helps. I don't need to tell you how to be creative or imaginative. Just don't go down the "traditional" path. The best item you can buy to corral your paper is an Everyday Sorter. It is like an accordion file box, those ugly brown ones your parents used to store receipts. This one has twenty slots that expand lying horizontally with no closure on the top or bottom. It can be put right on your desk, not in a cabinet, and it keeps your daily papers organized.

Try using plastic envelopes to hold assignments, or an expandable file folder that can accommodate specific items (e.g., receipts needed for tax returns). Keep it simple, easily transportable, and expandable. For example, a client of mine, Dan, loved binders. He would take things to the garage to work on—especially the household manuals. However, over time, it became a nuisance to continually punch holes, use sheet protectors, and so on. Guess where the binder ended up? Lost. When you feel like you are doing three steps when you could be doing just one, you are overorganizing, and that will most certainly hinder your progress. The maintenance of the system is the real element that must be conquered. If you get sidetracked and lose your focus, then likely you are undertaking too many steps.

Reference files can include anything that you may need to refer to at some later date—such as the ID file where you can store your passport and various travel documents or old tax returns. Normally, we would make a distinction between archival files and reference, but we won't in your case. Your reference files can either be stored in some horizontal baskets perhaps, two to four of them that are five inches deep located on a shelf, credenza, or in a drawer. Or you can just toss the various pieces of paper into a banker's box as mentioned earlier and store that in your closet. Remember that you are highly unlikely to go through this stuff. You can also create one box for important documents and a second for not-that-so-important documents. You know where they are and this works for you, so what else is there to discuss?

ORGANIZING YOUR OFFICE

A man paints with his brains not with his hands.
—**Michelangelo**

Your office is a place to work, not a storeroom or a place where you can't find a seat. And traditional filing cabinets don't really suit you. A great deal of flat surface to stack and pile projects on which you are currently working is much more compatible. Again, stacking wire baskets should be the ticket. Things can be together yet separate, and you can locate them easily because they are in plain sight. Keeping stuff in sight allows you to work with your ideas, see what still needs to be included, and track the big picture. If you have to return phone messages, it may be effective to use a giant paperclip that can hold the business card or note in front of you until you make that call. And certainly have a spiral-bound message pad to store all incoming calls. On the front use a black marker to put the date that you started to use the book.

You need cues (objects, colors, sounds) to remind you where things are and what has to get accomplished. Whether it's the sound of a bell every hour on the hour, or two huge wall calendars—one for the current month and one for the following month—anything that doesn't let you forget.

Doodling pads, flip charts, and large sheets of writing paper should be your best friends. Keep a sufficient supply so you can jot down (or draw, doodle, diagram) what's happening inside your head. I will allow you to have a bucketful of pens or markers on your desk. When you're brainstorming solutions or trying to come up with a new idea, use a flip chart or large sheets of paper and that can be taped or tacked to the wall. Viewing your work like this helps you visualize the big picture, and tap into creativity, problem-solving abilities, in a way that might not happen were you simply thumbing through stacks of paper. Remember, wall space is next best to counter space.

Since handling details can be energy intensive for you, spending hours labeling and filing away materials is often a waste of time. And it can be a challenge to try to recall the specific label you used for a given set of information. (The old "out of sight, out of mind" drill!) You know where everything is in your stacks (if no one has moved them), so leave them where they are until you are completely finished with that project and then decide if and where you will file the material for future reference. Remember that 80 percent of what is filed, most people don't ever need. If you must file, keep only the things you are sure to need in the future.

Your brain functions best in start-up situations, so you should develop an organizational system that matches that move easily. Your tendency is to go wild on an idea, get it off the ground, then move on to something else, leaving the project maintenance to others. If this is how you function best, allow for the remaining documents to be filed, shredded, or handled by your assistant. In other words, don't use up valuable stacking space with stuff you no longer need. If the project is finished, get rid of the piles so you aren't distracted as you move on to the next project.

Make efficient use of shelf space. Think of shelves simply as smaller flat surfaces. Shelving mounted onto a wall can add to visual stimulation and provide additional space for paper and objects, keeping them out of your immediate way. Try creating "project shelves." Projects can be stored horizontally in a basket as long as you can see them. Completed or incomplete assignments can be stored here. Avoid using drawers or cupboards. They are the last resort.

Your biggest asset is your assistant—if you have one (I pray you do!). If at all possible, delegate tasks that drain your energy. Your friend the Prioritizing Style does this as much as he or she can. When you hire employees, make certain that "detail-oriented" is an integral part of their job description. It can save your job and better yet, your life. If you had your druthers, I would try to encourage you to have an office with a door that closes so you can get more done and not be disturbed. This would be good both for you and your coworkers!

I also want to mention something that really affects your space—the desire you experience to read every printed piece of material that comes across your desk. Perhaps your brain has to do this in order to feel energized. According to Don Herold, a humorist, "The brighter you are, the more you have to learn." But I see you stressing out all of the time, worrying over magazines you haven't read and probably never will. Don't even get me going on catalogs, or the cooking and design magazines that pile up so quickly! If a new magazine comes in and you haven't read the old one—*out it goes!* Try it! The same goes for books. Donate them to the hospital. Or get to know your public library better. Save money and help save the planet.

#1. Electronic Organizing

Computers are a way of life, but how you go about organizing your computer can be a challenge. More than likely, computer stuff doesn't interest you that much either. You tend to use computers as a means to an end. If you don't find your computer intriguing, you won't use it. To solve this dilemma, you might find a Mac more desirable than a PC, since the Mac's style is more visual. Its outer and inner design is targeted for the more creative person who enjoys graphics and pliable software. Macs have a way of conveying ideas that might even render your thinking more imaginatively. Pause before you purchase extra computer paraphernalia.

All you really need to enjoy the electronic experience is some basic skills. You don't have to know the details of every program, since you aren't going to have to deal with the minutiae of software. However, you do need to be inspired, and specific programs can help you keep track of ideas and the people who can implement them.

Computer retrieval tends to be a challenge. If you are prone to misplace paper, what will you do with electronic files? Since you also tend to change categories every time you file paper, you may do the same with electronic documents. Computers can be a boom, however. I suggest you create a file for "names of documents," with short descriptions of what each contains. Going paperless can be wonderful as long as you have something to jog your memory about document names.

CONCLUSION

> The future belongs to those who believe in the beauty
> of their dreams.
> **—Eleanor Roosevelt**

It can be very challenging to be creative and still keep it all together. Organizing, as Samuel Beckett said, means "to find a form that accommodates the mess." It's no easy job, especially when there are thousands of other things that you would rather be doing. Organizing isn't for the weak, but you can conquer anything. It may be stressful when those around you don't understand your version of organizing and move things without you having a say. You tend to organize differently from others. That's okay. Perhaps you can learn from each other and design a system that works for both of you. All brain types are needed in our society. We usually hear, "Hey, my way is the best way, so why aren't you doing it my way?" The purpose of this book isn't to shame someone's behavior but rather to acknowledge and encourage it.

Notice when things begin to bother you because you now have the power to change them. Your brain knows what works for you, so organize *in whatever way* is workable and sustainable for you. If you begin to feel restless and out of sorts, it may be because your environment is not matched to what your brain does easily. Give yourself time to adapt, be flexible, and evaluate what you create. Your schedule may change and you may have to travel more than before, or there may be an addition to your family, or because you communicate well with those around you about your brilliant ideas for product X, you just landed a promotion and will be relocated in no time flat. Be open to planning your future in a nonstifling way. Yes, planning is essential, but allowing spontaneity and fun into that plan is a recipe for encouragement and hence success.

Let me repeat: Be assertive in reminding others to leave your stacks alone. You know what's in them. Going through them again because they were moved and/or dumped in one pile can be a huge waste of time, to say nothing of irritating and frustrating. Honor who you are innately and respect the organizational style that works for you. It's your brain, your things, your life, and your giftedness. Refuse to be shamed by pejoratives ("messy," "cluttered," "disorganized") and recognize that those are words often used by individuals who simply have an organizational style that differs from yours.

When a woman I knew was accused of having a disorganized space, her response was "I'm challenged when it comes to tracking bounded shapes. Having everything in sight, in stacks, works for my brain. I know it isn't your cup of tea—but that's okay." Then she serenely continued to address the topic at hand. How gracious and functional! No put-down of herself or others. Just acknowledgment and respect for "different styles for different folks."

Getting Started:
For Example—
Household Paper Clutter

1. It's time to get organized! Let's go wild and work until you are done. No time limits for you!

2. Start in the area that jazzes you up the most and stay there until papers are in order. Since you enjoy the stacking system, have a large flat surface space available. The dining-room table would work great.

3. Gather each pile from each room onto the table. Go through and create three new piles: "Toss," "Keep," "File." Don't spend a lot of time gathering. Set a timer, perhaps fifteen minutes for each 6-inch pile.

4. Consolidate these three areas. Don't leave the table and put something over here and something over there. Stay put until everything is presorted and consolidated.

5. Active papers must be placed in an interior file folder, labeled with a pen or whatever is easy for you. Depending on your space, store the file folder vertically on the desk in either a vertical stand or wall pockets.

6. Inactive papers must be placed together with a paperclip, binder clip, or in a hanging file.

7. What little paper you feel you must keep, either toss into a banker's box under your desk or use a 2-inch drop bottom hanging file set into a small filing drawer. (Notice that for you, interior files may not be needed at all.)

8. Keep containers loose and as much in front of you as possible. A hutch at the end of the desk to store cards, supplies, and active documents is great.

9. Since you are very spontaneous, try to sort paper often. Record in your calendar every 2 to 3 months to keep this up. You may catch yourself doing it more often.

10. Reward yourself. You can now give your full attention to something else for a while.

OVERVIEW OF THE INNOVATING STYLE

Purpose: To notice when things are changing and provide insight into the future.

Organization of Space: You must be able to see everything right in front of you. If it's out of sight, it's out of mind.

Strengths: When you decide to get organized, you are very hyperfocused, work quickly, and see the big picture.

Challenges: Very spontaneous and easily distracted. You tend to be a sporadic organizer, easily bored with detail or routine.

Time
Calendar: Must be fun and easy. Must be vertical or stored on available wall space. You may tend to use Post-its on a vertical calendar that can be moved around and changed every day. May need to be reminded of upcoming appointments.

To-do List: Can use to-do lists to help with task completion.

Goals: To accomplish tasks with minimum attention to time and detail.

Contacts: You tend to have pieces of paper all around. There should be one specific listing for all your contacts.

Paper
Incoming Mail: You tend to put mail down on any flat surface. Use one area where it can be contained.

Desktop: Stackers like you prefer all items directly in front of you or you forget they are there. Need extra flat space for stacking.

Filing System: Use a stacking system until finished with the project, so it can then be filed or discarded.

Closets

Closets: You prefer to hang rather than fold, in no particular order.

Drawers: May store by item but not in any great detail or matched by color.

Storage: Must try to store things visually as much as possible. Use clear boxes with lids so they can be stacked, or wire storage systems, where things can be seen. (Least amount of steps possible.)

Purging: Purge when you have completed the project or when the environment becomes unruly.

Memorabilia: Tendency to retain for a time and then purge for no apparent reason.

Chapter Four

Prioritizing Style

The less effort, the faster and
more powerful you will be.
—Bruce Lee

Greetings! I know you have many pressing deadlines to deal with and don't have a lot of extra time. If you can commit to quickly examining the way you go about doing things, scan this chapter and check out the organizing tips and systems that leap off the page. You'll enjoy discovering more about your distinct organizing style and learning shortcuts to make you lead more effectively. Plus, you can learn all sorts of new ways to make more time to explore those extra activities you've wanted to master since your college days.

Since I know you prefer your information brief and to the point, I'll honor your essential nature and tell it like it is. Your particular style is easy to sum up: *You want to win and are willing to do whatever it takes.* Your special genius lies in setting and achieving goals. You can take information, analyze it, and quickly determine the next step. Numbers, cost-effective strategies, and critical analyses speak to you. From making huge life-changing decisions to minor assessments about what documents need to be kept and filed, you are a leader. As "Biff" Jones, the college football coach, said about leadership principles, "Organize. Deputize. And Supervise." How are you going to manage better delegating if you were organized before? You prefer to delegate the actual job of keeping everything organized, however. This is your organizing lesson: You appreciate and deeply value organization, but have no interest in keeping it all together. Let me interject with a pointer on how you feel about this: "But I pay someone $35,000 a year to do it. Why should it concern me?"

Well, chances are that in today's world, you can't rely on someone, all the time, to help you make sense of it all. You absolutely, positively need to be in control, know where things are at, and be able to move forward—*effortlessly*. Filing was at one time considered a clerical job. No more. In today's world, it is your responsibility as well. Obviously making the tabs on the folders isn't your job, but knowing where a document eventually lands is. (Let's cross our fingers you have hired the right person as your assistant.)

Disorganization costs you money—and lots of it. If only one person at your workplace is inefficient, it can impact the efficiency of the entire organization. According to *Office Life Canada* (June 2003), most workers view themselves as:

1. 33% Neat Freaks
2. 27% Pilers
3. 23% Filers
4. 12% Pack Rats
5. 2% Slobs

To add insult to injury, the average time they spent organizing their office every week was 20.1 minutes. If you have 2 million paper documents at work, your company could stand to spend about $40,000 to $60,000 on filing cabinets alone! Organized electronically with clear classification systems, that information could be easily contained in less than ten CD-ROMs. Never mind the actual space it costs your company to store the filing cabinets. So, disorganization not only costs you money but time and space.

How about analyzing what you can do to improve? Obviously, in order to raise the bar, you must be even better organized than you think you already are. Even if think you are exceptional, you can improve your style. I have yet to meet one person with your Prioritizing Style who was organized to the best of their ability. You run here and there, often frantic, making sure everything gets done—by you. You normally don't delegate so well, so you end up doing a lot yourself. I recently worked with a CEO who asked me in one workshop why he still spent much of his time in the copy room. Since this really is not an organizational but a job description issue, you must sometimes wonder if lack of organization is the result of something else. Don't worry; we'll find out for you. Ultimately this will give you greater personal contentment and the self-assurance to make the right decisions.

My goal is to make sure that the time you invest in this chapter will give you the confidence that everything can work more easily in your personal and professional life. As you practice some solid organizational methodologies, you can maximize wins and minimize losses. You are always on the lookout for better means to get the job done without requesting the help of others. You would so much rather just do it yourself. We'll figure out tangible ways to help and motivate you. If you sprint through the other chapters, you can assess other people's strengths to help with your own. Remember, knowledge is power.

Here are some general characterizations of people with your brain type:

- You tend to keep your eyes open, working diligently around the clock, if necessary, to produce results that are derived from facts and figures.
- You relish the edge with facts, figures, precision.
- You tend to set and achieve goals and know at the end of the day that you accomplished everything on your to-do list.
- You view life as something to be mastered.
- Compulsive about improving upon things.
- React with logic not emotion.
- Work well under extreme pressure.
- "Control specialist"—perfectionist.
- Like things right—*your way.*
- Enjoy interesting ways of solving problems.
- Competitive rather than cooperative.
- Winning is part of what keeps you motivated.
- The chase to the goal holds your focus and helps drive you onward.
- You are able to analyze manipulate the situation to reach the desired outcome.

If even one of these statement matches who you are, welcome to your brain! Your fundamental focus and drive in life is goal attainment. Objects, things, even people may be lower on your list of priorities, unless of course they are needed to help you achieve the goal.

This poses a little bit of a conundrum with regard to organizing. You prefer to make quick, accurate decisions. You want instant access to information. However, the world doesn't operate like this 100 percent of the time. You need paperwork and reports for the task at hand. When you need a file folder, you need it right here and now. Either an assistant brings it to you or you have exactly what you require front and center. Since your brain type prefers streamlining, using only the minimum of everything (supplies, paper, belongings), you tend to believe that less is more. Still, you have to have support material ready and available for any given project. This is your ultimate challenge: To learn how to balance your desire to avoid clutter, yet remain in control with the realities of an active leadership position.

When I enter your office, usually I see a computer, a couple of fancy calligraphy pens, Mont Blancs, and a writing tablet. It is Spartan, so I know right off the bat I've landed in leadership territory. When possible, you dispense with the "extras." You are the antithesis of the pack rat. You may file the last page of a financial report rather then the entire report, knowing that if you ever need the details you can lay hands on them. One page is just right. In general, you save what is essential to help you analyze data, complete a project—and let the rest go. In your mind, anything else is superfluous.

Your brain type can provoke a tremendous amount of mystery, misinformation, and awe. Many of us don't quite understand how someone's fundamental passion could be to achieve success at all costs. You'd rather work than play? Wow! Other brain preferences sense your deep focus and intensity and secretly may look up to you, but they may not always be comfortable around such drive and determination. That's because people, emotions, and personal issues aren't tops on your list. You would rather deal with task problems than people problems. Let's face it: you are willing to do whatever it takes to get where you want to go. You show that you care about people by being responsible, not overly friendly. You care much more about being respected than liked. In chaotic situations you remain calm, cool, and collected where others tend to react emotionally. This is just who you are.

Your drive to be number one can leave little room for much else to happen. You are the quintessential CEO, the "leader of the pack," someone who knows where their organization is going 24/7 and is willing to work as hard as necessary. "Whatever it takes" is your motto! When I worked for Lance, a high-powered business executive (his wife gave him my organizing services as a birthday present!), it was daunting at first. Ms. Professional Organizer walked through the front door and heard, "I don't want you here. You are of no value to me." I didn't miss a beat but retorted, "Lance, I don't want any more chitchat from you until we finish organizing your home office. Let's go!" There was a pause, then he chuckled. He realized that I was dead serious. We immediately got to work. Mind you, we didn't stop until we were completely done. That meant no lunch breaks, no five-second water breaks, nothing but drive and perseverance. He later confided to me that he was a success freak. *Really?*

Sound familiar? You, like Lance, are an all-or-nothing person. No gray areas. Lance needed sound, proven, quick, intelligent, and above all convincing organizational solutions for every piece of paper, every financial binder, ever single thing in his office. I didn't bother him with the details about my methodology. And he got it. He was invigorated by the challenge and rose to the occasion. Moving his credenza two feet closer so he didn't have to reach every time to get a reference book was a revelation. I could tell he appreciated every little piece of information that might improve his life.

People with your brain type are admired and respected for their intense focus and ability to win. They are also feared for these same qualities. You accomplish your goals with courage, fervor, and accuracy. You have the tools, the right attitude, and the right management skills to make it all happen. As chief opportunists, you tend to assess life on a moment-to-moment basis, eagerly looking for whatever it takes to win. That edge or rush brings passion into your life and stimulates you. You have a tendency to analyze everything for functionality, evaluating the various parts and identifying how they relate to one another. You use diagnostic thinking and usually approach problems from an objective, unemotional, cost-conscious position. In developing an organizing system, you analyze what you need to know, select viable options, prioritize actions, and evaluate quickly. Then you take charge, make decisions, and head for the goal. "Onward and upward" is another one of your mottos!

You need functional space, both at home and at work. Functionality drives almost everything you do. The most effective way to "nail things down" in a timely manner is to have the tools, equipment, supplies, and necessary gadgets available in working order (I stress the word "working") and ready to go. Your tools need to be ready at a moment's notice. The effective organization system for you is one designed to offer functional support so you can relax and do what you do best: set and achieve goals.

Although objectivity supersedes subjectivity, you do want others to make the most of their time and money. Ask yourself, what are the strategies that can enable you to function more efficiently (doing things right) and effectively (doing the right things), with less stress? Let's look in greater detail at how you think and then at how you can reexamine the value you place on time, space, and the particulars about the way you set up your home and office. This should not seem like a chore. It is time that is going to be well spent learning how to adjust things. Normally, you are right on the money. But with the growing amount of people producing more and more stuff, even you can get a little out of control and find that not everything is well laid out and easy to retrieve. A positive mind equals a positive experience.

HOW YOUR BRAIN TYPE WORKS

> It is not enough to have a good mind; the main thing is to use it well.
> —Descartes

Your brain's strengths lie in the ability to take apart an entire structure and devise ways of understanding the parts' relationships to one another. Your keen ability develops a terminology, classifying systems, and coherent structures in a way that only a logical, mathematical mind can do. You are able to compare apples to crayons by using inductive and deductive reasoning to find a coherent relationship, so that dissimilar items appear to have a genuine commonality. You love the challenge of problem solving and can work alone in pursuit of theoretical topics. Using forms (such as $e = mc^2$) rather than symbols (such as a flower), you use your objectivity and critical thinking to get to the bottom line. Absolutely brilliant. Your talents can be used to run a company or lead a group. This quality is one that our society rewards over all others. Even if others don't understand how you approach things, they often envy or admire you.

Function is key for you. This applies alike to possessions, paper, and people. If things don't fit into your plan, they are done away with. You are the only brain type that has no difficulty whatsoever in throwing out stuff. I've seen several of you who, when I arrive, straightaway start filling garbage bags full of documents, old binders, college briefcases, etc. You go wild. However, you may fail to give yourself enough time to do this either well or regularly.

Figuring out how something works and dissecting it until you understand the overall relationship is what drives you in every situation, tangible and intangible. You are absolutely fascinated by mechanical stuff and the urge to take it apart and put it back, such as a clock or a radio. You work well under pressure. Your ability for in-depth mental analysis makes you enormously rational, objective, and gives you an edge over all others. You usually think things through before acting and can be a competent decision maker in residential or corporate environments.

You thrive when you can let others know that you are a strong leader and a powerful winner. That is actually your raison d'être. Emotional commitment doesn't at all matter; you are far more connected to how you think than how you feel. You prefer not to have to use emotions for a deeper understanding of something. You can manage willpower and know what works best and what doesn't. Because you value thinking over feeling, you stand behind your opinions 100 percent of the time. And since you tend to arrive at decisions based on available data, you carry tremendous influence. Thus, by personally making key decisions (or deciding to whom you will delegate), and by maintaining the final say in all matters, you try to ensure that success happens by design rather than default. You hate to be duped. And if an opponent tries to fool you, they'll be surprised that you also find confrontation and conflict something of a thrill.

You tend to design your life to be in charge, to be on top of the heap, to be number one. That's not good or bad, it just is. The drive to win is partly responsible for your many successes. It can result in rendering you a social loner at times, unless participating in the social event helps you achieve goals. But as Marc Chagall once said just before his ninety-seventh birthday, the aim is "To stay wild, untamed . . . to shout, weep, pray." He produced many works by staying true to his nature, his way, and his dreams.

If your organizing system is to be helpful, it must be streamlined so that things are accessible at the drop of a hat. Committing the necessary time to achieve this can prove an enormous health benefit as well. In a high-pressure environment, being able to relax and unwind knowing that you are ultimately in control at home and in the office pays enormous dividends.

WHY DO YOU NEED HELP?

> If a man has a talent and cannot use it, he has failed.
> If he has a talent and uses only half of it, he has partly
> failed. If he has a talent and learns somehow to use the
> whole of it, he has gloriously succeeded, and won a
> satisfaction and a triumph few men ever know.
> —Thomas Wolfe, *The Web and the Rock*

You may not like to ask for help—or to change, for that matter. Since you value inductive-deductive reasoning, want useful facts, and want to get to the point quickly (whether the topic is technical, financial, or operational), examining your organizational skills makes logical sense. It can yield excellent results and fuel your confidence even more.

You tend to evaluate everything from the perspective of doing it more accurately, more cost-effectively, more quickly—you name it. Naturally, you value organizing principles and want a system that is simple, cost-effective, efficient. You are also willing to do whatever it takes to get the job done. You are obsessed with completion. If that means being a workaholic, so be it!

I can sum up your organizing style in one sentence: "No clutter, no maintenance." But you love knowing that things are where they should be and available. Obviously, you want to keep your investment binders in order, but you don't necessarily want to do it personally. I was in the office of a CEO recently who had over sixty binders and was trying to sheet-protect every single piece of paper. This was an enormous task with an enormous amount of upkeep. He couldn't pull it off, so I suggested he delegate the task to someone else.

The bottom line is that keeping things minimal and maintaining order are what you are all about. Therefore, *how* you delegate the duties you do not want or need to do must be your focus. Since your own personalized organizing system usually works, things can get complicated when you bring in help. But learning how to delegate will free you up to do what you do best.

When I gave a lecture to a group of CEOs for TEC International (The Executive Committee, a company that educates CEOs), I demonstrated a new labeling device. One person was so overjoyed to learn how to label his documents that he devoted an entire weekend to the task. But this was a job that could have easily been done by his executive secretary. Admit it. Be flexible in your organizing approach. Sometimes your lifestyle changes, and then your organizing style must change as well. If you are frustrated by what you are doing, chances are you shouldn't be doing it. A manic approach can be harmful to your health. "All or nothing" is sometimes toxic and certainly drains energy. Fortunately, many of you have a partner or family to restrain you from putting in endless days at the office.

Your downfall as an organizer is *the failure to delegate*. You prefer to give orders rather than make requests and your temper can get out of hand. In addition, you aren't always aware of the feelings of those around you. You are much more interested in what you "think" is right. Because you truly want to win at everything, the things you say can intimidate your subordinates. You may come across as somewhat calculating, controlling, and a workaholic. Others don't always understand that your goal is not to be their best friend but to get the job done. This is a very challenging part of the organizing puzzle for you; but in all reality, it is the most important. Your organizing challenges include:

- Being willing to delegate
- Deciding what to keep
- Locating specific documents quickly
- Knowing how to space plan your various environments
- Taking time off to play
- Understanding that organizing has to be a component in your life if you are going to stay on top and must be done annually, at least

HOW TO MANAGE YOUR ENVIRONMENT IN YOUR OWN STYLE

> There is nothing more difficult to take in hand, more perilous to conduct, or more uncertain in its success, than to take the lead in the introduction of a new order of things.
> —Machiavelli, *The Prince*

So, how do you remain effective without the responsibility of maintaining everything yourself? That's the million-dollar question. Since you want to work quickly, and in control, in an environment that is uncluttered and where everything functions at tiptop speed, the first premise for setting up your space is *accuracy*. For example, you should clarify exactly which files are imperative on a daily basis. Everything you need must be at your fingertips and there still must be enough room on your desktop to work. You simply can't do the best job if you can't find the report on which to base your conclusions. Do you know where your passport is for tomorrow's trip? Are all of your ducks lined up in a row?

Hiring someone to help can be a huge asset. And a partner who can assist you on the home front can be enormously helpful as well. However, you should note that you won't be able to survive marching to another's drumbeat. It truly is "all about you" and there are very few areas of compromise. In hiring key staff you need to be discriminating in order to survive. That right person who really enjoys specific tasks can take care of items that you would consider a waste of your time. We all have talents. Use theirs and yours together and you will have a win-win situation. You walk a fine line between making important decisions and maintaining data. A difficult proposal but one that can be remedied. Letting go of mundane control can be a challenge. Remember the CEO who still found himself in the copy room? He now has an incredible support staff that can do the office work far better than he does. On a side issue, when we got right down to it, he confessed that he was more bothered by his garage than his key reports—he said that getting in and out of his car every day was something that stressed him out. Go where you think the strongest issues are and start right there, even though they may seem petty to others.

To do what comes naturally to you, it is *imperative* that you delegate. I have met several high-powered CEOs who just didn't get it, who had no idea how their energy proved to be so counterproductive in almost every situation. If you really are to be a leader and feel in control, choose your right-hand assistant very carefully!

THE STRENGTHS AND CHALLENGES OF YOUR BRAIN

> Not only do I knock 'em out, I pick the round.
> —Muhammad Ali

Strengths
1. Logical
2. Clear thinker
3. Focused
4. Decisive
5. Confident
6. Strong-willed
7. High-energy
8. Tenacious

9. Punctual
10. Loves a challenge
11. Problem solver
12. Objective
13. Efficient
14. Assertive
15. Ambitious
16. Perfectionist
17. Able to prioritize
18. Decisive
19. Disciplined
20. Manages time and money effectively
21. A natural leader
22. Good financial analyst
23. Strategic thinker
24. Mathematical
25. Good negotiator
26. Speedy
27. Practical
28. Prefers to work alone

Challenges

> Discipline is the soul of an army.
> It makes small numbers formidable; procures success
> to the weak, and esteem to all.
> **—George Washington**

1. Overcompetitive
2. Lack of communication
3. Opinionated
4. Critical of yourself and others
5. Compulsive
6. Impatient
7. Manipulative
8. Blows up when angry

9. Demanding
10. Argumentative
11. Temper
12. Weak at dealing emotionally with others
13. Weak at working with others
14. Inability to slow down
15. Judgmental

ORGANIZING YOUR TIME

Nine-tenths of wisdom is being wise in time.
—**Theodore Roosevelt**

There are 86,400 seconds to every day. How do you use them? You know the value of time. You tend to schedule appointments in your head rather than using a traditional calendar or day planner. Managing time effectively is one of the ways you guarantee personal success. You have no trouble staying on track, and you like to finish one job before beginning another. They say that one hour planned is four hours saved. This is truly your most valuable resource. You have the discipline it takes to get the job done. You are great at managing your time—and other people's as well.

Every book on time management uses you as an example of perfection. Maybe that is why you are so successful! Louis XVIII said that "Punctuality is the politeness of kings." You are renowned for sorting through duties, paperwork, and memorabilia in a timely and effective manner, making decisions quickly and decisively. Because you listen only to key information, you analyze speedily and take immediate action in any given situation. According to Susan Silver, author of *Organized to Be Your Best*, "When information is expressed in numbers rather than words, complex decisions can be made 20% faster."

How about this time saver? Rather than reading entire reports, request that your subordinates deliver individual summaries, using Excel rather than Word. I knew a VP of a Napa Valley winery who read over fifteen reports monthly. You can imagine the time this took her. But was it necessary? Could she avoid a report and contact her subordinate only if further questions arose, or did she even need to have that information? You react quicker to figures than words. You are on the fast track, the "edge," and prefer not to repeat anything because if it gets done right the first time, you are one step closer to achieving another goal. Your activities are organized around your goals—this is why you often inspire the other brain types. They appreciate the fact that you know where you are headed and that you will keep heading there until the job is completed. So, how do you do it?

More often than not, you schedule your day to accomplish whatever you perceive must be done during that period of time. Frankly, you don't give it much thought. I have yet to witness a traditional calendar for your type. You are not likely to have a wall calendar, a desk calendar, or even a pocket calendar. The best thing for you is a computer software program that can be hot-synced to your PDA. Some of you prefer to carry time commitments in your head rather than on paper—a potential problem for those around you, if not you yourself. Don't forget, effective memory can only get you so far. You naturally move from one topic to another without any obvious structure. It appears that you get it all done, but at what expense?

A schedule can be continually adjusted to accomplish daily tasks. According to Stephen Covey, "The key is not to prioritize what's on your schedule, but schedule your priorities." Like your friend of the Innovative Style, you work in a hyperfrenzied state; but whereas they don't finish one thing before starting something new, you do tend to complete one job at a time. You are a Zen Master of concentratation. You have the ability to stay heads down, focused, analyzing and evaluating the necessary data to make appropriate decisions. This ability is a huge advantage if you have to make important decisions and have very little time in which to draw conclusions.

Every second counts; no time is wasted. This is good but a little difficult for those around you. Try to internalize the truth: not everyone is like you. Others may have different work habits and utilize different strategies to cope with the ongoing pressures of the day. However, your staff's or family's strengths and weaknesses can play into your effectiveness during the day. It is important for you to establish your rhythm at the office or at home, but hopefully this isn't at the expense of others. Take note of their needs, too. This actually can help them to help you.

You may be so goal-oriented that you appear to be be a workaholic. Fun to you means achieving another goal. You should control the little "spice" that you put in your life. All work and no play can make you very dull. I know that for you work *is* play and that you have a hard time allowing yourself to relax and just chill out. But the truth is, you suffer from stress, and it can be a killer. Did you know that 80 percent of all doctor appointments are stress related? You need a way to reduce and manage stress. Give yourself one hour of free time per day, or draw up an external fun "to-do" list. This one tip can make an enormous difference in your life.

Here are some suggestions that can easily support your natural inclinations for time management and your preferred drive. If we are clearer on what your goals are, we will be able to schedule them for action so that your delegate can handle those details that don't interest you or that you haven't time to pull off.

#1. Goals

> Greatest productivity gains are made not by doing
> more work, but by eliminating unnecessary work.
> **—Harold Taylor**

You need to set goals. Writing them down will be your biggest time-saving tip. If you can equate goal setting with goal achievement and remain continually goal oriented, you will achieve more results in less time. Goals add purpose and give your life a specific direction. It is all about working smarter, not harder.

I have worked for several different businesses where there were no stated goals—no organizational or departmental goals. Key executives had no idea what they wanted to accomplish either. Since you are a leader, like the director of a movie, you need to set the tone. Your organization reflects you, and you can't ask something from people that you don't give yourself. If there is no genuine, concrete direction, your staff will flounder. So bear with me and let me ask you this question: What is your mission, passion, or vision for every area in your life? Don't be too demanding—there are only twenty-four hours in a day. But if you budget your time correctly, you can and will accomplish whatever you want.

Join me for a few valuable minutes. Quickly write down what you see as your short-term goals in the various areas below and the time frame for completion. You may even create a list for this year and a traditional five-year plan as well. Remember that goals are what motivate you. Use this experiment to activate your potential.

* Career
* Various department goals
* Personal
* Financial
* Relationship/Spouse
* Friendships
* Fun
* Mental health
* Physical health
* Children
* Travel/Adventure
* Charity work
* Community
* Organizing maintenance

Now, write a couple of sentences about your current short-term and long-term objectives in each area. First, what is your overall mission? These are some very big questions that you may have already read about or explored in a corporate seminar. What is happening now or tomorrow is very different to what may happen next year or five years from now. In order for you to max out your enormous potential, goals need to be determined annually. Give yourself a block of time to an-swer these questions and then immediately move to **#2 Day Planner** below so you can schedule them into your calendar. (Yes, calendar. Not your head.) Here are some extra little quick tips that can affect your life:

1. Ask yourself, "What is the best use of my time right now?" Try to do this continuously.
2. Block a time for vacations, quitting work on time, going out for lunch, and so on.
3. Daily reading time—preferred during downtime.
4. Let your involvement in any given assignment be determined by your personal and professional goals, not availability.
5. Check your calendar before you say yes.
6. Remember, you cannot do everything, nor should you.
7. Isolate the activities that produce the greatest results.
8. Avoid the tyranny of the urgent. Adrenaline is a killer.
9. Stack appointments—a fantastic commitment to ending on time.
10. Don't allow your assistant or partner to fill up your schedule.
11. "Got a minute?"—"No, I have a second!"
12. Question your work style. Are you working long hours, eating at your desk, never feeling caught up? Problem!
13. Do you have the same crisis every week?
14. Try to have online meetings. This increases productivity for dispersed work groups and you are able to share presentations and data.
15. Schedule some quiet time every day.

#2. Day Planner

> Remember that time is money.
> —Benjamin Franklin

I once had a high-powered lawyer tell me he knew what he needed to do—"It is all inside here!" And he pointed to his head, of course. Well, that would have been great thirty years ago, when there weren't such volumes of documents and information to handle, five different phone numbers for each law partner, and so on. No one escapes this ironclad rule: Your head only has so much memory. *Write it down!*

Shelly, an acquaintance of mine, who works for a large Canadian television company, said to me, "I love your organizing ideas, but I don't need a to-do list. I know what comes next." I asked her, "What is the quality of your life after work? Do you enjoy yourself? Do you spend time with people? Do you have a serious conversation with your husband?" She responded, "To be honest, I just continually play out in my head what I need to do tomorrow, over and over again." I asked her, "Then when are you actually present, living life?" She fell silent.

I think you feel embarrassed or weak if you carry around a little black book for notes and things to do. Just remember that your brain has only so much RAM space and if it is continually full, it is impossible for you to add anything new. Your thinking style can benefit from writing things down so that you can see what is really going on in your head. Why is it that writers keep a journal? They do it in order to provide a better context in which to think and grow. Did you know that Bill Gates spent $35 million to buy Leonardo da Vinci's notebooks several years back? How much are your thoughts worth? (Maybe enough for you to publish your memoirs for your grandchildren.) If thoughts are in your head, which I know they are, they will only stay there, spin around, and certainly clutter up future ideas. By writing things down, you free up your mind for other ideas or solutions to emerge.

The most important time management device you can purchase is a calendar or a PDA, so choose it wisely. Pick whatever works for you and is easy to maintain. I know you're a techno junkie and appreciate the latest gadgets. A daily calendar that can be expanded into a weekly one could be your best friend. If you decide to hot-sync it to your desktop, you will have immediate access to all of your contacts, schedules, and long-term goals. Checking off tasks completed today and this week can help you focus on what needs to happen for you to be successful.

Actually, a PDA may be the way for you to go. It looks fantastic and has the strategic flair you crave. Not only will you be able to condense all the information, but you will see how time-efficient it is to be able to say yes or no to an appointment request—immediately. A paper planner probably isn't for you. You need a mobile means of data entry and flexibility. Perfect for you, absolutely perfect.

In addition, a monthly or yearly overview calendar on the wall so that you can stay focused on long-term goals is helpful. Normally, you don't want people to see these goals as they tend to be somewhat private. But your calendar must have the capacity to record the long view in a way that can easily be integrated with daily tasks. Moment-to-moment living is great and you thrive in the Zen experience, but your daily accomplishments must correspond to the overall importance of your mission. If not, you will not feel fulfilled or happy at the end of the day—things that seemed like they mattered won't sustain you for future growth. Planning your day from the perspective of a long-term personal commitment is one strong way to ensure overall success. Try to be conscientious about this and you will experience enormous results.

A watch normally would be enough for you. However, since time is always of the essence, it's a great idea to make sure there is a timepiece in every room. Clearly, clocks enable you to manage time effectively. You might consider getting one that has a built-in alarm, or a stopwatch of some kind. There are times when that tool is a helpful adjunct to getting a job finished in the requisite time.

#3. Delegating

> Charisma knows only inner determination and inner restraint. . . . The charismatic leader gains and maintains authority solely by proving his strength in life.
> —Max Weber

You need to get off your high horse: "If I want it done right, I better do it myself." That may have worked when things weren't so hectic, when you actually had the time to do everything. Nowadays, you don't. The key to continued success is *delegating*. You basically don't like doing "insignificant" things. You are very particular about knowing who is responsible for what, and if it doesn't fall under your heading, you recognize it is most certainly a task for someone else. David Allen, who wrote *Getting Things Done*, says that if it takes more than two minutes to do something and you either don't have the time or the will, chances are you *have to* delegate to associates, assistants, family members, and whoever else comes into your day.

To do the job right, create a "delegation form." Write out what needs to be done, and then, when your helper arrives at your home or office, have them review and sign it. Their signature connotes a full under-standing of the tasks at hand. Answer questions. Make sure they hear you. Since we do so much repetitive work on a daily basis, this will en-able you to set up a consistent delegation structure and also help clarify whether you are giving the right job to the right person. Here are more points to consider when delegating:

* Know what you want done in the first place. Delegate with a clear objective in mind. Don't force traditional procedures on your assistants—allow their creativity and genius to shine.
* Be concise. Know what you are saying *before* you say it.
* Know what you are writing down *before* writing it down.
* Ask the person to repeat what you told them. This is not to belittle them. Try to encourage questions since you will save time and money if they know exactly what is expected of them.
* Agree to follow up together on a specific date.
* Be positive—encouraging, not discouraging.
* Be professional.
* Slowly increase your expectations when jobs are accomplished successfully.
* Slightly adjust your standards. This doesn't mean you have to lower them. Rather, don't judge or compare yourself to your assistants.
* It is their responsibility to report to you if they have any questions. You are not a babysitter.
* Last, empower people. Don't discourage or intimidate them. This sim-ply doesn't work, unless you are in the army!

You like to make a decision and then turn to something else. Dele-gate items that just don't interest you. Don't forget that when you dele-gate, people thrive. If you want to encourage them to assist in your life, give them a chance—as I suspect someone gave you a chance at one time. I knew a CEO in Vancouver who was a very successful IT person before getting into the food and wine business. When he launched his new company, he could perform all the electronic stuff, spreadsheet creations, and so on far quicker than anyone he hired. However, it wasn't appropriate for him to do those tasks any longer. Initially, he felt uncomfortable hiring someone else to take over. But later he recognized how much more time he had to be the powerful leader of his company. This could be the organizing tip that has the best possibility to change your life.

ORGANIZING YOUR HOME

> I had rather be the first man among these fellows than
> the second man in Rome.
> —Julius Caesar

After a hard day's work, nose to the grindstone, the last thing you want to do is entertain. Your home is fundamentally designed to encourage relaxation, peace, and sleep. Rejuvenation is what it's all about. From that perspective—even though your partner may have other things in mind—you desire a functional environment where everything should be maintained to perfection. In general, the equipment in your home is in tiptop shape. Your ability to analyze things and break them down is a big plus for maintaining any hardware or appliances around the house.

Home needs to be a place where you can relax, review what went on during the day, and prepare for tomorrow. As a competent and powerful decision maker, you need private space to nurture you. You normally make the decision when it comes to purchasing things for the household. Your nest doesn't have anything superfluous in it. Everything is there for a purpose. So, how do you design a home that can have that purposefulness as a main component, yet remain functional and livable for other family members?

Your natural tendency is to want a pristine, almost obsessive-compulsive environment. I don't want to misuse that term or treat it lightly, since over 5 million American have this disorder and it can be very serious. Under stress, these tendencies do flare up. I once read that Bette Davis would go home after a long day on the movie set, grab a toothbrush, and get busy scrubbing her bathroom tiles until the wee hours of the morning. You likely selected a partner who can help ensure that all goes smoothly so you don't have to contend with issues at home after work. Your belongings are polished and work well. However, you're gifted at delegating certain chores—such as bringing in someone to fix the security system. Remember, dealing with people isn't your strength; so delegating there would be perfect.

You want things to work well but you certainly aren't into having to take care of every little thing. You need to know where things are located. But if you have to find certain photos from a previous trip—chances are your partner has arranged them in a way that makes that retrieval easy. If you are on your own, then you will find the simplest way to store those photographs; more than likely, you will have discussed the unnecessary ones while waiting in line to pay for them, and even before that, have only taken pictures that are worth having in the first place!

You are certainly king/queen of your domain and desire the very best, searching out quality in every purchase. Unless someone knows you really well, you prefer to purchase supplies, tools, and clothing yourself. You tend to appreciate something that is well made. For example, buying a classic $2,000 suit of the best fabric makes sense to you. You prefer a leather in-basket for your mail at home rather than the acrylic or metal ones at work. Bottom line, you prefer things that reflect status, integrity, quality—and power. Storage, like everything in your life, must have style.

Last, you become very annoyed when someone in your household wastes things, and you truly despise people who waste money and resources. Since you work very hard for all that you have, you expect those around you to value things; by respecting those things, they are respecting you. And you are known to criticize. Yes, you set the rules and let them face the consequences.

#1. Design
"Functional" is the key word to remember in setting up your home. You want a place where you can unwind and thrive, but the look will be Spartan. The purpose of the design aspect is to foster a setting that helps you achieve goals. Therefore, clear desktops and key tools within reach are crucial. Stark, bold colors and clean lines work for you. Since you

have such a strong personality, your furniture doesn't need a loud presence. Your belongings must exude togetherness, composure, and success. When I worked for the movie producer, he wanted everything in chrome and leather, no frills, just the best that money could buy and the most minimal possible. You prefer monochromatic: black, silver, navy, even white. Think modern: steel, angular and cutting edge, Bauhaus perhaps, or a Mies van der Rohe look. With that you can't go wrong. Remember, clutter is your nemesis and style your friend. But displaying degrees, awards, or certificates around key entrances in your home or office might be a great energy booster for you.

You are a master of high-tech gadgets; you like the latest stereo systems, TiVo and HD televisions that are installed throughout your home. I knew a very prominent judge who had the largest flat-screen computer monitor money could buy. He thought it made him look powerful and in control! I have yet to meet someone like you who didn't have the best electronic stuff out there. Putting your DVD, CD, or other technical collections in perfect order—whether alphabetically, by artist, or genre—tends to increase your comfort level at home.

#2. Storage

As we have seen, your prime purpose in life is to make decisions quickly and accurately. You are objective and analytical about space, especially when it comes to retrieving items. You tend to get furious if you can't find what you are looking for. Therefore, the simpler the better, and the less stuff you have, the better. Since you are a continual purger, you tend to purchase items that reflect what you need at the time. If they eventually fail to serve you, they are disposed of. Being unsentimental about stuff, you are more than willing to recycle, move on, and purchase whatever you need later. Therefore, storing is a relatively simple matter for you. But stylish containers are imperative. The sleeker and easier on the eye, the better—from an electronic tie rack to acrylic boxes. No over-the-door shoe pouches for you.

So, how does this sound? A perfect prioritizer I knew would organize such stuff beautifully, with matching hangers for long coats, jackets, and sports jackets; gorgeous canvas sweater bags and drawer containers for underwear and socks, all color-coded, shelf-lined, and perfect. All in immaculate order. She thrived, able to find everything whenever she wanted it. I think you get the picture.

But suppose you are going to a birthday party; it is highly likely you would ask someone else to send the card. The drawback to this style of living is that you rarely have an excess of anything. This can be a problem—endless trips to stores to purchase last-minute items tend to get out of hand. You may wish to think about the future a tad when doing your shopping. Perhaps buy a nice storage container, and yes, purchase limited number of those items you noticed you keep making those odd dashes to the local mall for. Examine your life, then go out and buy the supplies you think you'll need. This will guarantee an added sense of security.

Your partner may not always want to live as you do. I have been in several homes where I had to act as organizing interventionist when two opposing concepts clashed. For example, Clair and Peter, a sensational couple, had very different ideas about the incoming mail. When Peter collected it first, it went right up to their shared office and was placed in a basket. However, when Clair collected the mail, it landed here, there, and everywhere. I had to encourage her to put a basket right where she walked into the house so her husband's mail could be sorted out. When she had the time to review it, she could then take it upstairs to their office. Sometimes habits are hard to break, but I do know they're still married! Strategizing at home can be very challenging if not done with clear, concise goals where everyone turns out a winner.

#3. Paper
This is an issue for most of us, but not for you. Normally, you just keep what you need where you need it. For example, if you are working on a particular file folder, there are no other folders on the desk.

A lot of these principles apply to your business office as well as the home office. Receipts or manuals are best kept with the actual equipment they refer to, or you may read the manual when you unpack the item and just throw it away. One basic file drawer for home-related stuff and one for personal financial records should be more than enough. Remember that subject drawers or categories work better for you than an A to Z system. Since you don't keep much, long-term storage of paper doesn't really bother you. The rest you probably have at the office where someone else can store it properly.

Purchase a personal shredder and a lock for your filing cabinets. I witnessed a prominent winery owner deal with the stress of ID theft because he didn't believe in using a shredder. Anything with your name and Social Security number *must* be shredded. If you find this duty a little dull, delegate it to someone else. Get in the habit of it. There are even companies that can shred on the premises—. Don't be paranoid, just be safe! And it is crucial to keep your files locked. You never know who your private information may appeal to. Privacy is number one in your affairs—don't tempt people. Really important papers need to be stored off site—away from work—or kept in a safety-deposit box or a safe at home.

You more than likely have topnotch electronic gear positioned perfectly on your desk and in your home office. You are big on the latest gadgets and probably have the top-running software in your organization or at home all figured out. Therefore, one database (preferably electronic) should satisfy your requirements at home and at the office. You need one place to go to find someone's contact information. Preferably, you are able to hot-sync this with your PDA and will be ready to rock 'n' roll! This will save you a lot of unnecessary grief in the future. Phone numbers, calendars, engagements, and anything else that requires immediate action can be kept in an address book or on a flat-screen monitor, or in your Palm. If you have a family, it is important to keep one calendar for them and one for your own personal calendar/database to contain all that growing information. You can check what is happening on theirs at the end of the day and then consolidate with yours. Keep it simple and expandable.

The paper issue is pretty straightforward. A few quick points will set you straight once and for all:

* Prefer to have paper filed away—except the project you are working on.
* Prefer to have an assistant do the actual filing.
* Prefer to file by subject, not alphabetically. What goes into the file folder is enormously important.

* Prefer manila file folders—keep extra ones in the filing drawer.
* Prefer traditional army green hanging folders. Depending on your occupation, letter size is always easier to handle.
* Prefer not to use hanging file tabs, if filing yourself. Therefore, a black Sharpie, not a pencil, would suffice in labeling interior tabs.
* Try purging at the start of the year. Having someone to assist can be helpful.

ORGANIZING YOUR OFFICE

Seest thou a man diligent in his business? He shall stand before kings . . .
—Proverbs 22:29

This is your domain—the place to be all that you can be. You thrive in an uncluttered and functional workspace, all the necessary tools at your fingertips, enabling you to do your job with passion and vigor. Because you work simply to get ahead—not to have your ego stroked—you prefer your office to have minimal clutter. Everything is there for a reason; it has purpose and meaning. For example, you don't need five hundred drawer containers to store office supplies in your desk. Normally, you're not a backup person. The traditional organizing systems, containers, and all that jazz don't matter to you. You tend to keep whatever you need on your desk and perhaps have an extra pad of paper in one of the drawers. The majority of work-related files are stored outside your office, and your personal files are very limited, more than likely located at home. It is not your job to maintain; rather, to direct and focus the efforts of those around you.

Your office represents power. Your tools and possessions are strategically placed to support you in making the right decisions for your organization, for your department, for yourself. You look responsible because you *are* responsible. The desk surface has nothing on it but a writing pad; there are two pencils and one pen in the writing utensil holder. You also prefer not to share office supplies with anyone.

When a CEO asked me to organize his office, I thought this was going to be a breeze. He didn't have hoards of papers or files and I figured we'd just do a little neatening up. I was wrong! His documents and various files were not well organized and certainly not aesthetically attractive. The interior file folders had dog-eared tabs; they were labeled in pencil and were not easy to locate when he needed to make a quick decision. Together, we relabeled and organized so that everything was at his fingertips.

Jenny, a high-powered computer programmer, hired me to fix up her beautiful home office. It was Spartan, but again, I noticed some things just weren't working for her. Her numerous financial investment folders were not laid out to function properly. For confidential reasons, she didn't engage her executive assistant in these areas and so she felt frustrated. She became very impatient when I explained to her what needed to be done. I had to put my foot down a couple of times, but by 6:00 p.m. she could see a new pattern: she was within reach of her documents at a moment's notice. The active financial binders on her credenza were replaced with hanging binders to be stored in the filing drawer. Jane's older financial investments were put into boxes, packed away, and filed annually.

Scanning is important for you. Asking an assistant to scan those documents into your computer, where you have easier access to such information, could suit you better than a paper-based filing system. The one caution here is that when you file something electronically, you must be very clear about the classification system and how long to keep something before you actually put it in an electronic file folder. Sometimes, technology looks like the answer; but improperly done, it could lead to more serious problems. Consult your IT person for solutions that fit your particular situation.

#1. Electronic Organizing

According to Jeff Davidson, author of *The Complete Idiot's Guide to Managing Your Time,* electronic parts have a shelf life of about ninety days; Peter Russell claims that computer memory capacity doubles every eighteen months. Don't think an electronic approach is always going to be the answer. One CEO made a comment that shocked me: he said that if someone in his firm couldn't find an electronic document in sixty seconds or less, they would be fired. To top it off, he declared that anyone who used emotional or personal comments in a professional e-mail would be fired. Yikes! He created the most intense, formal format for his e-mail communications. He wanted this template to be a time saver rather than a time waster. Obviously he was an authoritarian on how things should be done. How you use your computer and set up your organization depends on your personal style and your schedule. If you travel a great deal on business, your hardware buddy may be the cell phone rather than the laptop.

Your style tends to be "I need the best and I want the best." I worked with a CEO who had the largest flat-screen monitor ever created, hanging right there in his home office. He loved it and used it daily for all his personal communications. When he was out and about, he had the fastest, highest-end color-screen PDA that money could buy. Every year he updated all of his technological gadgets and liked to impress everyone with his new toys. I think Prioritizing Styles actually organize themselves better when they have the newest and brightest tools. It's your way of saying yes to your success and your personal power.

Sure, the better you understand how to operate all this new stuff, the better you can perform. Luckily, you don't need to spend time on computer classes, since you will have someone who is a master, and can train you in any new technology if need be. Remember, delegating is key for you, especially in those tasks that you would prefer not to do.

Your primary desire is to make quick and accurate decisions as information lands on your desk. Computer gadgets can make it easier on you so that you call the shots; but try to avoid being a slave to every new gadget in the universe. It's important you learn how to walk the very fine line between buying the latest and paring down stuff to a minimum to strengthen your specific needs.

CONCLUSION

> So little done, so much to do.
> —**Cecil Rhodes**

You are known for an intense focus and the ability to hit the bull's-eye, completely dedicated in your intention to succeed at all costs. Your work drive and enormously strong will help you accomplish most everything you set your mind to. You can be extremely intense and passionate about goals and the ability to succeed.

You may strike people as aloof or cold and don't usually engage in emotional conversations. Organizing is in your nature, but your challenge must be to spend time setting things up correctly first time around. Let's face it, you are not enthralled by keeping or maintaining an organizational system. So you must accept responsibility in finding the right person to do so for you. Since you thrive on getting the job done, no matter what it takes, keep in mind that there can be better ways of doing some things that you haven't necessarily thought of. Yes, even you can learn some new tricks. As Harold Taylor, Canadian organizing consultant, suggests, "Time isn't something you can control, but you can control yourself." And Henry Ford once said that "People who have no time, don't think! The more you think, the more time you have." So, when it comes to organizing, the only way you will save time is by focusing *prior to* undertaking it. Be like Bobby Fischer, the brilliant chess player, who sees twenty moves ahead.

Make delegation something you improve upon continually. This will give you time to develop new skills and talents, which will save you time for doing what you are good at. Practice does make perfect, and like your golf swing, there are no shortcuts. Clutter isn't your friend. You need to rely on others to store and maintain things for you.

Last, in order to be happy and healthy and live a life that benefits you and your loved ones, write down your organizing goals and plans of attack and keep that structure going year after year. With the aid of an assistant or partner, you can quite easily decide what you want and where you want it. Then let them do the finishing touches while you move on to something else. Your goal is to learn how to work with others. Once you master this—and you will—there's no stopping you!

Getting Started:
For Example—
Household Paper Clutter

1. If you are going to get organized, today is the day to get it done! In this instance, you may have no one to delegate the task to; just get it done yourself, quickly and accurately. Give yourself as much time as needed.

2. Gather all the paper in your entire home and put it on the table.

3. Use subject-related piles and toss what you don't need. Chances are you will purge a lot and keep very little. Don't be alarmed by this. It's just the way you think.

4. What remains should be stored for you to have easy access to and maintain if need be. Try to create a structured place for documents that require your daily attention, e.g., takeout menu binder in the kitchen, and so on.

5. What is left can be stored in binders, or large accordion file folders. Keep important documents close to where you do the necessary work and even locked if possible.

6. Knowing the categories and writing legibly or using a label maker, create labels for what remains active and inactive.

7. Create easy catch places for financial papers, newspapers, and all of your trade or magazine subscriptions.

8. Documents that remain must be filed thematically or by subject rather than alpha-organized.

9. Be familiar with what you store by remaining active in its maintenance. Not overkill, but knowing where things are at and how they are filed is a great tool.

10. Give yourself a reward! Managing any area by yourself isn't much fun. Go play a game of golf, or have a massage.

OVERVIEW OF THE PRIORITIZING STYLE

Purpose: To make decisions quickly and accurately.

Organization of Space: Objective and analytical about your space, you need to have logical access to data and prefer not to maintain but to delegate those organizing tasks.

Strengths: You tend to manage time and money effectively. You think logically about goal planning and attainment, working quickly and with great intensity.

Challenges: When there is no one to delegate to, you must manage space yourself. But when it's possible to delegate, do so with more attention to the feelings of others.

Time

Calendar: You prefer tools and gadgets for a calendar. Prefer to delegate maintenance duties as much as possible

To-do List: You tend to prioritize lists in your mind. May develop a list for delegation.

Goals: To achieve positive outcomes in a timely manner.

Contacts: Keep these in a electronic format ready to go—or have someone track that information for you.

Paper

Incoming Mail: Prefer to delegate sorting of mail based on predetermined criteria. Want to personally handle items perceived as important.

Desktop: Products denote power, quality, and authority. Only practical and needed supplies are on your desk.

Filing System: You will have a traditional filing system in place but prefer to delegate filing and maintenance. If you have no one to delegate to, may file by subject, then date, then last, alphabetically.

Closets

Closets: You prefer precise and functional style—hangers, hooks, etc.

Drawers: In functional order. What little you have is the very best.

Storage: You keep what is needed stored in attractive, functional containers.

Purging: Prefer to delegate this, but when no one is around, you undertake ongoing purges personally.

Memorabilia: You tend to retain the evidence of success.

Chapter Five

Sensory Preferences

Seeing stars, it dreams of eternity. Hearing birds, it makes music. Smelling flowers, it is enraptured. Touching tools, it transforms the earth. But deprived of these sensory preferences, the human brain withers and dies.
—**Ronald Kotulak**, *Inside the Brain*

How we take in information not only defines how we relate to what is outside us, but also determines how we communicate with others. Our brains filter the world around us through three key senses—sight; sound; and what is called the kinesthetic sense, which includes smell, taste, and touch. Although our experience of life is a confluence of stimuli from all of the senses, each of us tends to take in and decode this rich data more easily and efficiently through what is called our sensory preference. Knowledge then moves from sensory experience to concept formation. This simply means we prefer, say, seeing over hearing, or hearing over the kinesthetic. According to Arlene Taylor, W. Eugene Brewer, and Michelle Nash, the authors of *MindWaves*, "One type of stimuli tends to get our attention and register more quickly in our brain."

Ironically, in the sensory preference test that appears on page 54, if you gain a very balanced score, such as a 10 for auditory, 10 for visual, and a 10 for kinesthetic, you have more than likely accommodated your true preference—or hidden who you truly are—to relate to someone important in your life such as a parent, a teacher, or any other role model. When I started this work and took the test myself, my scores were nearly equal. I soon realized that my mother was visual, my father was auditory, and I was actually kinesthetic but had few objective realities to nurture who I really was. I have now become far more aware of what works for me in my living space and what makes me feel truly comfortable, energized, and organized.

I believe that it is crucial to identify your sensory preference in order to enhance how you organize time, home, and office. It really gives you more control in terms of efficiency and creativity when setting up daily routines and defining long-term goals. Learning what works best also helps to conserve your energy. If you don't enjoy your day-to-day environment, chances are you won't enjoy inhabiting your office and won't be as productive or as accomplished as you could. *Your sensory preference powerfully affects your life.* Having identified your primary system, you can use it as a motivational support in creating an organizing system and, more important, in sustaining one.

If you are a visual person, for example, but have somehow not honored that natural tendency, you will have problems maintaining all the hard work you put into organizing. Not only will you fail to "see" what you need to accomplish at work, but you may find yourself understimulated. Procrastination occurs in an environment that doesn't speak to you or support your sensory preference. Obviously, learning how to apply your knowledge of the dominant preference can help you make good choices.

When your brain and, more specifically, your sensory preference gets the appropriate, supportive environment, you are able to "hook" into ideas, take care of tasks more efficiently, and even approach clutter from a place that supports you. That means you have provided yourself with a visual, auditory, or kinesthetic link that motivates you from the outside in. It also colors your emotions. When you hear something you like, you feel better and can finish that report. When you see a colored file, you snap into focus and can write up that summary. When you feel the touch of a leather chair, you sense comfort and can make a solid decision. Learning to make conscious choices, first, by favoring your sensory preference, and then by responding to environments based on those choices, can make all the difference in the world.

To validate why I believe this is a crucial cornerstone often ignored in the organizing milieu, I want to mention the work of some groundbreaking scientists. Learning how and why we do things is so fascinating and important if we truly want to change. Patricia Wolfe tells us in *Brain Matters,* "Everything in memory takes the information coming into the brain through the sensory receptors and holds it for a fraction of a second until a decision is made about what to do with it." Torsten Nils Wiesel and David Hunter Hubel, 1981 Nobel Prize winners, for physiology or medicine, have shown how sensory preference is essential for teaching brain cells their jobs. They claim that we don't learn to our full capacity if the environment we are currently in doesn't speak to us innately. Dr. David A. Sousa, another famous scientist, suggests that cognitive research strongly reaffirms we learn best when we are actively involved in interesting and challenging situations that attract our senses. He also has researched how task-centered pursuits—basically knowing what comes first and needs to be done—is critical to the memory process because it helps maintain focus while enhancing sense and meaning. Last but not least, Leonardo da Vinci strongly believed that refining sensory awareness was the key to enriching human experience, claiming, "All of our knowledge has its origin in our perceptions." He coined the term *sensazione* meaning "in sensory appreciation," which embodies the value he placed on the power of the senses in helping us understand and engage in our world.

Let's discuss each sense briefly so you can understand the preference that best reflects your personal style. Then you will be able to apply this knowledge when undertaking any organizing task.

AUDITORY

Auditory stimulation involves sounds—noise, music, someone's voice—which affects our knowledge of what we receive from the outside world. It can be the most powerful sense and trigger more emotion and deep memories than the other sensory modes. Recent studies have coined the term the Mozart Effect. Studies have shown that listening to the music of Mozart can actually boost our intelligence and enhance our learning. When I need to concentrate, I put on Glenn Gould playing Bach's *Goldberg Variations* or certain Mozart pieces that not only center but inspire me. Wolfe claims, "There is little doubt that when information is embedded in music or rhyme, its recall is enhanced. Information embedded in music or rhyme is much easier to recall than the same information in prose."

Depending on the task at hand, listening to Handel, REM, or Alison Krauss can stimulate your mood and affect different levels of the many chemicals in your brain. Not only does music have documented benefits in helping us learn, but the stimulation and/or relaxation created by other nonverbal sounds (ocean, white noise, chimes, wind) move us in deeply personal ways. Awareness and sensitivity to listening—whether its nursery rhymes, rock 'n' roll, or laughter—are qualities that reflect an auditory preference.

VISUAL

Visual stimulation is probably the most effective way most of us take in data from the outside world. Some 60 percent of the population (and more men than women) are geared to this form of stimulation. According to da Vinci, who thought that this was the most important sense, "the eye encompasses the beauty of the whole world." Wolfe mentions that "The eye contains nearly 70 percent of the body's sensory receptors and sends millions of signals every second along the optic nerves to the visual processing centers of the brain. The capacity for long-term memory of pictures seems almost unlimited." If you have the ability visually to remember where you put something last, and can describe many experiences in total picture-perfect detail, chances are this is your preference. Just an important reminder here: light deprivation can lead to depression; therefore, full-spectrum lights are best. Less fatigue and eyestrain.

KINESTHETIC

Kinesthetics, which includes taste, touch, and smell, is the third sensory system. Kinesthetic types are sensitive to touch and often like the feel of something—e.g. petting a dog or cat. These individuals can be very sensitive to their overall environment, even how things are arranged. Their tactile system sends messages to the brain with information about how something feels. For instance, when you are unsure of the spelling of a word and write it down, you are relying on your kinesthetic sense to guide your hand—though you probably also rely on a visual check to see if the word looks right. You learn by touching and moving, not by hearing and seeing. Therefore, information is taken in most easily through your hands and through movement. Some suitable occupations would be chemist, clothing designer, or sculptor. Using an abacus is one way of helping you learn math with a kinesthetic preference in focus.

My own preference is kinesthetic, and I use it to help me in organizing. I have the ability to walk into a client's home and just sense where to begin. The therapeutic touch work I do when it comes to space planning is rooted in being very aware and sensitive to the quality of fabric, surfaces, touches, smells, and taste. Wolfe mentions that "Hands-on activities are extremely valuable as long as they are also minds-on." If you are influenced by the flavor of a particular food, sensitive to the quality of texture or an open space, or moved by certain aromas, you may have a kinesthetic preference. Keep in mind the effect that temperature can have on you. The cooler the room, the more relaxed your brain.

Last, smell is a powerful sense that can trigger memory and provide a keen association of experience and emotion. Wine tasters, perfume makers, even scientists use this sense to understand their current environment. Sometimes a familiar scent can be so powerful as to bring you back to the time you first experienced it.

Go through the quiz below and try to figure out which sense you operate from. As I said, when I first did this quiz many years ago, I scored very closely on all three. Later, I realized that my mother was primarily auditory, my dad visual, and I more kinesthetic. No wonder I was all over! It took a little time for changes to take place, but now I can't imagine how I ever lived without this knowledge.

Sensory Preference Assessment

"1984 by Arlene Taylor Ph.D.—Realizations Inc (Used by permission)

Instructions: Read each of the statements below and evaluate each as carefully and honestly as possible. It applies to you at least 75% of the time, place a check (✓) in the box. Otherwise, leave the box blank and move on to the next statement. Add the total number of checks in each column.

☐ I learn a lot about people from the sound and/or tone of their voices

☐ Sounds usually catch my attention quickly

☐ I talk to myself frequently, aloud, under my breath, and/or in whispers

☐ I keep up with current events by listening to radio news more than by watching television

☐ I would rather listen to an audiocassette or CD than read a book

☐ Others consider me chatty or sometimes say that I talk too much

☐ I tend to "hear" the voice of the author when reading a personal e-mail or letter

☐ Strange noises, rattles, or repetitive sounds in my vehicle or house annoy/worry me

☐ I talk to my pets as I would to close friends

☐ I use rhyming words to help me remember names, labels, dates, or other facts

☐ Jingles and acronyms help me to recall information

☐ I study for exams by verbalizing my notes and/or key points aloud

☐ I repeat new words to myself to help fix them in memory

☐ I enjoy humming, whistling, or singing (alone or in a group)

☐ I especially appreciate musical programs or concerts

☐ Talk shows and interview programs appeal to me

☐ I often enjoy verbal discussions including long telephone or ham-radio conversations

☐ I am usually considered an attentive listener

☐ I enjoy listening to audiocassettes, books on tape, records, and CDs

☐ I can't stand the sound of jangling keys or a dripping faucet

☐ I often use expressions such as: "sounds right," "I hear you," "keep your ears open"

Total # checked = ___ / 21

☐ I like to control the lighting in my environment (e g., dimmer controls, spotlights, uplights, mood lighting)

(continued)

☐ I purchase items primarily based on looks/visual appeal

☐ I tend to select clothes because they look good/sharp

☐ I avoid wearing clothing that is mismatched in color, pattern, or design

☐ I like to keep my vehicle washed, waxed, and looking good

☐ I prefer a map to receiving verbal or printed directions

☐ When eating, the presentation of the food/ table/environment is very important

☐ I learn a lot about people from their appearance

☐ I often see something before I hear, sense, or feel it

☐ I rarely bump into or stumble over objects that I didn't see

☐ I prefer to see people when communicating with them

☐ When shopping, I want the products to be clearly and attractively displayed

☐ I prefer pets that I can watch (e.g., fish in a tank, birds)

☐ I often say things like: "the light just went on," "I see what you mean," "looks okay to me"

☐ A picture or diagram is worth 1000 words when learning information or studying

☐ I prefer to watch TV/movies/videos as compared to reading the book or a script

☐ I prefer books/magazines that contain graphs, pictures, or colorful illustrations

☐ I really enjoy looking at photo albums

☐ It's important that my living/work spaces look visually attractive

☐ Mirrors are important fixtures in my home

☐ When selecting a place to live, the view from my abode is of major concern

Total # checked = ___ / 21

☐ I'm very sensitive to odor, taste, temperature, and texture

☐ I can usually recognize objects quite easily by touch in the dark

☐ I tend to select clothes because they feel good and are comfortable to wear

☐ If purchasing a vehicle, room and comfort are very important considerations

☐ I prefer frequent changes in body position and move often

☐ I often use expressions such as: "my sense is," "that fits," "I've got a handle on it"

☐ I enjoy getting physical exercise (e.g., walking, hiking, cycling, jogging)

☐ I like to work out and/or take jazzercise or yoga classes

☐ I'd rather participate in sports than observe others playing

☐ I enjoy soaking in the tub or basking in the warm sunshine

☐ I like to receive and/or give back rubs and massages

(continued)

☐ I enjoy touching and hugging my friends

☐ I readily learned the touch-typing method and/or data-entry systems

☐ I have good physical coordination

☐ I learn a lot about people from their handshakes, hugs, or touch

☐ I often tap my toes or feel like moving my body (e.g., dancing) to music/a beat

☐ I like to hold babies or pets that I can touch, stroke, and cuddle

☐ I especially enjoy making things with my hands (e.g., carving, sculpture, woodwork, crocheting, knitting, sewing, finger painting, various crafts)

☐ I prefer being outdoors over indoors whenever possible

☐ Above all, my furniture must be comfortable

☐ I prefer my home and vehicles to be climate controlled for comfort

Total # checked = ___ / 21

Explanation: Sensory preference refers to the type of sensory stimuli that register most quickly in your brain. Early in life we use the five senses almost equally. Usually by the age of five or six the brain begins to select a preferred sensory system, although we can decode data from any system (assuming we're free of sensory impairment). Unless you have adapted, the column with the highest score usually represents your overall sensory preference (first column = auditory; middle column = visual; last column = kinesthetic).

If two scores are tied, one likely represents your sensory preference while the other represents skills you developed in order to relate to or please someone significant in your life. If one of the tied scores is kinesthetic, consider the strong possibility that your innate preference may be kinesthetic, but you have pulled back from it. Try to identify possible reasons why this might have occurred.

If all scores are equal, recognize that this is not a naturally occurring pattern. Use this clue as an opportunity to evaluate your sensory history. Try to uncover and identify factors (e.g., lack of opportunity, abuse, shaming) that may have influenced you to repress your sensory preference.

MAINTAINING STYLE

> The five senses are the ministers of the soul.
> —**Leonardo da Vinci**

Auditory

With an auditory preference, you appreciate what sounds accurate and clear, and will want to design a space that accommodates writing, filing, and putting things away (in order, of course).

YOU:

—Like to choose your words carefully.

—Respond well to others who speak to you in a tone that is soothing and accommodating.

—Appreciate precision and learn quickly when you are told something in a very clear, 100 percent, accurate manner.

—Tend to remember names better than faces.

—Would rather listen to the radio than watch television.

—Appear rather unassuming but need to make sure you communicate to others in a consistently clear way. This will alleviate all kinds of potential mishaps and misunderstandings.

—Have an amazing memory and will retain facts and figures most of us would forget.

Tools and strategies that can help you strategize and be more productive:

- Need to provide clear verbal explanations.
- Prefer directions written down rather than explained on the phone.
- Top-of-the-line computers, printers, phones, and faxes, with the most accurate numerical printout and features.
- Soothing, relaxing rings or sounds from hardware and clocks.
- All reference books (manuals, instructions, policies and procedures) must be labeled perfectly and filed in alphabetical order. Words are important.

- A master list of important telephone numbers, account numbers, and anything else you may need filed away safely.
- Marching music at work that lifts your spirits.
- Tape recorder for staff meetings—to ensure accuracy.
- A relaxing fountain to balance out your style.
- Books on tape to keep you learning.

Visual

With a visual preference, you appreciate what looks right, in balance, and design a space that encourages things to be seen and also put away, in perfect order.

YOU:
—Want things filed, labeled properly, and easy to find.
—Prefer consistency.
—Remember names better than faces.
—Find the appearance of your handwriting important.
—Are distracted by visual disorder or movement.
—Organize your thoughts by writing them down.
—Respond better to utility over beauty.
—Work better in natural lighting.

Tools and strategies that can help you strategize and be more productive:

- Label maker or **Avery** labels to help you identify everything with the same system, font, and placement.
- Filing cabinets with room to grow into and a file for master lists of what is inside.
- Manila file folders with army green hanging files.
- Clear-colored tabs all labeled and in a row, not a zigzag placement.
- See-through organizing containers.
- Drawer or shelf organizing containers perfectly measured in each cupboard or drawer.
- Different-colored hangers for different family members.
- Desk containers that fit pens, file folders, and paperclips.

- Calendars set in strategic places.
- Full-spectrum bulbs rather than traditional fluorescent lighting.

Kinesthetic

With a kinesthetic preference, you appreciate what feels right and design a space that encourages things to be touched and used.

YOU:

—Prefer to use your hands in fixing and putting things together, so if there is a worktable with high-end tools, you are inclined to work diligently.
—Prefer not to share your stuff with those around you.
—Get more done when you have ease of movement from one project to the next.

Tools and strategies that can help you strategize and be more productive:

- Furniture that feels good and encourages movement.
- A plastic mat beneath your chair for easier movement.
- A typewriter or word processing system that has wrist guards and padding for extra comfort.
- Space and comfort is important in any room you are in.
- Handling filing, typing, and touching papers yourself.
- Using a labeler for the hands-on approach.
- Room temperature is important where you work.

HARMONIZING STYLE

> All our knowledge has its origin in our perceptions.
> **—Leonardo da Vinci**

You have one beautiful mantra—harmony, harmony, and harmony. Your brain is always attempting to harmonize everything from the outside world, whether it's with words, sounds, or images. You crave connections and love to communicate, so much so in fact that you need this to feel alive and comfortable.

Auditory

With an auditory preference, you are sensitive to the voice, so *how* you hear things is more important than what is being said. Any jarring sound or high-pitched voice will cause discomfort or anxiety. When setting up your environment, here are some things that will help:

- Easy-to-use but not necessarily top-of-the-line computers, printers, phones.
- Music that is soothing, inviting, and relaxing.
- Various sounds that are inviting yet encourage work performance, e.g., soft music.
- A Zen fountain for comfort and harmony.
- An appealing ring to your cell phone or landline.

Visual

With a visual preference, you need to *see* things in harmony with one another. Because you don't view them as independent units but synthesized, you also need to think about the harmony of all the colors in your home or office, rather than putting one color here and another there. You are extremely sensitive to relationships of all kinds, whether between a table and a chair or a man and a woman. So, you must always choose things you believe are beautiful in order for relationships to blossom.

Here are some tips that can help you stay organized while keeping comfortable:

- Decorations that stimulate you to be a successful conversationalist and generate a homey environment.
- Soothing yet vibrant color combinations.
- Coordinating the colors of furniture with prints to accentuate.
- Easy access files and office supplies. Don't store them.
- Big, attractive organizing containers for your home/office.
- Photos of everyone you love to decorate home and office.
- Artwork that encourages you to occupy a room.
- Plants and other natural items to support relaxation.

* Mementos that generate a sense of peace and calm.
* Fresh flowers.
* Using colors to your benefit:
    Red—creative thinking/short-term energy spurt.
    Green—for productivity and long-term energy.
    Yellow/Orange/Coral—conducive to physical work, exercising, positive moods.
    Blue—slows pulse, lowers blood pressure, conducive to deep thinking, concentration, and insight.
    Purple—tranquilizing, good for appetite control.
    Pink—restful, calming.
    Light colors—provide minimum disruptions across all moods.

Kinesthetic

Kinesthetics enjoy being touched by people they care about and learn by using their hands. Since our society doesn't give us acceptable access to touch, you must create an environment that feels yummy, sensual, and warm. This will keep you feeling alive and at ease. Combining texture, spatial planning, lighting, and ease of movement at home and in the office creates harmony.

Some things that will help you:

* Office supplies that are easy to use and feel good—e.g., data entry systems. Ergonomics should be key for all electronic purchases.
* Clothing that feels great.
* Furniture that allows you to nestle and feel nurtured.
* Containers for magazines and books that are easy to reach.
* Organizing containers that reflect the feeling of a room—e.g., wicker for the living room, plastic for inside cupboards and closets.
* Proxemics—the study of how people use and structure space or spatial arrangements.
* Aromatherapy—to keep you motivated and centered.
* Keeping the temperature just right. No drafts, no hot pipes.
* Handling organizing supplies if they appeal to your sense of touch, such as a cloth notebook, fluffy photo books, leather day planners, and so on.

INNOVATIVE STYLE

> Artists say: Stop, look and see what is real. In our rushing world, no one has time for this.
> —Langdon Gilkey

You can easily "visualize" in your mind's eye. The right brain, but especially yours, is very sensual and operates much of the time from a gut level. You analyze things first and foremost by how they *feel*. You are intuitive and have a hard time organizing a room or a cabinet with ruler and paper. But when you envision what it will feel like when the task is completed, you can do just about anything!

Auditory

> I am not a human being. I am dynamite.
> —Friedrich Nietzsche

With an auditory sensory preference (approximately 20 percent of the population), you are sound sensitive and quickly learn about the environment through verbal and aural cues. You have a love of pleasant music and natural sounds such as running water, wind in the trees, and birdsong. Nature nurtures and comforts you, and you love to include it in your home and office. Ensuring you have soothing sounds supports you, especially when you are tackling something you don't want to do—*like organizing*. You prefer verbal explanations of how things need to be done and resonate strongly with people's voices. Sound stimulates your actions and intentions; and listening to new ideas, solutions, as well as friendly conversation and good humor really gets you going! Let's not forget, too, that you like things to be out in the open. You respond to written communications, words, and language of every kind, especially if it's a compliment or recommendation highlighting something you've done that merits a little applause.

Things that enhance the auditory performance include:

* Reference books that clarify words and pronunciations.
* A conscientious attempt to create labels for file folders, containers, and whatever else you need to retrieve on a daily or weekly basis.
* Talking through a problem.
* Expansive music, like jazz, that reflects your love of variety; creative, uncommon music is a strong motivator.
* Working with music on, especially when doing anything you consider drudgery.
* A clock that makes sounds (e.g., cuckoo, Bavarian).
* Positive sounds to alert you that time is up or someone is coming.
* Objects that make pleasing sounds (e.g., musical chimes).
* The use of jingles and mnemonics to help you remember things.

Visual

> My nature is orderly and observant and scrupulous,
> and deeply introverted.
> **—Joyce Carol Oates**

With a visual sensory preference (perhaps 60 percent of the population), you are engaged in seeing on all levels. When you have a chance to *see* how something is done, you learn remarkably fast and have no trouble remembering faces or physical descriptions of people. Also, you tend to remember where things are by visualizing them, eyes closed, in the last place you left them. (And you are usually 100 percent right.) You are extremely concerned about your own appearance as well as how everything looks, from the smallest detail to the largest. Naturally, one of your deepest desires is for your environment to be attractive and to support your mental pursuits. When you are creating space, aesthetics is the key to a comfortable and creative environment.

Things that can help a visual preference include:

* Colorful supplies for home and office, such as baskets, file folders, storage containers.

* Any container that is see-through or simply clear plastic—perfect for storing seldom-used items or seasonal clothing.
* Spaces with lots of posters and pictures.
* Thinking in imagery.
* Geometric or modern wire storage containers that help the mind easily recall where items are stored—"Design Within Reach" kinds of things.
* Hanging calendars and an unusual clock to refresh your memory of appointments and upcoming events.
* Chalkboard or corkboard in locations where the eyes automatically locate it.
* Beautiful containers to store incoming material, works in progress, and outgoing material—all placed strategically on a desk or shelf, in plain view.
* As many shelving units as possible.
* Signs located in strategic positions.
* Eye-catching important objects (e.g., watch, brightly colored telephone, unique wallet). The Levinger Company has numerous such items.
* Inspirational artwork.
* Plants and flowers as stimulants to the eye.

Kinesthetic

> I have become aware of this: the earth breathes,
> smells, listens and feels in all its little parts.
> —Egon Schiele

With a kinesthetic preference, you are alert to what smells, tastes, and feels right. This includes room temperature and the position of furniture and other objects. You often sense where objects are rather than locating them first by sight. You want to be able to reach out and touch books, papers, or files, quickly decoding stimuli that relate to smell, taste, touch, and position. Kinesthetic Innovating Styles can often recall where things are by their location in relation to other things, or by recalling how the objects felt when they were last handled. If the environment "feels right," including odor and especially texture, you work more effectively and for a longer period of time. Preferring to learn in a hands-on style and to use your hands to produce a desired result, you ultimately value an environment by how it feels and whether it stimulates your creativity.

Strategies that can help a Kinesthetic preference include:

* Organizing gadgets that feel right.
* Comfort as number one.
* A climate-controlled environment that has a pleasant smell.
* Fabrics and textures that feel good to the touch.
* Placement of belongings in ways that are easy to reach.
* Objects of inspiration in the home and at the office.
* Avoidance of excess supplies.
* Things arranged in reasonable order, though not a rigid one, with plenty of space for additional items.
* Simple, uncomplicated organizing solutions.

PRIORITIZING STYLE

> All my genius resides in my nostrils.
> —**Friedrich Nietzsche**

Auditory
With an auditory preference, you value sounds that are functional and structured.

YOU:
—Enjoy traditional classical music (e.g., Bach, Beethoven) that is composed of a beginning, middle, and end.
—Prefer directions, reports, and instructions (verbal or written) to be precise, brief, and to the point.
—Tend to remember names better than faces.
—Rely on hearing and reading data, summary drafts, e-mails, memos, and letters.

—Like collecting project paper trails so that you have data available to validate decisions or delegating.

Tools and strategies that can help you strategize and be more productive:

- Top-of-the-line computers, printers, phones, faxes.
- High-end sound systems and tape recorders to record thoughts or dictate instructions to others.
- CD-ROMs or Internet sites that house information (e.g., famous quotes).
- Bells, whistles, or alarms that resonate one clear sound.
- Books or seminars on tape to make use of commute time.
- Stationery and business cards that clearly display your position, professional title, and/or degrees.
- Written summaries of the latest news from around the world.
- Excerpts from key talk shows and interviews.
- Tiny tape recorder for any of your many creative thoughts.
- Current events sources available online or on the radio rather than on television.
- Avoid uncomfortable sounds, like your cell phone ring, which will annoy you and make you uneasy or even angry.

Visual

With a visual preference, you have very high standards, and an elaborate vision of what you want to achieve. Possessions that look good and are topnotch contribute to the overall picture of a winner.

YOU:
—Prefer neutral color on walls and furniture.
—Want top-of-the-line quality and efficiency in everything, from work supplies to home furnishings. Even a label maker must be the very best.
—Prefer to read a story rather than listen to someone tell it.
—Dislike clutter and prefer minimalism as a style for decor.

Tools and strategies that can help you strategize and be more productive:

- Finest craftsmanship for all material objects.
- Mirrors in key places that capture your movement and help you to feel in control of your space.
- Office space that contains all the latest informative, up-to-date supplies that look great and are clean, working, and maintained.
- Files located in a circular file stand; simple but handy.
- Home furnishings that are beautiful, practical, and encourage you to relax, but not necessarily entertain.
- An abundance of pictures, images, and charts to support you in making quick decisions.
- A fish tank or birds in a cage to give you access to nature that is beautiful but controlled.
- Keep your perfect fashion sense up to date with every new fashion flare.

Kinesthetic

With a kinesthetic preference, you are sensitive to taste, odor, temperature changes, and touch. You are usually very aware of your body and concerned about the way in which your clothes feel against the skin.

YOU:
—Love to pick out your own furnishings, which must be comfortable and efficient.
—Are the most sensitive to your environment of all the Prioritizing Styles.
—You like being outdoors and active—biking, hunting, fishing.
—Like to make models or other handcrafted items.
—Learn a lot about others by the quality of handshakes and may draw inferences by observing people's actions.

Tools and strategies that can help you strategize and be more productive:

- Office supplies that are easy to use and feel good to the touch—e.g., data entry systems.

- Appropriate ergonomics—key for all your electronic purchases.
- Furniture that is comfortable as well as functional.
- Clothing or any personal items that portray a winning attitude.
- Physical exercise equipment at home or at the office—encouraging you to feel great.
- Tools of every type for anything that might require assembly or repair.

CONCLUSION

> What we have to learn to do, we learn by doing.
> —Aristotle

Being aware of your own sensory preference can greatly enhance the way you relate to the world, what you receive, and also what you give back. Establishing an organizing routine that reflects your sensory preference can make your surroundings come alive and will contribute to a lifetime of organizational support. Using your sensory preference (whether visual, auditory, or kinesthetic) to keep you on track will also contribute to your feeling nurtured and at ease, whether performing tasks that you love or find a tad tedious.

Organizing can seem like a challenge for the best of us. There are a million ways to get things done, but connecting with your sensory preference—an essential element of organic being—can bring you more practical success as well as more joy and fulfillment. A little consciousness goes a long way!

Chapter Six

Different Strokes for Different Folks

No amount of training can produce innate giftedness, although practice can build competencies and hone skills.

—Arlene Taylor, W. Eugene Stewart, and Michelle Nash, *MindWaves*

Organizing is a formidable enough task to master on your own. But when you live or work with someone who has a different brain type than your own, you are faced with a whole new set of challenges. We all know how uncomfortable and sensitive this situation can be. Moving out of your home or getting a new job to avoid your clutter nemesis is usually not a viable solution. I have worked with highly successful clients who are embarrassed to call me to assist them in the first place. But when they admit that they also have some dicey issues with coworkers or spouses about where to put what and why, they really get uneasy. I have learned how much potential and real conflict can arise over how two people mange differently. Let me tell you that this is a genuine and very important area for discussion.

So far, I have given you information to help you transform your relationships with time, paper, and possessions. We are now going to focus on other people's styles. Remember that there are no best styles; each has its pluses and minuses. Remember too that *organization is a direction, not a destination*. Once you have things in reasonable order, you are able to work at it—just a little—to keep the initial investment of your time and money going. The more often you go through things and remind yourself what you possess, the less waste of money, and the more time you will have. Working together is a big solution to this somewhat monotonous and endless game of organizing.

With more control, fine-tuning, and contentment, organizing is an investment in your life, but also in the life of others. You are now ready to develop valuable insights into handling those people who have a different preference. In this chapter you will develop important techniques for successful communication, negotiation, and resolution, no matter the brain type or situation. You'll also cultivate a dose of kindness and compassion, which will certainly make life easier and happier as well.

Janice, a business owner, has a Maintaining Style that wants everything in meticulous order. She'd wait until her husband, an Innovating, more broad-stroked style of guy, went out of town, and then she'd purge fanatically. Here was a man who couldn't part with his precious stuff, but this woman knew it was crucial to take a stand for her own sanity and peace of mind. Last time he went away she eliminated over twenty banker's boxes brimming with old newspapers, receipts, trade journals, magazines, and catalogs from their home office. She confessed she was petrified that he'd come home and go berserk!

I helped these two come up with a system that worked, could be maintained, and most important, honored both of their styles. I sat down with them and had each one explain why they did things the way they did and how the other person's style truly bothered them. In this organizing therapy session, both shared the pangs of domestic disorganization. I suggested that both needed to give something up in order to gain something. Once on the same page, we could begin to change old habits and open new strategies to work together.

Then I explained to Mr. Innovating Style that his wife's Maintaining brain type was an asset in keeping things totally organized. I helped him see that her need to impose a more meticulous order wasn't a power trip or a critique of his pack rat habits; rather, it was her way of expressing her innate style. There was a tremendous shift in the healing process for this couple and it actually brought them closer together.

On a lighter note, I worked with another couple where the wife, an extreme Innovating organizer, left her dirty clothes all over the bedroom. She would try to pick them up at the end of the week, but the husband was pretty fed up and ended up buying her two of the most expensive laundry baskets I've ever seen. He put one in the closet near the entrance of their bedroom and one in the bathroom of their master bedroom. "If the container is close by, she'll use it," he thought. I've noticed over the years that people tend to be a little lazy. Everyone is more likely to choose the sweater at the top of the pile than the one at the bottom; 80 percent of what we own we wear 20 percent of the time. The husband later told me how that one defining moment saved his marriage: *two laundry baskets!* So easy, yet so difficult to see sometimes. She put her clothes away and he wasn't walking into a dirty laundry pile after a long day. My point is that it can be so simple, so easy to make a world of difference. It doesn't have to be earth-shattering. It's all about learning to accept people in a way that does not threaten your own innate style.

You are well aware by now that there are four innate organizing preferences, each expressing their own unique talents. Let me stress that all of these styles need to be celebrated and tweaked, never discouraged or dismissed. I want to make very clear that I'm not advocating that you adapt to someone else's style in order to fit in. If your lifestyle makes you feel unhappy, unfulfilled, or tired, the first step is to deal with and accept *yourself* first and foremost. This is a very sensitive issue. Most people lack the courage to explore their own style or evaluate their stuff first. As the authors of *Mind Waves* suggest, "Every adult should understand his/her brain's preferred functions. Then the trick is simply to use them as much as possible."

Looking at others' brain types and organizational expression, or lack thereof, can bring up so many issues. This is an area that is emotionally charged and can be filled with criticism. However, you must remember that our world couldn't survive if there was just one type. We need to depend on each other and value our differences and strengths or we won't be entirely happy. Although we often want to blurt out, "My way or the highway," it is not an option. We need to learn how to accommodate our different styles so we can work together. It is that simple. Again, the authors of *Mind Waves* claim: "Each of our four cerebral divisions has its own built-in scanner. Each perceives the environment somewhat differently and focuses on specific interests. Stretching the metaphor just a bit, one could say that each is a specialist in its own field. Think of each as having a purpose and containing functions that can help you manage specific situations in life."

By now you recognize the strengths that become apparent when you identify your own brain preference. You realize how much easier it is and how much energy you experience when you act in alignment with your type. It gives you more focus, power, and satisfaction as you tackle all kinds of activities. Now it's time to learn how to apply this approach to other areas in your life, which will give you the ability to encourage and support those around you.

As Ned Herrmann, a former researcher at General Electric, claims in *The Whole Brain Business Book*, each brain quadrant has its own distinct plateau and focus for optimum performance: Form centered (Maintaining Style); Feelings centered (Harmonizing Style); Future centered (Innovating Style); Facts centered (Prioritizing Style).

The types tend to clash over these main tenets that rule our world. Becoming better aware of other people's general needs, issues, and orientations will assist you in understanding how we all are motivated and can work and live together. It will also show you how to support others as they set up their environment for optimum ease, and how you can go about living, working, even loving together. I encourage you to spend time reading through this entire chapter. It will help you identify and appreciate all of those talented folks in your circles of work, friends, and family who bless you with their differences.

Everybody basically uses all four brain preferences to one degree or another; but according to Arlene Taylor, in order to thrive, you must match at least 51 percent of your daily activities to your own brain type. That means we all lead from one quadrant, but we have access to the other three. It also means you can learn from the other brain types and strengthen a weak mode or cultivate those areas where you find affinity to give you additional skills. But be careful. At the end of this chapter, you don't want to spread yourself equally thin and come from 25 percent of each brain preference. That would not only be unproductive but very energy intensive. I'm also not advocating trying to live from a brain preference that you believe society would reward more, or choosing one brain preference for work and another for home. I've tried it and it nearly wiped me out! Ultimately, it won't work. The idea is to stimulate yourself to open up your mind to the other three types and their wondrous workings. Everyone benefits!

Focus on self-knowledge and understanding others so that you can get beyond clichés and differences and learn how to relate successfully whether working or playing with the people in your life. This goes way beyond conquering clutter. As D. H. Lawrence suggested, "Be a good animal, true to your instincts."

MAINTAINING STYLE—"THE PERFECTIONIST"

> We come into the world with a given genetic complement of cognitive capabilities, options, and mental strengths and weaknesses. As we respond to life's learning opportunities, it's natural that we learn to go to our strengths first.
> —**Ned Herrmann**

What concerns me about you is that you strive for total perfection. If things are out of place and people are tardy, you find yourself stressed out. People's actions and attitudes, particularly when it comes to organization, are often very different from yours. So you tend to want to control both people and your environment, and you need this control in order to feel safe. You abide by the rules and expect everyone else to. When people start to push you to take a new, unknown direction, you become resistant and stubborn. Therefore, learning how be successful without demanding that others change will actually strengthen your position in life, as well as bringing enormous relief to coworkers, friends, and loved ones.

Maintaining Style + Prioritizing Style
You two tend to work well together. You recognize each other for your competencies and expertise. You both share similar traits, such as great follow-through, an appreciation of organization, and a reliance on data for decision making. You also thrive on using logic to solve a problem.

You and your Prioritizing coworker's basic needs are very complementary and you certainly appreciate that he/she isn't the "let's just wing it" type. What a relief! Although the Prioritizing Style prefers calling the shots to keeping the paperwork, your different roles sync rather nicely.

Both of you know what you need and want from each other, and both of you are decisive and respectful enough to honor and value each other's time. Neither of you wants to waste a moment fretting about something. Since you and Prioritizing types appreciate communication via e-mail, your connection really works, with an almost automatic division of labor that serves you both. You become the keeper of documents, filing systems, and whatever else the Prioritizing Style has no desire to keep, and you get to interact with him/her in a way that feels comfortable for you. Don't be offended if your coworker doesn't notice all the work that you do behind the scenes. When he/she needs something, you will have it ready, and that will be the biggest pat on the back that you will get.

It would help if you can develop a tight and consistent timetable for your relationship with the Prioritizing Style. For example, have a meeting, open the mail, and be in the office at the same time every day. This will provide the structure you crave and help you flourish as you maintain all of the stuff they'd rather not know about. Let them know ahead of time how you want to organize your time: they'll listen and you'll feel good about what you do.

You are not happy with conflict of any kind, so make sure to give yourself plenty of scheduled time to prepare and seek alignment between people and procedures. The Prioritizing Style can handle adversity far better than you, so let them take care of people issues. (Even though they can be cantankerous much of the time.) Remember, people are not your forte; papers and possessions are. You and the Prioritizing Style will rarely get into disagreements or arguments. Like yourself, the Prioritizing Style doesn't take things all that personally, nor does he/she care for lengthy or emotional conversations. You two communicate just great, best in written and brief e-mails, no need for face to face. You certainly prefer and actually enjoy this to-the-point behavior rather than the endless chatter of a Harmonizing Style, who always wants to hang out for a few more nonproductive minutes at the water cooler!

Maintaining Style, you not only provide the gift of a well-oiled machine at work but keep the domestic front running like a tight ship. You are certainly the most together spouse imaginable. Dinner on the table nightly at six. Laundry done every Sunday between two and four. This behavior, although a tad rigid, proves endlessly comforting for the Prioritizing person, who doesn't have to bother doing things they don't want to do. And if they want something, you most certainly know where it is! Prioritizing Styles do appreciate things working perfectly all the time, so they appreciate you. The Prioritizing person is a master at purging, no sentimentality here, but in the end they may need to locate something they tossed out. (This is where you come in, again.) Since their closets, drawers, and cupboards are all reasonably organized, their mess won't overwhelm you. But you'll need an annual purge to ensure and maintain a happy home life for both of you.

Mind you, the Prioritizing Style has a few things to tell you. They may insist you ask for their guidance when it comes to making new decisions at home or at work. You need to remind them that you don't want to see the "big picture." It's just not your style. The Prioritizing Style thrives on a sense of controlled adventure and creating alternative working solutions. You, on the other hand, thrive on the nitty-gritty nuts and bolts of a project. You prefer labeling, filing, answering calls, and sticking to a schedule. It's your comfort zone. Change can terrify you, whereas the Prioritizing Style often welcomes it. Why? Not because they are such risky people, but because they have already made tons of calculations to feel secure about what lies ahead. I assure you, you can trust them to pull off just about anything. But also continue to emphasize that "God speaks through the details" and to remind them that they do need you.

Maintaining Style + Innovating Style

Of all the brain types, the Innovating Style, who often maintains that you have "no imagination whatsoever," presents the biggest organization and communication challenge. Since you are fact centered and they are idea centered, you are traditional and they are innovating, you most certainly think and work in exactly opposite styles, making you the least complementary combination of brain preferences. Don't worry. There is much to gain from your relationship and you can learn a lot from each other.

Innovating Styles need everything all over the place and work hours that are not "scheduled" but rather in tune with their own system. This can be very unnerving for you since you normally don't speak up until you have all the facts in front of you. They value their gut reactions, follow their intuition, and will act immediately once they get a feeling for what they need to do. They may try to teach you something about spontaneity, taking new risks, even about trying new things, but that isn't you *at all!* You can learn to appreciate them for who they are, and when you feel comfortable, you can put your big toe in to test the water, but not most of the time. If you can clearly define responsibilities for them in an easier manner, identifying tasks and setting obvious deadlines, you may feel more comfortable. Even though they thrive on opening your mind to other possibilities, you need an agenda, a careful plan of attack that has been written down and thought through thoroughly before you act. So, how can you ever work or live together? The answer is: Very carefully!

Since you are fundamental opposites, sometimes this works and sometimes it doesn't. The Innovating Style is both space- and time-challenged. This can drive you nuts! If you go into their office or bedroom, you may have a heart attack. It looks like total chaos to your Maintaining Style. However, they usually know exactly where everything is and I would strongly advise you not to touch anything without their permission. Keep in mind that they don't need things like reference files or documents of any kind in any particular order. A lot of them really live by "out of sight, out of mind" when it comes to a filing system. And putting things in "perfect" order is something they wouldn't understand, let alone consider doing.

I worked with a fanatical Maintaining Style individual who for the last twenty years wrote down every single thing she did every single day in this itzy-bitzy calendar she got free from her bank. While we were organizing her garage, she suddenly got hysterical. She thought she had lost this precious artifact and proceeded to scream at her Innovating husband, who couldn't bear to waste his time looking for what he deemed a silly obsession. This man had no clue about his wife's Maintaining brain preference and had a difficult time being in any way compassionate. Luckily, she found her paper treasure, and I suggested she explain to her husband why this calendar was so important to her. She listed all of her reasons, including how crucial it was for her to note down and keep a reference of the details of her life. It made her feel in control. This is just a short anecdote about Maintaining and Innovating styles, but you can see how dramatic things can get when we don't understand one another's differences. The Innovating husband was unable to support or understand his Maintaining wife's behavior and fears until he learned more about how she basically functions.

So, how do you deal with such types where organizing isn't even a word, let alone an item on the agenda? You need to be fully supportive. You may have to loosen up your organizing style to accommodate their needs or simply feel that organizing them is part of your job, period. Since you also enjoy *supporting* everyone on his or her journey, it's really not such a stretch. If you do dare help them, set up a system so that they can flourish, not fail. Please be reasonable in your expectations as well. You will never convince them to fold their socks three ways and then line them up in perfect color coordinates as in your exemplary drawers.

Another warning. To the Innovating Style, paper is an enemy. To you, it is your treasure. If you are helping, working with or for an Innovating person, you've got to know how they think. Rather than creating a filing system in which every single piece of paper is located in one manila file folder accompanied by its own hanging file folder, all perfectly labeled, try to leave a banker's box under their desk or on top of a credenza where they can drop errant pieces of paper, freeing up their desk space. Or ask them to put a colored piece of paper between the piles. They probably won't look at those sheets, but at least you'll know where they are, and it won't be such an eyesore. When it's time to purge, they'll probably first take a peek before dumping the entire box out. If you still can't swing that concept, then devising a filing system with big, broad categories that could easily be stored in a 2-foot 2-inch drop bottom hanging file would work quite nicely. Don't forget that color is their passion, even though it isn't yours. Don't go overboard, either. Less is more in this case. If they wish you to file, then let them have a filing basket where you can do your magic after they're gone.

In order to keep your relationship working, you need some basic organizing structures in place. It may not be perfect, but if it causes less animosity between the two of you, then it is working. This is compromise time for you Maintaining people. At home, it is a little easier to keep things in order. Innovating Styles can manage to hang up their clothes, while you prefer to fold yours nicely. Creating a laundry spot right where the Innovating person changes will encourage them to use it. You need to keep the systems easy, fun, with exciting new products that they will love to use. Changing it every now and then will add spice and encourage teamwork on all fronts. Remember, you enjoy maintaining things, so you will probably get stuck with most of the work. If you are ever feeling exploited and not celebrated for your drive at keeping it all together, then you need to bring that up in a civil discussion. Your seriousness can scare them away from issues that bother them. Don't forget that humor is their greatest gift. Use it and you will be applauded, adored, and actually come out a winner.

As for managing time, try to place clocks at their workspace or home office in strategic places. They can quickly get lost in their thoughts and forget about time altogether. You won't need to make it your job to remind them if you buy lots of cheerful, fun clocks. Also, remind them at breakfast what is happening later in the day, and remind them again later on as well. Riding them a bit, in a supportive and encouraging way, should prove the right mix for both of your skills to flourish.

Maintaining Style + Harmonizing Style

You love getting organized, so why not assist someone who values what you do but has a hard time doing it on their own? The Harmonizing Style is also a relatively easy ally. They too enjoy maintaining organizing systems, but express their talents in a less methodical, far more organic, connected kind of way than you. They value people and interaction over detail work; just the opposite of you. They see you as a tad too picky and often think you do a lot of unnecessary work. Hmmm . . . It is obvious that what you each contribute to a work or social situation is very different. Harmonizing Styles give you access to interpersonal relationships. You give them the guidance to stay on track. Harmonizing Styles cannot give you any of the specifics about people, places, procedures, and things that you crave in order to feel informed and secure. And you cannot give the Harmonizing Style the incentive to keep organized.

So, how can you get a Harmonizing person on your bandwagon? Your best bet is to speak to them face to face, and from a more humanistic perspective than you are used to. That is challenging for you, but it will make them comfortable and you will come off as trustworthy. When you do supervise, if you are helping organize their office or home, you need to keep them on a short leash since they tend to wander off. Babysitting these folks might feel like a huge energy drain, but keeping a watchful eye will ensure that the job gets done properly, with your specifics in mind.

Harmonizing Style's spaces tend to be covered with all the things that matter to these people personally—photos, memorabilia, and the like. To them it feels cozy; to you it feels cluttered and may even drive you berserk. You will notice that very little real workspace exists on their desk, in their office, or family room. Don't forget, Harmonizing Styles desperately need things that make them feel connected. If you can't assist them in keeping a comfortable nest, or if you cannot accept what is important to them, you and they will have a tough time getting anything accomplished.

At home, Harmonizing Styles also need their own area to build their nests. They may still have their stuffed animal collection from when they were children! You could suggest they store this in a closet where the clutter doesn't upset you too much. Or photos, like so many other things that they enjoy collecting, rather than being in a zillion individual frames, can be placed in a photo album or on their desktop that is just as easily viewed. Keeping their stuff around them (to make them happy) in a noncluttered kind of way (to make you happy) is what makes for a successful relationship.

Last, they thrive on maintaining things, like you, but don't care for the specifics. Being motivated to get organized, to clean out the attic, for instance, would be wonderful if both of you could do it. They need a little company, and you can assist them in making a final concise purge of what they do and don't need. Sure, it may be challenging for you to be in their space; but I guarantee that some of their warmth and humor will make you feel better in the long run.

Let's keep in mind ten major things that you can do to bridge the differences with the other brain preferences. They are:

- Try to be spontaneous.
- Try to explore new possibilities.
- Try to give up the words "No," "Never," "Why?" and "Perfect."
- Try to be less critical—yes, look the other way!
- Try not to analyze everything that comes your way.
- Try new ways to do things.
- Try to loosen up.
- Try not to worry.
- Try to take some risks!
- Bless others' imperfections.

HARMONIZING STYLE—"THE HUMANIST"

> Agitation in body and mind creates dis-ease and ac-
> celerates aging. Deep rest in the body and mind re-
> verses biological age.
> —Deepak Chopra and David Simon,
> *Grow Younger, Live Longer*

Like your Innovating Style buddy, your traits do not necessarily feed the
organizing bug. You are more interested in group approval than anything else. You are certainly not big on logic or practical implementation
of any kind, but your interpersonal skills, whether working or playing,
offer such huge gifts. You encourage all of us to express our best selves,
to feel good about our ideas, and to relish being alive. If someone
needs you, you are always concerned with his or her well-being and
will instantly stop whatever you are doing to help. This can sometimes
work against you when you are actually on task. Let's look at how you
can take your amazing strengths and communication skills and apply
them to working and living with others in a more organized fashion.

Harmonizing Style + Maintaining Style

Maintaining Styles find you too touchy-feely for their conservative
selves. If you want to connect with them at all, you need to keep a re-

spectful distance, at least at first, and present yourself as a little more serious. This can be challenging since you thrive on being close, both physically and emotionally. Avoid emotional outbursts if you can help it. You will get so much out of aligning with their meticulous organizational skills. Send them an e-mail and tell them the exact day and time you would like to meet. Don't waste their time with lengthy explanations. The briefer the better. Remember, no surprises! Make them comfortable by spelling out your organizing needs prior to getting together. That way they'll feel more prepared to talk about specifics. Don't forget, these folks rely heavily on planning and structure. So, do your share, ensure a little preparation ahead of time, and don't be late. A bit of a stretch? Maybe, but you'll get a lot back for your efforts. You'll be pleasantly surprised to see the kind of support team you can create when you combine Maintaining Style's flair for extraordinary organizing with your talent for connecting successfully with people.

Maintaining Styles are well aware that organizing is their domain, and not yours! They will assist you in every way possible, as long as you promise to remain focused and can take their direction. Don't pass up this opportunity for help. Write "Get Organized" on your schedule, and once there, stick to the task at hand. This means you do not answer the door, you do not return phone calls, and you do not engage in much personal conversation. I know, it's not your style, but you will impress these serious souls with your commitment to something that they really enjoy doing. Then they'll do all of the work you don't want to do and you can delight in all of the time freed up to socialize and help others.

There are other ways the two of you can work together to complement each other at work and at home. I have seen many couples that divvy up duties, switching off who leads and who plays the supporting role. It helps each execute the tasks less appealing to the other. As a Harmonizing Style you feel more focused and comfortable with a Maintaining Style by your side, and have consistent, well-orchestrated partnership. They benefit of course by getting to rub up to some of your warmth and personal charm.

Harmonizing Style + Prioritizing Style

The Prioritizing Style sees you as a tad gullible, and your intuitive style makes no sense to their fact-based, logical way of thinking. Where you are people centered, they are task centered. Where you are more laid-back, emotional, and helpful, they are more hardworking, practical, and controlling. Prioritizing types act more quickly and decisively than you, and always look to the bottom line for determining outcomes, rarely worrying about how anyone feels. They are much more interested in your respecting them than in paying you compliments. They actually *enjoy* conflict, relish a good debate, and thrive on a feisty disagreement revolving around pertinent issues. Because you have difficulty tolerating conflict, you often feel serious discomfort in their presence. Avoid emotional outbursts. Do not use emotion as a means of controlling them— they will sense it and retaliate. If you want to help them get organized, let them know the financial benefit, without your little personal stories. They don't want to know the process; they would much rather see the result. There is hope for you two, but caution and not being overbearing are essential.

Prioritizing Styles like to save time, money, and space. Working with them, it is advisable to find your focus and limit your desire for stories or chitchat. I'm not suggesting that you hide your personality or deny who you really are. But the Prioritizing person will respond much more positively if you exhibit a more serious, down-to-earth side, which can assist them in getting closer to their goals at the end of the day. What you get out of this is an enormous sense of helping them in all of their needs. You love making other people feel good about themselves.

At home, you both can thrive because much of the time the Prioritizing person is delighted to let you take care of all of the household chores and maintenance, and you actually enjoy doing so. If you are willing to make sure their closet is in good order and the garage neatly organized so you both can park your cars, most things will be just fine. A combination of everything working perfectly at home plus your empathetic self guarantees that your Prioritizing partner will have a wonderful working platform so that he/she can be their best, most successful authoritative selves!

Harmonizing Style + Innovating Style

Innovating Styles see you as a Chatty Cathy or Chatty Chuck, talking, talking, talking. They love to interact, but sometimes prefer the company of their ideas over other people. They can be quick to judge, and if you come off as less than introspective, they might consider you superficial and shut down for a while. But they, like you, thrive on creativity, and are overjoyed when they try out a brand-new gadget or test a new idea to see what works. It's advisable to be somewhat cautious when you approach them with your novel organizational ideas. Don't be fickle or exhibit mood swings. Be sincere with your compliments—they will know if you are lying. They'll warm up to your sense of humor and you'll discover how enjoyable it is to work and play with one another brain type.

When it comes to organizing, neither of you are exactly naturals! So make sure you turn a usually tedious cleanup session into more of a social event. You both enjoy a bit of spontaneity, so rather than scheduling a regimented "Let's get organized" every other Friday, try to be more spur of the moment. Afterward, reward yourselves with a great big pizza and celebrate what you have accomplished.

Neither of you can offer much support when it comes to your almost mutual lack of time management skills. Working together in a way that allows for freedom, in a structure that is loose and enjoyable, may help. Both of you need to respect the person you are living or working with to make sure you are considerate and not regularly tardy. Do whatever it takes . . . from setting five alarm clocks to ring twenty minutes early to posting sticky notes everywhere in sight. Remember, this has been and might continue to be a bone of contention for both of you.

In the office, make sure you set time limits for the Innovating Style to keep them focused when they are needed to receive or put away important documents and files. Since you both operate from the right side of the brain, creating boundaries is a must. Make sure you come up with rules about how long things need to be stored and where they should go. And do it all prior to getting organized. This will really help you out. Even though you will probably do most of the organizing work, ask the Innovating Style the most specific questions to ensure that the work you do is the right work, and you are not just spinning your wheels.

At home, you both can have so much fun. You'll want lots of color on the walls, music, candles, and a spiritual vibe to boot. It's possible things can get a little out of hand, and your shared enjoyment might create a slightly unruly home. Assign each other duties, with you in the supporting role, and I assure you the jobs will get done. Since Innovating people thrive on creativity and love planning the spatial arrangements of their home and office, they will come up with ideas that you can implement. That kind of combination spells a winning relationship. Don't feel slighted if they don't assist you in your more mundane duties and don't get caught up trying to be everything to everyone. Make sure at the end of the day you aren't totally burned out and that you have some time and energy to pamper—just you.

Let's keep in mind the ten main things that you can do to bridge the differences with the other brain preferences. They are:

- Try to take care of yourself before you take care of someone else. Remember that you are number one. Fight for what you believe in.
- Trust yourself, your abilities, and don't feel you must give gifts or even your time to be liked. Try to be more independent.
- Assert yourself; don't be afraid to express your thoughts. Be confident. Your ideas are just as important as anyone else's.
- Meet deadlines—set goals and do what it takes to achieve them.
- Try to be more punctual.
- Work more, talk less.
- Try not to be too sensitive or prone to personal upsets.
- Work faster and speed up tasks by staying focused.
- Make commitments only after you consult your calendar.
- Be professional in all that you do.

INNOVATING STYLE—"THE EXPLORER"

> Difference does not mean inferior. It doesn't mean superior. It just means unlike.
> —Taylor, Brewar, and Narle, *MindWaves*

You are a forward thinker, a risk taker, a dreamer, visionary, visualizer, and a holistic being who thrives on generating new ideas. You can see all of the possibilities many of us are blind to. The big picture inspires and drives your idealistic hunches, leading beyond thought models to tangible outcomes. Taking the initiative, being spontaneous, playful, and extremely open does not get in the way of cultivating deep, sometimes hidden but solid values and beliefs.

Unfortunately, of all the four brain types, you face the biggest organizational challenge. As long as you can find what you need, why should you care how it looks? You just love new stuff, new procedures, and new ideas, and cannot bear repetition. That means systems that keep things in order might prove too boring and you'll want to invent new ones. That's great in some areas, but can wreak havoc in an office that you share with others. Obviously, administrative or financial details wear you out. Even though you may feel pretty organized in your own space, it doesn't always appear that way to the other brain types and might make your coworkers or spouse a tad nervous. Let's look at how you can learn to work and live with people who lead with a very different style than your own.

Innovating Style + Harmonizing Style

Harmonizing Styles are highly emotional and love interacting with people. Even though you are both highly intuitive, you tend to be far less interested in communicating how you feel. However, if you are able to share you emotions or needs with them, you may be surprised by what you get in return. Since you are a big picture person, who prefers ideas rather than relating to others, you may even get angry when the chatty Harmonizing Style wants to talk about Joe's mother or Sally's sister. You both share an enjoyment of your belongings, but the Harmonizing person connects to his or her possessions to feel emotionally connected to memories or stories about friends and family. You, on the other hand, see your stuff as a creative resource—something that inspires or feeds an idea, enriches your imagination, or becomes material for another innovative project.

You seem so different from each other. How can both of you help and not hinder each other's progress and pleasure in the world? Yet, sharing the knack of people-related stuff and creative implementation, together you can conquer the world.

In the working environment, you'll find Harmonizing Styles aren't quite as speedy as you'd like. You need to work with people who are quick both in thought and action. While you are trying to find a document, the Harmonizer will definitely not scurry over and drop it into your outstretched hand. Instead, she worries about how you are feeling and wants to engage you in conversation. You see, Harmonizing Styles are always concerned with people over ideas. You, on the other hand, are always dreaming up some new scheme or plan. While you are coming up with a unique way to handle a problem, the Harmonizer will feel displaced; and instead of reveling in your genius, she might express hurt, sadness, or disappointment, or all three. What do you do with such a feeling-based person?

The most important thing to a Harmonizing Style is not just how he or she feels but how everyone else feels. The good news is they always want to please and will try their hardest to make you happy. Use this wonderful gift, defining clearly, but warmly, exactly what you need done. Neither of you is big on the details. So, rather than trying to ask them to put every little thing into impeccable order, laugh a little, keep loose, do your best, and find the way. The sum is more than the parts in this equation. In time, if you remain friendly and kind, you'll discover your mutual companionship helps each of you tweak the other's strengths a notch while diminishing your weaknesses.

At home, you are able to build a creative, funky little nest. The real issue is how you go about maintaining it, since neither of you is too specific about the location of most of your belongings. Because the Harmonizing person really aims to please and make others happy, he/she will probably pick up the slack with regards to domestic duties. Appreciating them, letting them know how much you value what they do, and creating easy systems so you can contribute to helping store things is the route to take here. For example, use big catchall baskets for your stuff when you arrive home. Of course, the baskets must interest you and be beautiful in your eyes. Coats and jackets should be stored on a coatstand or hooks on the wall rather than hung up in the coat closet or stored a mile from where you arrive. Since this is all about working together, devise strategies that can keep you in line and still leave them feeling respected.

Innovating Style + Maintaining Style

You scare them! It's as simple as that. The Maintaining Style sees you as reckless, wild, out of control, downright frightening. You terrify them because your dynamic and enthusiastic style is unpredictable, proving to them, in some way, that you are unreliable and inconsiderate. Basically, you thrive on change, not structure; you live for new possibilities, not conformity. Don't expect them to change completely. Where you are idea centered, changeable, a rule breaker, and flexible, they are fact centered, structured, rule followers, and above all, sequential. You couldn't be more opposite in your functioning styles. Since the Maintaining person prefers predictability and doesn't necessarily see new possibilities, you both need to work to make this connection sing.

The Maintaining Style can assist you enormously with most of your concerns. All he or she needs is for you to spell it out, in a checklist, preferably written down neatly, so that they can take care of it, check off what's been accomplished, and then report back to you on their success. You need to learn how to speak their language. See if you can stop judging them for their seeming lack of liveliness and instead appreciate the fact that these folks have a low tolerance for chaos and instability. If you really communicate with them in a way that they understand, you will receive endless benefits and they will feel secure and respected. Before you know it, they will organize and maintain all of those things you felt were just unimportant or couldn't bear to face.

Here are more specifics about how a Maintaining person can simplify your life. Since you really don't like to file or keep up with up-to-date contacts and calendars, have them set up an appointment to meet with you every day *when you first arrive* in the office. Storing paper is another bone of contention. Since you may need things filed, create a basket where you just toss paper in and let them deal with it at the end of each day or at a scheduled time that they prefer. Also, let them assist and support you in your basic office organization. Get together with them at the end of each week, where they can tidy up and get things better organized for you—even though you will probably undo it all again next week. Don't worry. They will gladly be back willing and able to do a job that you really despise.

I once knew of a couple in which the wife was a traditional Maintaining Style person and her husband, a developer of children's products, had a real challenge on his hands. He had one office at work, but he had another huge office at their home, and that is where the problems emerged. His wife was the one ultimately responsible for all the stuff at home, and she needed to have enormous patience. She created a shelving system in his office that went all the way up to the ceiling, with a library ladder that afforded him access to all of his creations. He was able to see everything. And when she walked past his office, she didn't have to see stuff on the floor or outside his door!

Your differences will become apparent quite quickly. By using curtains, or just keeping the closet door closed, you can store stuff the way you like it and not have to see their belongings every time you go into a room. Really easy storage that is not an eyesore for you is the solution. Since this is your organizing nemesis, avoid conflict by giving them more time to do things, providing accurate information, respecting their routine, and valuing their intelligence. Try to honor your very different tendencies in a way that pleases both of you. It's a bit of a challenge, but wouldn't you like to be even more creative, with less maintenance involved? Absolutely!

Innovating Style + Prioritizing Style

The Prioritizing Style sees you as being undisciplined. Ouch, that hurts, but that's how they see your passionate creativity. Well, not all of the time. Their financial figuring and almost always rational thinking can run contrary to your risk taking, energizing leadership style. They need to take time to reflect before they act. Not you! But you have an ally with the Prioritizing Style. As they are quick in thought and action, you can draw on their problem-solving abilities. Again, the differences are dramatic. You aren't one to structure your epiphanies. They, on the other hand, are masters of time management. You tend to get upset at meetings that don't go your way, while the Prioritizing person tends to be both self-righteous and cautious. It's exasperating. Just don't force them into making decisions without adequate time to think them through.

Let's look at ways you can come to terms with your innate gifts and work together. Basically, neither of you was ever meant to organize or maintain anything—without help, that is. But you as a Innovating person have more of an appetite for putting things in order than the Prioritizing person, so accept that you may have to coax them into it, or just leave them alone.

I recently meet a big-shot Prioritizing CEO and his highly respected Innovating fashion designer wife. She was excited when I arrived, and we worked together, all day long, with gusto and much success. Her husband, on the other hand, was reluctant to give me more than six hours to get his entire office organized. His idea was to just toss out as much as possible. Yes, Prioritizing Styles can purge! He was terribly controlling about time and made things very unpleasant. She was so much fun and free, but willing to do the work.

At first I was surprised they were still married after twenty years! They have completely different styles that really make it challenging to rely on each other for much of anything. Yet they are still able to have a great relationship because where he keeps nothing, she keeps everything, and every so often he encourages her to tackle her organizational issues. He requires a systematic look at it. With her creative bent, both are able to live comfortably; but the Prioritizing Style, who tends to be controlling and likes to vent, may find some of the creative quirks a little hard to take.

A total compromise must be enforced in order to make this work. If you both can handle the little things that annoy you, you will be able to avoid allowing them to become bigger things that might drive you apart. For example, maybe the Prioritizing Style will handle the bill paying and the incoming mail while the Innovating Style handles basic household maintenance like laundry or grocery shopping. A division of labor, which ultimately becomes a workable team effort, might do the trick. If you can afford it, your best bet is to hire an assistant (i.e., a Maintaining Style), who can do all of the nitty-gritty stuff that both of you can't envisage doing day in and day out.

Let's keep in mind ten main things you can do to bridge the differences with the other brain preferences. They are:

- Appreciate facts, details, structure, rules, and error-free work.
- Try to commit to something and stay the course. Don't shake things up just for the sake of it.
- Try to finish what you start.
- Think before you speak.
- Try to avoid extremes by slowing down and finding a balance. This may seem strange at first but give yourself time to adjust.
- Be more professional in your work and personal environment.
- Try to be more punctual and considerate of those around you.
- Once a home has been created for your belongings, go the extra step just to return them.
- Proofread your work before you hand it in or discuss it with colleagues.
- Try to be more responsible to your work, standards, and routines.
- Pay more attention to the needs of others.

PRIORITIZING STYLE—"THE LEADER"

An organization without the balance of all four quadrants is by design an organization in conflict.
—Ulf Caap, CEO of IKEA, North America

Since you learn by acquiring and quantifying facts, and applying logical thinking to ideas and new theories, you need 100 percent support and commitment from the other brain types to help you put together your masterpiece. Even though you prefer uncomplicated relationships, *be nice, they can help you!* You need the other brain types' ability to give you key points for your groundbreaking report, to supply you with clear-cut data-based content, and to do everything to help you process numbers quicker, faster, and with dead-on accuracy. You'll get what you need in a concise, positive, and effective way, and those other brain types will be eager to provide you with the right information. You need the facts, without chaos (Innovating Style finds this intriguing), without emotions (Harmonizing Style can't help it), or without overly detailed reports (Maintaining Style loves these). You have to create a team that responds to your particular needs. Delegation is the primary organizing issue that you must master in order to emerge even more triumphant. Remember Harold Taylor's injunction: "Be ruthless with time but gracious with people!"

Your organizing style is impressive. You usually don't have a lot to do since you purge like a pro and/or have learned how to delegate infrastructure activities as much as possible. You ultimately need to feel great about all of your accomplishments. How? By keeping less stuff around and by relying heavily on everyone else, especially the Maintaining Style to whom you can delegate all those details that don't interest you and certainly would not be a very efficient use of your time. Let's look at how you can work more effectively and, yes, more politely to create a powerful support team.

Prioritizing Style + Innovating Style

The Innovating Style is a person who values experimentation and exploring synergistic opportunities when problem solving. They are your opposite in so many ways. They aren't great at follow-through and hover in the abstract or conceptual zone of ideas over action. They view you as a number cruncher, and see you as far less creative than you actually are. They pose numerous mundane challenges for someone like you. They don't always appear competent; they don't even make a point of showing up on time! However, don't forget that at the end of the day you may need their insight in understanding future trends and creative solutions. Try not to treat them impersonally or criticize them in front of their peers. Draw them into projects where fresh ideas are needed. Remember, although they come at problem solving from a completely different perspective, they are big picture thinkers like you. That's where you can link up and make magic!

Innovative Styles march to the beat of their own drummer. Because they honor the creative process, ideas, and their imagination over facts and numbers, they may seem a tad off the wall to you. Combine their eccentricities with the fact that they don't like being told what to do, don't respect schedules all that much, and question authority—what can you do? They listen and answer to themselves only, work from pure gut instinct rather than the latest economic formulas. How, then, can you two work effectively together?

First, don't judge them too harshly by the appearance of their office or the fact that they tend to be a little tardy. Surely they need to be considerate and should be reminded about how disrespectful it is to hold people up. But yelling and blowing your top is one sure way to shut them off from you completely. What to do? *Don't go into their offices, ever.* You don't need to, it will make you uneasy, and you'll never believe that in all that seeming clutter, they actually know what's what. Don't be impatient with them because they don't adhere to your standards of neatness. Also, try to be a little more flexible around schedules. If you know that a certain time of day isn't to their liking, don't schedule things then. Give them ample notice as to what you need and when you need it. Remind them a day before, and don't expect them to remember when you mentioned you wanted something a week ago. Sure, you may have to ride them a little, and you'll find yourself pulling your hair out now and then; but you cannot underestimate their innate skills and talents. You really cannot survive without their ability to foresee future trends. You need them. So breathe and regroup a little.

If you share a home with an Innovating person, their relaxed style may be too much for you to take. Giving them a certain closet, or even a room you never enter, may be a workable solution. Of course, if you do share a space—and let's hope you do—some serious compromise needs to happen on both fronts. Look at your DVD collection, for example. You prefer each disc housed in its appropriate case, once viewed, you want it put back promptly. Consider yourself lucky if the Innovating Style even puts it back in the right case, let alone on the shelf in alphabetical order. Since you thrive on delegation and have no interest in doing the nitty-gritty, and they are the big picture person, without a bone in their body for regular maintenance, you need to find a compromise. This is difficult for both of you. Okay, you've got to loosen your standards in some areas a little. Something's gotta give. And either your dear Innovating Style needs to get someone to keep things organized for him/her or you need to encourage organizing in a playful manner. It's possible to accommodate both of your styles, but it will take real dedication and a shared vision of the common goal.

Prioritizing Style + Harmonizing Style

You are primarily a numbers, not a people person. You may be a little standoffish and often leave your emotions at the door. Harmonizing Styles are all emotion personified and exactly your opposite on the brain wheel. They might be the most difficult brain type to understand, let alone work or play with, and yes, chances are you may be married to one! You see things so differently, but yet you have the possibility of being complimentary. Where you are independent, hardworking, and controlling, they are very much team players, relaxed and helpful to everyone they encounter. Don't easily dismiss them. They have organizational qualities that you need, and vice versa.

The Harmonizing Style can make a great spouse or partner since they value feelings, humanistic pursuits, and companionship, which on some level you crave but innately don't really value or have time for. They see you as calculating and judgmental. They believe you primarily care for people only when they are working hard, and they would prefer you to just relax and forget about the right everything 24/7. "Take a break," they say. "Hang out." Feelings over facts are what this is all about. You both communicate so differently. You are extremely straightforward (completely overlooking people's feelings) and lead by a personal forcefulness that may be too much for them. If you must criticize, be extra-sensitive to their feelings. Don't make them feel rejected. That may come back to bite you. It may be torturous for you actually to ask this Harmonizing Style how they are doing when you arrive home after a long day at work or at the water cooler with a coworker. But in order for any conversation to take place between you two, you need to actually acknowledge the Harmonizing person's feelings initially. How?

First, take the time to chat with these people in your lives. I know a CEO in Vancouver who had to force herself to talk to people by setting up her computer printer at the other end of the office. If she needed something printed, she had to walk across the office, which forced her to approach people and connect with her staff in a way that wasn't too terribly intimate and uncomfortable. You thrive on common sense, but again, the Harmonizing Style thrives on personal relatedness. They love to feel appreciated and desperately need your stamp of approval rather than a promotion or pay raise. The extra five minutes of chitchat will go a long way.

Second, tell your Harmonizing Style what you need to get done. Don't wait for them to come up with the answers. Since your styles are completely opposite (you purge, they can't; you're quick to the punch, they are more sensitive and need to think things over), learn to give them some space to come to their own conclusions. Meaning: don't rush them, don't yell, minimize pressure, look for the positive, show understanding, and especially, *don't embarrass them*. Living and working with a Harmonizing Style is a blessing in disguise. They bring a richness of perception and humanity that warms up the room.

Finally, if you live with a Harmonizing Style, please let them have the run of the house. They are nest builders and love to have piles of mementos of everything they have ever seen or done all around them. This may be a bit much, but I guarantee it will make them happier in the long run. I have met several high-powered business executives who lived in ample spaces and said their Harmonizing spouses were always complaining how small their homes were! If this story sounds familiar, before blowing up and pointing out the actual square footage of the house, listen to their feelings. Then suggest ideas and let them make the next move. And try not to judge them while they do all the work. They'll feel more encouraged and you can go off and develop a new business plan.

Prioritizing Style + Maintaining Style

The Maintaining Style is your closest ally. These people are very task-oriented, on time, and total perfectionists in all that they do. They are slower than you, but your organizing styles mirror one another and you won't need to make many changes to your natural style of doing things if you work with a Maintaining Style. They will upgrade everything you set out to accomplish and will even garnish you with more free time, once you know that their allegiance is to keeping things in perfect order.

Maintaining Styles might see you as being "power-hungry." Try to avoid arguments using aggressive behavior and power struggle tactics. They might think that a bit rigid. But be nice. Be straightforward in your answers. You need to respect their obsession with schedules, order, and routine, so that if you decide to change something, they'll get enough lead time to be prepared. They are not good at short notice. If you learn how to honor their schedule and respect their need for regularity with as little novelty as possible, an ideal relationship is guaranteed.

If you live with a Maintaining person, you need to make sure you dedicate a specific time to discuss what stuff you do and don't need to keep, and they'll happily go about getting it done. Maintaining Styles don't like clutter, either. Plus, it's really great that they love doing what you cannot bear to do. So, create some clear-cut direction and boundaries (they have a hard time with that) and let them go at it.

Since they are the keeper of all things important that you may someday need, they are devoted to spending time making their home or office orderly and efficient. Although this task doesn't seem too earth-shattering, they deserve your attention and some kudos. You will find you are not able to dictate exactly when they should do all of this work, by the way. They will work their scheduled hours, no more, no less, and will stick to what has always been expected of them from day one. But they will do a great job. Maintaining Styles can assist you and keep you in line like no other brain preference. Honoring them and valuing what they do will make a world of difference.

Let's keep in mind ten main things that you can do to bridge the differences with the other brain preferences. They are:

- Try to be diplomatic when dealing with people's emotions and be sensitive to others' needs.
- Enjoy people, not just your victories. Helping someone is a good thing!
- Listen first, talk second. Take five before you open your mouth and are ready to argue and shout. Being explosive is good way to make others less willing to share their opinions with you—opinions that could easily benefit you and your company.
- Relax—remember the Tortoise and the Hare.
- Inspire and empower those around you. Don't worry. Your power will not diminish because of this: it will strengthen *your* team.
- Value the process and numerous work styles, not just the end result.
- Try to let your needs take a second place to those around you.
- Try to be more patient, more understanding, and less hotheaded.
- Ask others for their feedback and ideas.

- Pitch in and help—don't think you are too important or too big for a job like filing.

CONCLUSION

> We must learn to live together as brothers or perish together as fools.
> —**Martin Luther King, Jr.**

We all need to work together. It's time to admit we just cannot do it all by ourselves. According to Carl Honoré, the author of *In Praise of Slowness*, "We seek to cram in as much consumption and as many experiences as possible. . . . The result of this obsessive behavior is a gnawing disconnect between what we want from life and what we can realistically have."

This contradiction naturally feeds a common attitude that we never have enough time or energy to live the way we would like. You might find yourself feeling afraid, frustrated, and alone in this process. This is when you can discover that the whole is greater than the sum of its parts. Whether you are part of a company or a family, being aware of other's brain types and how their inherent strengths help you work and play together is the key to success and fulfillment.

Here's a description of dynamic brain flow to help you see how it all comes together: The Prioritizing Style is the industrial side of the brain. It generates energy and focus and is able to extrapolate advantage from the information gathered by the Maintaining Style. The Maintaining Style takes that thought or theory and verifies it, checking for accuracy, then hands it over to the Innovating Style for review. From that point on, the Innovating Style incubates the thought, sees all of the possibilities and nuances, then passes it on to the Harmonizing Style. There it is brought forth into the world and the best people can implement it. Working together creates the synergy of an idea, from inception to final delivery. Pretty impressive!

Now to get a little more detailed, the Prioritizing Style is all about performance; the Maintaining Style is about production; the Innovating

Style is willing to take imaginative chances or leaps of faith; and the Harmonizing Style is value driven. We need to ascertain the brain styles of each of the people we come into contact with. As we determine their innate preferences, we are better able to understand how they go about their tasks, prioritize, and organize their thinking and doing. Knowing who you are dealing with really helps you discover viable solutions to ease the tension in every situation—be it personal or professional.

I admit, life gets in the way and can make organizing difficult. Our growing population produces more and more information for us to take in, digest, and make sense of. Each of us has fewer traditional support systems, such as an extended family. And when you finally decide you need to get organized, you often lack solid guidelines to help you. Organizing isn't rocket science, but a few people have learned and developed skills that can make these quotidian tasks less threatening, and this can have an enormous impact on the quality of your life.

Hopefully, you have discovered your own brain style and now find your strengths at your command. As you learn to understand other people's styles, you will practice interacting in ways that do not diminish either of you, but instead enhance your talents as you cultivate working together. Once you tackle and master your own situation, you can finally make space—literal three-dimensional and psychic space—to cultivate human connectedness. According to Alexis de Tocqueville, "He who has set his heart exclusively upon the pursuit of worldly welfare is always in a hurry, for he has but a limited time at his disposal to reach, to grasp and to enjoy it."

With megastores crammed into every nook and cranny of our landscape, overflowing with material goods to lure us into consumerdom, there is a glut of stuff and an overabundance of choice. It's time to slow down, quit stockpiling things and worrying that your life is going to come to an end if you haven't got the latest, the newest, and the best thing in town. Having ten bottles of cleansing cream on hand aren't really going to make you feel better. Everyone take a breath. It's time to ask, "What *really* motivates me?" Why burden your already tedious schedule with endless shopping, thousands of tasks, and growing agendas? The author of *Choosing Simplicity*, Linda Breen Pierce, sums it up: "Our hunger for material things is a substitute for emotional cravings that go unsatisfied." Organizing is a genuinely healthy antidote to this dilemma. Organizing gives you access to what is inside of your head as well as to seeing what is inside of your cupboards. It affects how others relate to you and, therefore, how you go about being in the world and what you ultimately get from being alive. It gives you your life back—and a renewed quality of life.

Remember, organizing isn't about being a control freak; it is about essential survival in a world that is rapidly expanding and moving forward. Gary Thorp, a Zen practitioner, asserts that "The joy comes not from trying to keep things forever. But from keeping them well." Enjoy a little amount, but kept in a way that gives you enough security and sustenance. What all of us want is to feel that we're living a deeply satisfying life that we enjoy and that liberates us. Success for world survival depends on lightening up our spirits by lightening up our stuff. As George Carlin sums up so nicely:

> The paradox of our time in history
> is that we spend more, but have less.
> We buy more, but enjoy less.
> We have bigger houses and smaller families,
> More conveniences, but less time.
> We have multiplied our possessions, but reduced our
>   values.
> We plan more but accomplish less.
> Life is not measured by the number of breaths we take,
> But by the moments that take our breath away.

Acknowledgments

I once thought that if I ever did anything major in my life, I would have no one to thank but myself. My innate perseverance that knows no boundaries, God's blessings, and even good karma can get me through almost anything! Luckily, I have realized over time—especially in writing this book—that many people have contributed not only to my writing but also, more important, to my life, thus making this book possible.

The most important person in my professional life was my very first organizing client, Palmer Jaffe, who eventually became a wonderful friend, my American mother, and my guardian angel. She supported my work from day one and led me to Dr. Arlene Taylor. And she and her family have given me a special place in their hearts while I was frantically working away. Without her, there would be no book. She is definitely the right-brain anchor here.

The one and only Dr. Taylor (whose thesis I've extrapolated from) has had a major influence on my work: an intellectual mentor and a shining example of what I want eventually to become. Her highly energized mind has overseen the manuscript from conception to delivery with tender criticisms, insight, and encouragement. She is the anchor.

Another frontal right, Ilene Segalove, must be acknowledged for her editorial strengths and comments throughout this endless "eleven rewrites per chapter" saga. Her intelligence, humor, and true "soul sister" conversations were deeply appreciated and always much needed. She's not only my cosmic sister but also a total superstar!

Other Innovating and Harmonizing individuals who should be thanked are: Patti Bloomfield, Rhonda Bowen, Jennifer Butler, Debbie Davies, Reverend Janet Garvey-Stangvik, Tim Guetzlaff, Leslie Jonath, Ken Hamlet, Suzie Heller, Isabella, Barry Izsak, Gary Jaffe, Vida Jaffe, Peggy Liles, Professor James Mullens, Barry Robison, Lisa Sarasohn, and Amy Siu.

On the left side of the brain are those wonderful prioritizing and maintaining folks. My agent, Stephanie Kip Rostan, at Levine Green-berg Literary Agency, who really believed that this book was such a great idea from day one and who was there 24/7, answered my juve-nile questions with kindness and professionalism. A true gem! My editor, Julie Mente, at St. Martin's Press, did all the things that I didn't want to do with ease, clarity, precision, and especially enthusiasm at the end of it. You're a keeper! Finally my copyeditor, Ann Adelman, who really worked diligently and gave my manuscript a good working over. What a true talent and blessing you are. The readers will be indebted to you. Thanks, also, everyone at Levine Greenberg and St. Martin's Press who worked on this book. In their own way. Thank you so very much.

Continuing on the Maintaining quadrant is Christine Palen—the first professional organizer I ever met—who introduced me to the organiz-ing world and especially to NAPO. To my other left-brained friend, Jenny Kane, for her unbelievable support and daily discussions of "writ-ing brilliance." A friendship money couldn't buy. Also Vicki Howie, who gave me the spiritual grounding and insight into the nature of all of this writing stuff. Other support from the left-brain quadrants includes: Elsa Alonso, Dean Bowen, Lee Crawford, Mary Edano, Carolyn Hamlet, Lauren Jaffe, Lea Ann McClendon, Net-Flow, Denise Mertz, Greg Price, Susan Scott, Christina Tabora, Sarah Trester, Renee Vincent, Judy Wag-goner, Carol Wright, and everyone at Copperfields bookstore in Calis-toga and in Napa at the St. Helena Public Library. I would also like to thank fellow NAPO members and the professional organizers who participated in my workshop at the NAPO 2002 National conference in Atlanta. You gave me a lot of insight and support in this radical new ap-proach to a somewhat dry topic. Thanks, guys! And thanks, too, to the NBOC (North Bay Organizers and Coaches), who offered me much en-couragement and support through all of this.

Also, my Canadian family, my sister Shane and brother-in-law Michael, and my brother Ward, who supported me, and were already planning the celebration when I was just finishing the book proposal.

Last, and just as important as those mentioned above, are the clients that I have worked with throughout the years, who have colored every-thing I write and who gave me valuable insight into the pains and joys of getting organized. Whether you reside up and down the California coast or in another country, your openness in allowing someone to come in and organize your personal belongings, and your desire to stay focused and on top of things, warm my heart. Thanks for letting me into your space—your world.

Lanna's Favorite Organizing Supplies

No, this isn't another excuse to go shopping! Yes, you may need to purchase a few things once you see what is left after you purged. Now I want you to learn how to focus when you shop for supplies. It's important to try to stick with one or two brands, especially for long-term storage. As you scan the list below, you'll notice a number of suggestions. Some appeal to and work for your brain type better than others. Just make sure you stick to your new routine in the category that fits your type. That way you will discover the right items to support your day-to-day needs.

Some organizing supplies aren't all that great, and many are really troublesome. Try to stay away from over-the-door shoe bags, or cardboard storage under the bed. Even hangers that attach to other hangers can be more of a nuisance than a solution. The biggest new gimmick is the "squeeze the air out" plastic bags for storage or travel. Yikes! These require more work on your part, your clothes look horrible after you take them out of the bag, plus how much space do you really save? And please, forget about those plastic storage systems with the zillions of teeny drawers. Sometimes, the creators of organizing products produce products that don't ultimately work—that actually disguise the problem. Again, try to buy less, but choose items appropriate to your style and your needs. Below is a list of some Web sites that will give you a sense of your organizing supply options.

THIS IS FOR EVERYONE!

www.avery.com
www.bedbathandbeyond.com

www.containerstore.com

www.creativememories.com

www.dayrunner.com

www.dwr.com (dwr-design within reach)

www.dymo.com

www.eldonoffice.com

www.expandashelf.com

www.fellowes.com

www.filofax.com

www.franklincovey.com

www.frontgate.com

www.gladiatorgw.com

www.holdeverything.com

www.horchow.com

www.ikea.com

www.improvementscatalog.com

www.lizell.com

www.levenger.com

www.lillianvernon.com

www.llbean.com

www.longaberger.com

www.meadwestvaco.com

www.momastore.org

www.neatnix.com

www.officedepot.com

www.oriacdesign.com

www.potterybarn.com

www.potterybarnkids.com

www.rubbermaid.com

www.russellandhazel.com

www.scullyandscully.com

www.shopgetorganized.com

www.smead.com

www.snapware.com

www.staples.com

www.sterilite.com

www.target.com
www.topdeq.com
www.ultoffice.com
www.universityproducts.com

RESOURCES: PROFESSIONAL ORGANIZERS

For further information, please feel free to reach me at:

Organized World
Inakone@organizedworld.com
P.O. Box 457
Rutherford, CA 94573
Work: 707-524-9896
Fax: 707-963-1179
www.organizedworld.com

The National Association of Professional Organizers (NAPO)
4700 West Lake Avenue
Glenview, Il 60025
USA Information: 847-375-4746
USA Fax: 877-734-8668
International/Canada Fax: 732-578-2636
www.napo.net

Recycling

When you get out of spring training and onto the organizing playing field, you will quickly notice how much stuff you really don't need. Don't worry. In the midst of organizing, things can look like a tornado just hit, but as you keep on, you'll be amazed how soon you'll feel in control. Every year, 4 million tons of paper junk mail pours into our homes. It's time to examine our social responsibilities to each other and to the planet as we learn how to reduce, reuse, or recycle the stuff we don't want or need. Here are five ways to make recycling an easy part of your organizing lifestyle:

1: Use the Recycling Services Your City Provides

I'm always surprised that in this day and age, so few people in America actually recycle obvious things like paper and plastic, never mind bigger items like old kitchen appliances or clothing. Depending on where you live and the criteria for recycling plastics, you can recycle most things. Most communities have garbage services that provide different-colored cans for different items. Make it easy on yourself. Put all of the garbage cans together. In your garage, put a can right by the door so you will be able to toss junk mail before it gets into the house and piles up. Also, try to schedule your organizing dates around the time of neighborhood garbage pickup days. Remember, once you make the decision to discard something, get rid of it as soon as possible. Things have a magical way of creeping back into the house if you don't look, toss, and walk away.

Here some additional resources for things you may need help to recyle:

- Cell phones—www.wirelessrecycling.com
- Computer floppy disks and video tape—www.greendisk.com

- Peanut packing filler—Mailbox companies take it
- Holiday cards—St. Jude's Card Recycling, 100 St. Jude Street, Box 60100, Boulder City, NV 89006
- Eyeglasses—The Lions clubs or New Eyes for the Needy, 549 Millburn, P.O. Box 332, Short Hills, NY 07078. In Canada, send glasses to The Low Vision Clinic, 1929 Bayview Avenue, Toronto, ON M4G 3E8

2: Think of Other Ways to Use Your Stuff

It's time to get a little creative. Lots of stuff can be reused. For example: use old belts to tie up tree branches when tossing out cuttings from gardening; use old film canisters to store buttons, pins, and nails; make bookmarks out of used greeting cards, and reuse the other side of printed paper. But once you decide there is nothing else to be done, please, *donate it*.

3: Buy Less

When you buy less, you not only save money but time, space—and the planet. Ask yourself: *Do I need this again and again or do I just want this?* All of your future organizing challenges stem from these two basic questions. Once you acquire anything, you have to figure out not only how to enjoy it but also how to maintain and store it. Sometimes this can become a real burden. Do you want to spend time with your stuff or your friends? Simply reducing the amount of what you purchase can probably get your life back on track without much struggle. "Even though junk mail can often be recycled, recycling is second best to reducing need"—www.obviously.com.

5: Getting Rid of Stuff Is Liberating

When you look around at all the boxes or garbage bags filled with stuff you are tossing or giving away, you will feel good. But come up with a clear strategy of what you want to do with all of it. Don't feel like you have to find a home for every little thing. It's often best to phone a local donation center and set a pickup date. It's simple and it will happen! Otherwise you could end up waiting for months and the bags never go away! Typical donation centers are waiting to help you:

- Salvation Army
- Goodwill Industries
- Hazardous waste
- American Waste System
- Bulky trash pickup

4: Stop the Paper Glut in Your Home

Here are some tips to help you keep you from drowning in your own living room:

* Filling out warranty cards often results in your name being placed on a direct mailing list. Call the company first to find out if they require the card to secure the warranty, and make sure that if you do need to fill it out that they don't use the information for marketing purposes.
* When you order from a catalogue, state: "Please do not sell my name or address." By law, they must oblige.
* Your credit card company sells your name the most. Call the following companies to stop companies from selling your name.
    Credit offers—(1-888-567-8688) 24 hours a day
    AOL (America Online)—1-800-605-4297 (24 hours)
    Publishers Clearinghouse Sweepstakes—1-800-645-9242
    Local businesses and flyers—ADVO, comes with pictures of missing children 1-860-602-1600, or write to ADVO Consumer Assistance, P.O. Box 249, Windsor, CT 06095-4176
    Local newspaper/supermarket flyers—look for a phone number on flyer. If that doesn't work or for other junk mail, contact Mail Preference Service, Direct Marketing Association, P.O. Box 643, Carmel, NY 15012-0643.
* Eliminate Spam—Never reply to a spam e-mail. Use spam filters. If worst comes to worst, contact your senator or government representative. Spam filter—spamrecycle.com

Bibliography

General

Bits & Pieces. Chicago: Lawrence Ragan Communications, August 2004.

Byron, Christopher. *Martha Inc.* New York: John Wiley & Sons, 2002.

Chopra, Deepak, and David Simon. *Grow Younger, Live Longer.* New York: Harmony Books, 2001.

Dinnocenzo, Debra A. and Richard B. Swegan. *Dot Calm.* San Francisco, CA: Berrett-Koehler Publishers, 2001.

Fretwell, Sally. *Feng Shui.* Novato: New World Library, 2000.

Fromm, Erich. *On Being Human.* New York: Continuum, 1994.

———. *To Have or to Be?* New York: Harper & Row, 1976.

Gelb, Michael. *How to Think Like Leonardo da Vinci.* New York: Dell Publishing, 1998.

Goldman, Daniel, Richard Boyatzis, and Annie McKee. *Primal Leadership.* Cambridge, MA: Harvard Business School Press, 2002.

Healing Environments. *The Journal of Hope.* Palo Alto, CA: vol. 6, no. 3, 2001.

Honoré, Carl. *In Praise of Slowness.* San Francisco, CA: Harper, 2004.

Kasser, Tim. *The High Price of Materialism.* Cambridge, MA: MIT Press, 2002.

Kornfield, Jack. *After the Ecstasy, the Laundry.* New York: Bantam Books, 2000.

LeGuerer, Annick. *Scent.* New York: Turtle Bay Books, 1992.

Linn, Denise. *Sacred Space.* New York: Ballantine Books, 1995.

Maisel, Eric. *Affirmations for Artists.* New York: Penguin/Putnam, 1996.

McGraw, Phil. *Self Matters*. New York: Free Press, 2001.

Norman, Donald. A. *Emotional Design*. New York: Basic Books, 2004.

Ritberger, Carol. *Your Personality, Your Health, and Your Life*. Carlsbad, CA: Hay House, 2000.

Science of Mind Magazine. UCRS: Burbank, CA: July 2004.

Turner, Diane, and Thelma Greco. *The Personality Compass*. Boston: Element Books, 1998.

Tzu-Lao. *The Tao Te Ching*. New York: Shambala, 1998.

Weiss, Michael. *The Clustered World*. Boston: Little, Brown, 2000.

Brain Preference

Amen, Daniel G. *Change Your Brain, Change Your Life*. New York: Times Books, 1998.

Benziger, Katherine. *Thriving in Mind*. Dillon, KBA Publishing, 2000.

Blakeslee, Thomas. *The Right Brain*. Garden City, NY: Anchor Press, 1980.

Bloom, Floyd E., Arlene Lazerson, and Laura Hofstadter. *Brain, Mind, and Behavior*. New York: W. H. Freeman Co., 1985.

Bragdon, Allen D., and David Gamon. *Building Left Brain Power*. Bass River, MA: Brainwaves, 1999.

Buzan, Tony. *Make the Most of Your Mind*. New York: Fireside, 1988.

———. *The Brain User's Guide*. New York: E. P. Dutton, 1983.

Herrmann, Ned. *The Creative Brain*. Lake Lure, NC: Brain Books, 1989.

———. *The Whole Brain Business Book*. New York: McGraw-Hill, 1996.

Howard, Pierce J. *The Owner's Manual for the Brain*. Austin, TX: Leornian Press, 1994.

Kotulak, Ronald. *Inside the Brain*. Kansas City, MO: Andrews & McMeel, 1996.

McCarthy, Bernice. *About Learning.* Barrington, IL: Excel, 1996.

Newberg, Andrew, Eugene D'Aquili, and Vince Rause. *Why God Won't Go Away.* New York: Ballantine Books, 2001.

Pinel, John P.J. *Biopsychology.* Needham Heights, MA: Allyn & Bacon, 1993.

Ratey, John J. *A User's Guide to the Brain.* New York: Pantheon Books, 2001.

Restak, Richard. *Mozart's Brain and the Fighter Pilot.* New York: Harmony Books, 2001.

Sousa, David A. *Learning Manual for How the Brain Works.* Thousand Oaks, CA: Corwin Press, 1998.

Springer, Sally P., and George Deutsch. *Left Brain, Right Brain.* New York: W. H. Freeman & Co., 1981.

Taylor, Arlene, W. Eugene Brewar, and Michelle Nash. *MindWaves.* Siloam Springs, AK: The Concerned Group, 2003.

Williams, Linda Verlee. *Teaching for the Two-Sided Mind.* New York: Touchstone, 1983.

Wolfe, Patricia. *Brain Matters.* Alexandria, VA: ASCP, 2001.

Wonder, Jacquelyn, and Priscilla Donovan. *Whole Brain Thinking.* New York: William Morrow, 1984.

Organizing

Ahlgren, Toni. *Organize Your Stuff the Lazy Way.* New York: Macmillan, 1999.

Allen, David. *Getting Things Done.* New York: Simon & Schuster, 2002.

Back office. *Office Life Canada,* June 2003.

Bernstein, Nina. "So Much Clutter, So Little Room," *New York Times,* December 31, 2003.

Better Homes and Gardens. 301 Stylish Storage Ideas. Des Moines, IA: Meredith Books, 1998.

Cherniss, Cary, and Daniel Goleman. *The Emotionally Intelligent Workplace.* San Francisco, CA: Jossey-Bass, 2001.

Culp, Stephanie, *Streamlining Your Life.* Cincinnati, OH: Writer's Digest Books, 1991.

Davidson, Jeff. *Complete Idiots Guide to Managing Your Time.* New York: The Penguin Group, 2002.

Glenwell, Malcolm. "The Social Dysfunction of Paper," *The New Yorker* (March 2003).

James, Jennifer. *Thinking in the Future Tense.* New York: Simon & Schuster, 1996.

Kingston, Karen. *Clear Your Clutter with Feng Shui.* New York: Broadway Books, 1998.

Kolberg, Judith. *What Every Professional Organizer Needs to Know About Chronic Disorganization.* Self-published, 1999.

Lehmkuhl, Dorothy, and Dolores Cotter Lamping. *Organizing for the Creative Person.* New York: Crown Publishers, 1993.

Luhrs, Janet. *The Simple Living Guide.* New York: Broadway Books, 1997.

McGee-Cooper, Ann. *Time Management for the Unmanageable People.* Dallas, TX: Ann McGee-Cooper & Assoc., 1983.

Merkel, Jim. *Radical Simplicity.* Gabriola Island, BC: New Society Publishers, 2003.

Morgenstern, Julie. *Time Management from the Inside Out.* New York: Henry Holt, 2000.

Ordesky, Maxine. *The Complete Home Organizer.* New York: Grove Press, 1993.

Passoff, Michelle. *Lighten Up!* New York: Harper Perennial, 1998.

Phillips, Carol. *The Household Inventory Guide.* Emeryville, CA: IPP Press, 1991.

Pierce, Linda Breen. *Choosing Simplicity.* Carmel, CA: Gallagher Press, 2000.

Pollar, Odette. *Organizing Your Workspace*. Menlo Park, NJ: Crisp Publications, 1992.

Robyn, Kathryn L. *Healing the Space Within by Beautifying the Space Around You*. Oakland, CA: New Harbinger Publications, 2001.

Sapadin, Linda, and Jack Maguire. *It's About Time*. New York: Penguin Books, 1996.

Segal, Jerome, *Grateful Simplicity*. Berkeley, CA: University of California Press, 2003.

Silber, Lee. *Time Management for the Creative Person*. New York: Three Rivers Press, 1998.

Silver, Susan. *Organized to Be Your Best*. Adams-Hall, 2000.

St. James, Elaine. *Simplify Your Life*. New York: Hyperion, 1994.

Summers, Marc. *Everything in Its Place*. New York: Jeremy P. Tarcher/Putnam, 1999.

Sunset Books and Sunset Magazine. *Sunset: Complete Home Storage*. Menlo Park, NJ: Lane Publishing Co, 1984.

Taylor, Harold E. *Getting Organized: Increasing Personal Productivity*. Willowdale, Ontario: Harold Taylor Time Consultants, 1992.

Thorp, Gary. *Sweeping Changes*. New York: Walker & Co., 2000.

Winston, Stephanie. *Getting Organized*. New York: Warner Books, 1978.

———. *The Organized Executive*. New York: Warner Books, 1993.

Wolfman, Perie, and Charles Gold. *A Place for Everything*. New York: Clarkson Potter, 1999.

Yager, Jan Dr. *Creative Time Management for the New Millennium*. Stamford, CT: Hannacroix Creek Books, 1999.

www.clutterersanonymous.net

www.drweil.com

Index